Bilingualism in Schools and Society

This book is an introduction to the social and educational aspects of bilingualism. It presents an overview of a broad range of sociolinguistic and political issues surrounding the use of two languages, including code-switching in popular music, advertising, and online social spaces. It offers a well-informed discussion of what it means to study and live with multiple languages in a globalized world and practical advice on raising bilingual children.

Sarah J. Shin is Professor of Education and Co-Director of the M.A. TESOL Program at the University of Maryland Baltimore County.

Bilingualism in Schools and Society

Language, Identity, and Policy

Sarah J. Shin

Routledge
Taylor & Francis Group

NEW YORK AND LONDON

First published 2013
by Routledge
711 Third Avenue, New York, NY 10017

Simultaneously published in the UK
by Routledge
2 Park Square, Milton Park, Abingdon, Oxon OX14 4RN

Routledge is an imprint of the Taylor & Francis Group, an *informa* business

Library of Congress Cataloging in Publication Data
Shin, Sarah J., 1970–
    Bilingualism in schools and society : language, identity, and policy /
    Sarah J. Shin.
        p. cm.
    Includes bibliographical references.
    1. Bilingualism in children—United States. 2. Education, Bilingual—
    United States. 3. Language acquisition—Parent participation.
    4. Hispanic American children—Education. 5. Child development—
    Cross-cultural studies. 6. Sociolinguistics. I. Title.
    P115.2.S48 2012
    404′.2083—dc23   2012011332

ISBN: 978-0-415-89104-2 (hbk)
ISBN: 978-0-415-89105-9 (pbk)
ISBN: 978-0-203-82867-0 (ebk)

Typeset in Minion
by Keystroke, Station Road, Codsall, Wolverhampton

Printed and bound in the United States of America
by Edwards Brothers, Inc.

For my family

Contents

Illustrations

FIGURES

TABLES

Preface

This book is an introduction to the social and educational aspects of bilingualism. The idea for this book grew out of a graduate seminar on bilingualism that I have been teaching at my university. I decided to offer this course some years ago upon realizing the growing need, especially among educators, to better understand bilingualism and bilingual speakers. With a profound demographic shift currently underway in the U.S. and the realities of contemporary multicultural populations around the globe, more and more programs in teacher education, applied linguistics, and literacy studies are responding to calls for coursework on how to better address the educational and social needs of linguistically diverse student populations. This book addresses this need.

I will begin with an overview of a broad range of social and political issues surrounding bilingualism. Various definitions and descriptions of bilingualism will be explored, and some common misperceptions clarified. While this book covers all the main bases that educators need when dealing with linguistically diverse students such as bilingual identity, code-switching, language shift, and language policy, it also explores bilingualism in popular music, advertising, and online social spaces. It will examine some of the opportunities and challenges of globalization and make a case for preserving minority and endangered languages. I will also discuss issues related to educating English learners and raising children bilingually in the family, as well as program options for educating students in two or more languages.

This book can be used as a main text or as a supplementary text in courses on multilingual education, literacy and social context, second language acquisition, and language policy. Written primarily for upper-level undergraduate and graduate level students, this book is organized around reviews of important and up-to-date research and is grounded in the analysis of empirical work with bilingual children and adults from around the world. At the end of each chapter, **Further Reading** and **Online and Video Resources** (where relevant) will direct readers to additional resources, and **Study Questions and Activities** can be used to guide classroom discussions and suggest ideas for investigating bilingualism in schools, families, and communities. The **Glossary** lists key words and phrases, which are bolded the first time they are used in the text. In addition, the **Out of the Mouths of Bilinguals** boxes found in every chapter feature "voices" from the field, first-hand accounts of what it's like to live with two or more languages.

ORGANIZATION OF THE BOOK

Chapter 1: Facts and Myths about Bilingualism

This introductory chapter will discuss common myths about bilingualism. Some of the questions I will address include: Who is bilingual? What criteria should be used to define a bilingual? Should bilinguals be only those people who have equal competence in both languages? Are there different degrees of bilingualism that can vary over time and with circumstances? Where does the notion of the "ideal" or "full" bilingual come from and how does it affect our perception of bilingual individuals? When is the best time to learn a second language? Should immigrant parents be advised to speak English to their children at home? Is bilingualism linked to academic difficulties?

Chapter 2: Bilingualism in a Globalized World

Globalization presents both exciting opportunities and new challenges for educators and language professionals. Technological advances of the last few decades have made it easier for people from distant corners of the globe to come into contact with one another. Since this contact increasingly involves people accessing and exchanging information across national and linguistic borders, there is an ever increasing need for bilingualism. We will see that while the forces of globalization have produced a thoroughly interconnected world and leveled the playing field for billions of ordinary people, the same forces are threatening the existence of local cultures, identities, and languages. We will also see that language is increasingly treated as a commodity, a cultural capital that is required for success in a "flat world" (Friedman, 2005).

Chapter 3: The Politics of Bilingualism

This chapter discusses the politics behind people's language choices in multi-lingual societies. Bilingual societies come about as a result of contact between groups of people that speak different languages. Such contact always produces a power differential—speakers of one language have more political, economic, and social capital than those of another. This power differential is perhaps most obvious in diglossic societies where one language (called the "High" variety) is reserved for use in formal domains such as school, government, and the media while another language (the "Low" variety) is used in informal settings of the home and the community. We will examine the official language policies of several countries, and see that there is often a mismatch between policy and actual language use.

Chapter 4: Heritage Language Education

Nearly one in five Americans speak a language other than English at home. In this chapter, I make a case for promoting the bilingualism of these individuals and why doing so makes economic and political sense for the mainstream American society. Community-based language schools are sprouting up in cities and suburbs across America, and in some school and college language departments, the number of heritage language learners exceeds the number of foreign language learners. I describe the current state of heritage language education in the U.S. and the benefits and challenges of developing heritage language programs. I will argue that the languages that are learned and used by immigrant and indigenous populations in their communities are a national asset, a resource that must be protected and cherished.

Chapter 5: Bilingualism and Identity

Language and identity are inextricably linked. In this chapter, I will show how identities are reflected in the way bilinguals use their languages and how people construct new identities through language. I will discuss the role of essentialist frameworks such as Social Network Analysis (Milroy, 1987) in predicting the language behavior of bilingual speakers. These theories try to correlate bilinguals' language choices with predetermined categories such as the degree of ethnic social ties. I will show that essentialist models, though insightful in their own right, do not adequately explain the negotiated, constructed, and often conflicted nature of identity. What is increasingly preferred are the more interpretive, constructivist accounts which conceptualize identity as fluid and dynamic. We will see that this view of identity is more and more adopted by educators who are committed to improving the education of linguistically and culturally diverse students.

Chapter 6: Social and Conversational Aspects of Code-Switching

This chapter will examine the social and conversational attributes of code-switching, the alternating use of two or more languages within the same conversation. Bilinguals most often switch languages in ordinary conversations when they are in the company of other bilinguals. Code-switching is perhaps the most obvious indication of one's bilingual abilities, since very few bilinguals keep their two languages completely separate. But people often have negative attitudes toward code-switching and think that it indicates language incompetence. In this chapter, we will see that code-switching is a communicative option available to the bilingual speaker in much the same way that switching between styles or dialects is an option for the monolingual speaker. We will see how bilinguals use code-switching as a resource to communicate their meanings and why insisting on strictly separating two languages is counterproductive.

Chapter 7: Educating English Learners

In this chapter, I discuss some of the major policies and pedagogical issues related to educating English Learners (ELs), the fastest growing segment of the American school-age population. I will provide a brief history of the policies that have guided the instruction of language minority children in the United States and discuss some state-level educational policies that have restricted the use of languages other than English in the classroom. We will see from the ample available evidence that English-only instruction neither leads to faster learning of English nor produces better academic results for ELs. I will argue that what ELs need in order to be successful in school is an explicit instruction in the structure of academic English. I will show how academic English is different from everyday spoken English and what teachers can do to draw students' attention to linguistic form within a meaning-driven study of content area texts.

Chapter 8: Educational Models that Promote Additive Bilingualism

In this chapter, I discuss the so-called "strong forms of bilingual education" whose goal is to develop high levels of bilingualism in students. There are mainly two types of strong forms of bilingual education: (1) enrichment programs, which serve relatively privileged language-majority speakers learning through the medium of another language, and (2) maintenance programs, which help language-minority speakers maintain the use of their mother tongues while learning a second language. I will introduce two enrichment programs (Canadian French immersion and the European Schools) and two maintenance programs (Indigenous language immersion and Developmental bilingual education). I will also discuss Two-way (dual) immersion, in which language-majority and language-minority children help each other in learning both languages in the same classroom.

Chapter 9: Multilingual Families

More and more parents are interested in the idea of raising bilingual children. This chapter will address questions such as the following: Why do some children become bilingual and others don't? What kind of language exposure is necessary and for how long? What does it take to raise children bilingually in monolingual societies? Could bilingual input confuse children? I will review the research on children who acquire two languages simultaneously from birth (i.e., simultaneous bilinguals) and those who acquire a second language later in childhood (i.e., successive bilinguals). I will introduce case studies of three families that have employed different strategies to achieve bilingualism. I will also discuss the effect of birth order on bilingual experience and how children move in and out of bilingualism throughout their development.

Acknowledgments

I wish to thank the many people who have helped me in writing this book. I am grateful to Christine Mallinson for introducing me to Ivy Ip, my editor at Routledge, who believed in the potential of this book and supported me throughout the writing process. My heartfelt thanks also go to the seven reviewers of the book whose comments and suggestions I found immensely helpful. I have benefited greatly from the expert assistance of the editorial staff at Routledge: Mike Andrews, Elysse Preposi, Louisa Semlyen, and Leah Babb-Rosenfeld. Many thanks to you all.

Parts of this book draw on material I have published elsewhere. I would like to acknowledge my article, "Birth order and the language experience of bilingual children" published in 2002 in *TESOL Quarterly*, and my book, *Developing in two languages: Korean children in America*, published in 2005 by Multilingual Matters.

I am grateful for the support of my colleagues at the University of Maryland Baltimore County, particularly my department chair, Eugene Schaffer, and my colleagues in the M.A. TESOL Program, John Nelson, Jodi Crandall, and Mary Tabaa. I also wish to thank Alex Sheffrin for compiling the indexes for this book. The students in my bilingualism course have directed me to some of the quotes found in "Out of the Mouths of Bilinguals" and shared with me their own experiences with bilingualism. Their insightful questions and comments in class discussions have honed my arguments and formed the basis for many of the examples I included in the book.

Finally, this book could not have been written without the love and encouragement of my husband, Yoon Ki, and our sons, Isaac and Joshua. Thank you from the bottom of my heart.

Sarah J. Shin

1

Facts and Myths about Bilingualism

INTRODUCTION

Bilingualism is a fact of life for the vast majority of the world's populations. It is estimated that as much as two-thirds of the people in the world are bilingual (Crystal, 2003). There are anywhere between 6,000 and 7,000 languages spoken in the world today and only about 190 countries in which to house them, which suggests how widespread bilingualism (or multilingualism) must be. Bilingualism involving two or more languages is quite common in many of the historically **multilingual** societies of Africa and Asia. For example, some 25 languages are spoken in South Africa and 20 in Mozambique (Kamwangamalu, 2006). Bilingualism is an integral part of the cultural fabric of India where 216 languages have at least 10,000 speakers each and 24 of them are recognized by the national constitution (Bhatia & Ritchie, 2006b).

Pandit (1977), as cited in Gargesh (2006: 91), provides an apt description of the functional multilingualism of an Indian businessman living in a suburb of Bombay (Mumbai). His **mother tongue** and home language is a dialect of Gujarati; in the market he uses a familiar variety of Marathi, the **state language**; at the railway station he speaks Hindi, the pan-Indian **lingua franca** (a common language used by speakers of different mother tongues); his language of work is Kachhi, the code of the spice trade; in the evening he watches a film in Hindi or in English and listens to a cricket match commentary on the radio in English. As this example illustrates, a whole range of languages are available to Indians, who choose each language purposefully to perform particular social functions.

Even in many of the world's so-called "**monolingual**" nations, one can find substantial numbers of bilingual individuals and communities. For instance, nearly 55 million Americans—or roughly one in five Americans—age five and older, speak a language other than English at home (U.S. Census Bureau,

2005–2009). France is home to the biggest Muslim population (4.7 million) in Europe (Pew Forum on Religion and Public Life, 2011), and more than 15 million people living in Germany (18% of the total population of 82 million) have an immigrant background (Facts about Germany, 2011). Many people in officially monolingual countries know someone who is bilingual even if they may not use two or more languages regularly.

Although there are more bilingual than monolingual people in the world, bilingualism has traditionally been treated as a special case or a deviation from the monolingual norm (Romaine, 1995: 8). Most linguistic research has tended to focus on monolinguals and has treated bilinguals as exceptions. For instance, Chomsky's (1965: 3) theory of grammar is concerned primarily with "an ideal speaker-listener, in a completely homogeneous speech community, who knows its language perfectly." Given the emphasis on describing the linguistic competence of the ideal monolingual speaker, bilingualism has necessarily been regarded as problematic, an impure form of communication by people who do not seem to know either language fully.

One of the ways in which people display their bilingual abilities is through **code-switching**, a change of language within a conversation, usually when bilinguals are in the company of other bilinguals. Code-switching is perhaps the most obvious indication of one's bilingual abilities, since very few bilinguals keep their two languages completely separate (Gardner-Chloros, 2009). However, monolinguals who hear bilinguals code-switch often have negative attitudes toward code-switching and think that it represents a lack of mastery of either language. Pejorative names such as "Chinglish" (Chinese-English), "Konglish" (Korean-English), and "Franglais" (French-English) are often used to refer to the mixed speech of bilinguals, and bilinguals themselves may feel embarrassed about their code-switching and attribute it to careless language habits or laziness (Grosjean, 1982: 148). However, a great deal of research in the past few decades has shown that code-switching, far from being a communicative deficit, is a valuable linguistic strategy (see Chapter 6 for a review of the research on code-switching).

Strictly speaking, it would be difficult to find someone who thinks bilingualism is downright bad. After all, to most people, having proficiency in two or more languages is considered a desirable attribute—one can reasonably argue that knowing two languages is better than knowing just one. Indeed many people think that bilingualism is a sign of intellectual prowess and sophistication—those who have competence in several languages are often regarded with envy and admiration. However, attitudes toward bilingualism and bilingual people vary widely depending on who the bilingual is and the circumstances of his/her bilingualism. For example, while the bilingualism of a Haitian immigrant to the U.S. may be frowned upon as evidence that he has not yet fully integrated into mainstream American society, the bilingual abilities of a native English-speaking Anglo American who has learned French as a foreign language may be prized as a valuable asset.

In this book, I discuss the social contexts that make certain kinds of bilingualism desirable and others not so desirable, and how these influence language and educational policies at various levels. The languages involved in any bilingual situation almost never have the same status—one variety is perceived as having greater prestige and value than another. We will explore how these unequal perceptions shape and color the ways in which people—bilinguals and monolinguals alike—identify themselves and others. We will also see how parents' and teachers' educational decisions are driven by larger sociopolitical forces as well as by personal motivations for achieving bilingualism. I will discuss the advantages and disadvantages of different models of bilingual education programs and research-based best practices for promoting bilingual development in children from both majority and minority language backgrounds. Throughout the book, I aim to show that bilingualism is a resource to be cultivated for all kinds of populations, not a problem to be overcome.

OUT OF THE MOUTHS OF BILINGUALS 1.1

Multilingualism as the Norm in Malawi

"My father is Tonga by tribe and he has always spoken to me in Chitonga, Chitumbuka and English, with a bit of Chichewa. My mother is Sena by tribe, but she has always spoken to me in Chitumbuka, Chichewa and English, with a bit of Chitonga. . . . I acquired Chitonga, Chitumbuka and Chichewa as mother tongues simultaneously, and English as a second language."

(Kamanga, 2009: 115)

At the heart of much debate on language in schools and society are certain myths about bilingual processes and people. In the following, I disprove five such myths by providing the relevant facts and research evidence:

Myth #1: A bilingual is fully proficient in two languages.
Myth #2: Immigrants are reluctant to learn English.
Myth #3: Children need early exposure to a second language if they are to learn it successfully.
Myth #4: Immigrant parents should speak the societal language to their children at home to help them succeed in school.

Myth #5: High dropout rates of Hispanic students in the U.S. demonstrate the failure of bilingual education.

The following discussion of the myths and facts about bilingualism introduces the reader to some of the major topics that are covered in this book.

MYTH #1: A BILINGUAL IS FULLY
PROFICIENT IN TWO LANGUAGES

One of the most common myths about bilingualism is the view that a bilingual is completely fluent in two languages. It is often assumed that "true" bilinguals are those who are equally proficient in their two languages, with competence in both languages comparable to those of monolinguals of those languages. Figure 1.1, which illustrates this myth, shows three individuals—a monolingual speaker of language A, a monolingual speaker of language B, and an "ideal" bilingual speaker of languages A and B. This is a crude and over-simplified diagram that does not accurately depict the changing needs for a bilingual's two languages in different situations with different interlocutors, but it nonetheless illustrates my point. Notice that the size of the circles (which indicate the level of proficiency in each language) is the same for monolingual A and monolingual B speakers as well as for the bilingual A-B speaker.

In reality, however, bilinguals will rarely have balanced proficiency in their two languages. Terms such as "full" bilingual and "balanced" bilingual represent idealized concepts that do not characterize the great majority of the world's bilinguals. Rarely will any bilingual be equally proficient in speaking, listening, reading, and writing both languages across all different situations and domains. In other words, a bilingual is not the sum of two monolinguals. However, the monolingual view of bilingualism is so entrenched in popular and scholarly thinking that bilinguals themselves may apologize to monolinguals for not speaking their language as well as do monolinguals, thus accepting and reinforcing the myth.

Most bilinguals in the world look more like those in Figure 1.2, which shows four A-B bilinguals. Notice that the relative sizes of the circles are different in

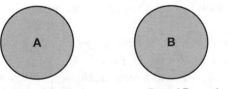
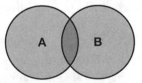

a monolingual A speaker   a monolingual B speaker   an "ideal," "full"
                                                        bilingual A-B speaker

FIGURE 1.1 A Mythical View of the "Ideal" or "Full" Bilingual

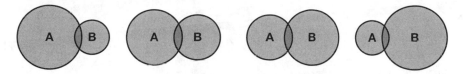

FIGURE 1.2 More Realistic Conceptions of Bilinguals

each, indicating that the bilinguals have different proficiencies in the two languages. The bilinguals' proficiency in each of the two languages may be lower than that of monolingual speakers of each language, but taken together, the bilinguals' two languages are bigger than a monolingual's only language in terms of vocabulary, syntax, and range of expression. Most bilinguals have different proficiencies in two languages because the two languages are often learned under different conditions for a range of purposes, and are used in a variety of situations with different people.

As an illustration, I will describe my experiences as a bilingual. I am a native speaker of Korean who started learning English as a second language at the age of 13 when I moved to the U.S. as an immigrant. As a newcomer student in a local junior high school, I had to skip one class each day to go to a separate ESL class where I learned English grammar and pronunciation with other immigrant students. Learning school subjects in English was enormously difficult, and I remember often coming home frustrated and exhausted from having to hear, speak, and read English all day. I spoke in Korean at home with my family but slowly my two younger brothers and I included bits of English in our otherwise Korean interactions. We watched TV programming in English, made friends with kids from other countries in our ethnically diverse neighborhood in New York City, and tried to keep up with schoolwork in English.

While my English skills developed both academically and socially throughout high school and college, my Korean skills stagnated since I used it only at home. I would say that my current reading and writing skills in Korean are at about an eighth-grade level which is when I stopped going to school in Korean. Although I have no trouble communicating informally in Korean, I find giving an academic lecture in Korean quite challenging because I never learned the advanced discipline-specific vocabulary and syntax in Korean to be able to do so. I am married to a Korean American and we have two American-born sons who, despite our many efforts to teach them Korean, are mostly English-speaking. Spousal communication at our home is a mixture of Korean and English but we find ourselves speaking more and more English as our children grow up. I do almost all of my reading and writing in English now and rarely pick up a Korean newspaper. Since the uses for my two languages are very compartmentalized (English for work, Korean for home and ethnic community), I do not have the same proficiencies in both languages. Overall, my

FIGURE 1.3 What a "Semilingual" Child Might Look Like

bilingualism has been an evolving phenomenon and is continually changing with shifting circumstances and communicative needs in my life. The same is true for many bilinguals in the world.

In educational circles, the term **semilingual** has been used to describe bilingual students who appear to lack proficiency in both languages (Martin-Jones & Romaine, 1986). Figure 1.3 shows what a semilingual child might look like. Compared to the "ideal" or "full" bilingual in Figure 1.1, a semilingual falls short in both languages. Before the 1960s, there was an overwhelming number of studies that highlighted the negative effects of bilingualism on children (Romaine, 1995: 107). Observers noted many problems with language development of bilingual children, such as restricted vocabularies, limited grammatical structures, unusual word order, errors in morphology, hesitations, stuttering, and so on. Some have even argued that bilingualism could impair the child's intelligence and lead to split personalities.

Valadez, MacSwan, & Martínez (2000) quote a 1996 *Los Angeles Times* article which reported that in the schools of the Los Angeles Unified School District there were 6,800 immigrant students who have been labeled "**non-nons**" or "clinically disfluent," that is, children who allegedly do not know English, Spanish, or any other language. The district's educational response was to place these children in separate classrooms and provide them with intensive language instruction. Supposing that this many students could not all be linguistically deficient, Valadez et al. (2000) systematically compared the oral language proficiencies of children who were labeled as "clinically disfluent" by the school psychologist and children who were identified as having "normal" or "high" ability. They found that the group of children labeled "clinically disfluent" or "semilingual" did not have an impoverished knowledge of morphology, nor did they make frequent errors in syntax. Contrary to the school evaluations, these students were not inexpressive. In fact, the authors found that the "semilingual" children have the same command of language as do the children in their control group. Valadez et al. (2000) conclude that labels like semilingual or non-non are extensions of a **deficit-based model of bilingualism** for language minority children and must be used with extreme caution.

Research comparing monolingual and bilingual children on a wide variety of linguistic and cognitive tasks often includes a measure of receptive vocabulary, usually the Peabody Picture Vocabulary Test (PPVT) (Bialystok, Luk, Peets, & Yang, 2010). PPVT is relatively easy to administer, and the task requires children to point to one of four pictures that best represents a word spoken by the experimenter. The items become increasingly difficult and detailed tables convert children's raw scores to standard scores based on their age. Many studies have reported lower vocabulary scores for bilingual children than for monolinguals (Romaine, 1995), but each study is based on a small sample so it is difficult to determine whether the vocabulary difference is due to sampling error (Bialystok et al., 2010).

To address this problem, Bialystok et al. (2010) analyzed the PPVT scores of 1,738 children between three and ten years of age recruited from multiple studies. They found that there was indeed a significant difference in the vocabulary sizes of monolingual and bilingual children. However, the difference was largely confined to words that are part of home life—a reasonable result given that English is not used as extensively in bilingual homes as it is in the homes of monolinguals. When the researchers looked at the school vocabulary for children in the two groups, they were more comparable. Bialystok et al. (2010) conclude that bilingual children are thus not typically disadvantaged in academic and literacy achievement in school because the linguistic basis of school activities is well established.

Aside from vocabulary, there is evidence that young immigrant children *momentarily* lag in grammatical development in both of their languages when compared to their same-age monolingual peers (Pfaff, 1994; Shin & Milroy, 1999; Verhoeven & Boeschoten, 1986; Verhoeven & Vermeer, 1984) *but the errors usually disappear as they grow up*. However, findings such as these have been misinterpreted as saying that it is counterproductive to the child's welfare to develop and maintain proficiency in more than one language. Similarly, tests that are designed for monolinguals are often used to compare bilinguals' proficiency in either of their languages with that of monolinguals. These assessments often do not take into account the fact that bilinguals use their two languages with different people, in different contexts, and for different purposes. They also do not take into account the fact that bilingualism is never static and that children are continuously developing in their two languages.

So, who is a **bilingual**? François Grosjean, a leading authority in bilingualism, provides the following definition:

> The bilingual is a fully competent speaker/hearer; he or she has developed competencies (in the two languages and possibly a third system that is a combination of the two) *to the extent required by his or her needs and those of the environment* [italics mine]. The bilingual uses the two languages— separately or together—for different purposes in different domains of life and with different people. Because the needs and uses of the two languages are usually quite different, the bilingual is rarely equally or completely fluent in the two languages. Levels of fluency in a language

will depend on the need for that language and will be extremely domain specific.

(Grosjean, 1985: 471)

Grosjean's definition emphasizes that bilingualism must be understood in its own right and that monolingual competence should not be used as a basis for assessing bilingual ability.

MYTH #2: IMMIGRANTS ARE RELUCTANT TO LEARN ENGLISH

When people visit ethnic enclaves in big cities (e.g., East Los Angeles, Little Saigon, and Chinatown), they often get the impression that these are **linguistic ghettos** where only Spanish, Vietnamese, or Chinese is spoken generation after generation. It may seem as though some people in these communities do not speak English at all and are not interested in learning it. However, contrary to the popular assumption that immigrants are staying in language ghettos, they are learning English, and in fact, losing their **native languages** in the process.

In her book, *Why don't they learn English?: Separating fact from fallacy in the U.S. language debate*, Lucy Tse (2001) observes that these ethnically concentrated communities get started and perpetuated with influxes of new immigrants. She notes that when adult immigrants arrive, especially without significant financial resources or English skills, they tend to gravitate toward communities where they are likely to get assistance in settling into their new surroundings. These communities provide the new arrivals with the ability to survive without significant English ability, and may provide formal or informal networks for getting a job, finding housing, and navigating life in a new country. However, second and later generations are less likely to live as adults and raise their own families in such communities, especially since immigrant enclaves tend to be in poor neighborhoods. Once people have the linguistic and financial means to move out of such communities, many do so.

I have never met an immigrant who does not want to learn English. This is true even for my 75-year-old mother-in-law who has been learning English ever since she first came to America in 1980 and is still taking classes. Immigrants know full well the value of knowing English. The inability to speak English forces many immigrants to take low-paying jobs or perform menial tasks despite having high levels of education and training from their home countries. While immigrants in earlier days could labor on farms, work in factories, and build railroads without speaking much English, today's service-oriented economy requires English ability for all but the lowest paying jobs. Immigrants know that mastering the societal language is their ticket to success in the new country.

Furthermore, lack of English skills is a source of a great deal of stress for the immigrant family as parents must rely on their school-age children to translate simple documents in English or to inquire about credit card bills or bank statements. It is embarrassing for parents to depend on their children for things that they should ordinarily be able to do, and frustrating for the children whose parents are so dependent on them for even the very basic tasks. Working long hours in one or more low-paying jobs limits the opportunities for immigrants to improve their English by leaving them little time and energy to attend English classes. It is enormously stressful to manage long working hours, family responsibilities, and children's education, all in a linguistically and culturally foreign environment.

Free or low-cost **English as a Second Language (ESL)** classes usually fill up quickly and often have long waiting lists. According to a U.S. Census report, the foreign-born population of the U.S. has continued to increase in size and as a proportion of the total population during the last four decades: from 9.6 million (4.7%) in 1970 to 38.5 million (12.5%) in 2009 (Grieco & Trevelyan, 2010). Of the 38.5 million foreign-born residents, only 921,548 adults were enrolled in federally funded, state-administered ESL programs in program year 2009–2010 (U.S. Department of Education, Office of Vocational and Adult Education, 2011), which means that the unmet need is enormous. In addition to federally funded programs, English instruction is offered by volunteer and faith-based organizations, museums, libraries and other community centers, private language schools, and academic institutions (Center for Applied Linguistics, 2010). Even with these programs however, the demand for low-cost ESL classes far outstrips supply.

Many immigrants wait months or even years to enroll in government-financed English classes, which are often overcrowded and lack textbooks (Santos, 2007). The National Association of Latino Elected and Appointed Officials conducted a study to examine the wait times associated with popular adult ESL programs across the country (Tucker, 2006). Among 176 adult ESL providers surveyed, 57% reported that their waiting list was from a few weeks to more than three years. In some parts of the country, such as New York City, waiting lists have been abolished, because the wait has become too long. Rather than put students on waiting lists, some programs place students in available classes that may not meet the students' specific goals or are not the appropriate instructional level, in the hope that space in a suitable class will open up.

Although many first-generation adult immigrants struggle to become proficient in English, English language proficiency increases dramatically with each subsequent generation. For example, the Pew Hispanic Center surveyed 14,000 Latino adults on their ability to speak English (Hakimzadeh & Cohn, 2007). The study found that while only 23% of first-generation Latino immigrant adults reported speaking English very well, 88% of second-generation,

U.S.-born Latino adults reported speaking English very well, and 94% of subsequent U.S.-born generations of Latino adults reported speaking English very well.

Observations of different communities that come into contact with a **majority language** have shown that there is almost always a complete **language shift** within three generations (Fishman, 1989). In the typical scenario, the first generation speaks the native language, while the second generation is bilingual to some degree followed by the majority-language-speaking third generation. However, recently, an increasing number of language minority communities are undergoing a complete language shift within two generations with no intervening bilingual generation (Wiley, 2001). This accelerated shift creates major communication problems, as parents and children living in the same household do not understand each other. In Chapter 3, I will explain why the U.S. is sometimes referred to as a "language graveyard" and how the pressure to become monolingual in English has led many immigrant individuals and communities to abandon their native languages (Portes & Rumbaut, 2006).

MYTH #3: CHILDREN NEED EARLY EXPOSURE TO A SECOND LANGUAGE IF THEY ARE TO LEARN IT SUCCESSFULLY

We often hear that when it comes to learning a foreign language, it is better to start earlier than later. Compared to adults, children seem to have a much easier time learning a second language. For example, it is common to see young immigrant children speaking pretty good English within only several months of being placed in American schools whereas some adult immigrants struggle to put together simple sentences in English even after many years of living in the U.S. Moreover, younger children seem to have an easier time learning another language than older children and adolescents. Observations like these have led people to believe that there is an age-related point beyond which it becomes difficult or impossible to learn a second language to the same degree as native speakers of that language. This view is known as the **Critical Period Hypothesis** (Gass & Selinker, 2008). While second language researchers have grappled with this issue for several decades, there is currently no consensus as to whether or not the acquisition of a second language is constrained by a critical period.

Various empirical studies show that there is a decline in performance in different language domains among older learners of a second language, especially in the area of pronunciation (Butler & Hakuta, 2006). Some researchers have shown a significant negative correlation between the age of arrival in a country and grammar knowledge in a second language. For example, Johnson & Newport (1989) gave a grammaticality judgment test to English learners who arrived in the U.S. between the ages of three and 39 years and found that people who came to the U.S. at an earlier age generally performed better than those who came at a later age. However, no correlation was observed among those who arrived in the U.S. after 17 years of age, and large individual differences were observed.

Other researchers argue that age of initial exposure to a second language is not a critical factor in second language acquisition. Instead, they suggest that individual variables—learner motivation, language learning aptitude, level of anxiety, and amount and quality of second language input—have a bigger influence on the acquisition of a second language (see Gass & Selinker, 2008 for a summary). Moreover, researchers disagree as to what is exactly meant by a critical period. Different scholars have suggested different times for closure of the critical period ranging anywhere from five to 15 years of age, and no clear explanations have been offered as to the reasons for the specific timing of the closure of the period (Butler & Hakuta, 2006). In addition, studies on age and second language acquisition have been mostly limited to grammar knowledge and pronunciation while other aspects of language (e.g., language usage and pragmatics) have not been investigated to the same extent (Butler & Hakuta, 2006).

With regard to second language acquisition in school settings, Genesee (2006) notes that the findings on the effects of starting to teach children through the medium of a second language in kindergarten vs. secondary schools have been varied. Whereas some report that older students in bilingual programs can make impressive progress toward second language learning (Genesee, 1988; Krashen, Long, & Scarcella, 1979), others find that students starting in kindergarten do better (Genesee, 1981; Wesche, Toews-Janzen, & MacFarlane, 1996). But even some scholars who claim that starting earlier produces better results (e.g., Wesche et al., 1996) observe that the differences between early-onset bilingual and late-onset bilingual students tend to diminish as the students approach the end of secondary school. Other researchers (e.g., Singleton, 2001) also show that early second language learners are neither more successful nor more efficient in acquiring a second language than late second language learners.

When we consider the social and educational settings in which children and adults find themselves, we can explain a lot of the differences observed in child and adult second language acquisition. For instance, being schooled in a second language for six to seven hours a day is a significant source of language input for immigrant children. Schools provide children with structured opportunities to develop both spoken and written language through a wide range of academic and social activities. Most adults, on the other hand, do not have the luxury of being in school for six to seven hours a day. Immigrant adults often have limited second language input on the job and little time and energy to study the language systematically when they are not at work. Children's communicative needs are also less complicated than those of adults, and children's language practices are often supported through gestures and visuals whereas the same kind of help is normally not available to adults.

But given adequate time, effective instruction, motivation, and support, adults are quite capable of becoming bilingual. For example, the U.S. Defense Language Institute provides resident instruction for U.S. military and other government personnel "in 23 languages and two dialects, five days a week, seven hours per day, with two to three hours of homework each night" (Defense Language Institute Foreign Language Center (DLIFLC), 2012). The language courses last between 26 and 64 weeks, and the school's website states:

> To further advance student knowledge in a particular language, DLIFLC has designed an immersion program which consists of an off site facility where students spend from one to three days in an isolated environment with their instructors and are not allowed to speak English. The facility is equipped with kitchens and sleeping quarters, while the program con- sists of real-world exercises, from bargaining for food and clothing at a market place, to going through customs, or making hotel reservations. DLIFLC also sends a number of students on 30-day in-country immer- sions to countries such as Egypt, Korea, China, the Ukraine, etc.

With this kind of intensive, full-time language training, adults can become quite proficient bilinguals. Most adults, however, do not have opportunities like this, which is why we get the sense that they are not as good as children in learning a second language.

So does age matter in developing bilingual abilities at all? The answer is yes, for certain populations. For example, for language minority children, earlier exposure to the societal language may actually prevent them from becoming bilingual. Research shows that immigrant children who are exposed to the societal language at an earlier age tend to have lower proficiency in their mother tongues than those who are exposed to it at a later age (Hakuta & D'Andrea, 1992; Shin, 2002; Wong Fillmore, 1991). For most immigrant children, system- atic exposure to the societal language starts when they begin schooling in the majority language. Many start using the school language at home and soon shift entirely to that language (Wong Fillmore, 1991). Thus, instead of becom- ing bilingual, the children go from being monolingual in the home language to being monolingual in English. This is an example of **subtractive bilingualism**, a situation in which the socially dominant language replaces the weaker ethnic language (Baker, 2007). For language minority children, achieving **additive bilingualism** (i.e., learning the second language while continuing to use the first language) may actually require postponing exposure to the majority language for some time (for more on bilingual education models that promote additive bilingualism, see Chapter 8).

MYTH #4: IMMIGRANT PARENTS SHOULD SPEAK
THE SOCIETAL LANGUAGE WITH THEIR CHILDREN
AT HOME TO HELP THEM SUCCEED IN SCHOOL

There is probably no professional advice that is more harmful to language minority families than this. In many monolingual societies, immigrant parents are routinely advised by doctors, speech therapists, teachers, and counselors to stop speaking their native language to the children so as not to "confuse" them with input from two languages. The so-called **linguistic mismatch hypothesis** is the notion that in every situation where there is a switch between home language and school language, students will encounter academic difficulties (Cummins, 1996). The argument that bilingual input confuses children is not valid, however, since most children growing up in bilingual or multilingual societies (e.g., India, Singapore, as well as many Asian and African countries) learn to use two or more languages with no apparent negative consequences to their cognitive development. This view is not supported by empirical sociolinguistic evidence either.

Much of the policy regarding the education of language minority students in the U.S. has been driven by a hypothesis called "maximum exposure" (Cummins, 1996). The **maximum exposure hypothesis** posits that if children come to school lacking proficiency in English, they require maximum exposure to English in school in order to learn it. This hypothesis has led to the claim that immersion in English is the most effective means to ensuring the learning of English. It is also assumed that, under these conditions of immersion, language minority students will learn sufficient English in about one or two years to survive academically without further special support.

Cummins (1996) notes that the maximum exposure hypothesis fails to account for the success of students enrolled in **enrichment bilingual education** programs (e.g., Canadian French immersion programs). He notes that countless evaluations have shown that students in French immersion programs make good progress in acquiring French fluency and literacy at no cost to their English academic skills despite considerably less instructional time spent in English (more on French immersion programs in Chapter 8). This is because, in a French immersion program, French instruction that develops French literacy is not only developing French skills, but it is also developing a deeper conceptual and linguistic proficiency that is related to the development of English literacy. This is called the **linguistic interdependence principle** (Cummins, 1996).

Research suggests that literacy skills transfer between languages, especially when the two languages have the same writing systems. Bialystok, Luk, & Kwan (2005) compared three groups of bilingual (Cantonese-English, Hebrew-English, Spanish-English) first-grade children with a group of monolingual

English-speaking first-graders on early literacy tasks. All the bilingual children used both languages daily and were learning to read in both languages. The children were given decoding and phonological awareness tasks, and the bilinguals completed all tasks in both languages. Bialystok et al. (2005) found that the Hebrew and Spanish bilingual children's ability to read in English was more advanced than that of the Cantonese bilingual and English monolingual children. The Cantonese bilingual children showed some advantage compared to the monolingual children in the decoding task but their performance on the phonological awareness task was at the same level as the English monolinguals and significantly lower than that of the other two bilingual groups. Thus, the Hebrew and Spanish bilingual groups (whose two languages were both based on an alphabetic principle) had the advantage of applying the literacy concepts they learned to their two languages. The two languages are in an interdependent relationship—improving skills in one language helps improve skills in the other.

Bilingualism is an asset for immigrant children, and parents should be encouraged to speak their native language with their children. If parents do not speak the native language at home, children will most likely never learn it. What happens when children never learn (or lose) their native languages? In a study of Korean American college students, Cho & Krashen (1998) report that loss of Korean significantly interfered with the students' ability to communicate with their parents. All of the subjects either were born in the U.S. or came to the U.S. before they started school and reported that they spoke Korean fluently before entering elementary school. However, all of them became more comfortable in English once they started school and used English with their siblings and friends. The following excerpts from Cho & Krashen (1998: 33–36) poignantly capture the participants' sense of frustration in communicating with their parents:

> My parents and I do have a communication gap, a communication problem. Not in just a sophisticated way. I can't even hold a normal conversation with my parents. I just say my thoughts once and I repeat it constantly until they understand. . . .
>
> I see barriers between my mom and my sister. I can explain what I want . . . like when my sister wants something, if she says it directly to my mom, my mom just doesn't get it, and they get frustrated with each other and they are like fighting, tension. . . . I can just say "Mom, this is what she meant" and my mom says, "Oh, why doesn't she say so . . . okay . . . go to the movie." . . .
>
> It is frustrating when I'm speaking with my parents and we can't fully comprehend what we're trying to say to each other. I hate it when I eat dinner with my parents and they always carry on their own conversation

that I can only half understand. . . . I hate having something to say but not being able to say it.

As these excerpts show, significant costs are incurred when parents and children cannot communicate with one another due to a language barrier. Telling parents who are not proficient in English to speak in English to their children is like taking away their parental rights and responsibilities. More than teachers, parents need to teach values to their children—they need to show children why it is important to work hard, respect others, and be honest. They need to talk to their children about setting personal goals and persevering when things get difficult. Because parents need to do this in the language they command, they must be encouraged to speak their native languages to their children. Children's development in the home language helps ensure strong parent–child communication and improve family relationships, which also benefits the larger society.

MYTH #5: HIGH DROPOUT RATES OF HISPANIC STUDENTS IN THE U.S. DEMONSTRATE THE FAILURE OF BILINGUAL EDUCATION

Bilingualism is often wrongly blamed for the poor academic performance of language minority children. Groups opposing **bilingual education** in the U.S. such as "English for the Children" claim that bilingual instruction leads to educational failure of immigrant children. They argue that millions of mostly Hispanic immigrant students are hurt by being taught in Spanish, which prevents them from learning the English they need to succeed in school. They have used this argument to help pass legislation in California, Arizona, and Massachusetts to end bilingual education as an instructional option for immigrant children (Chapter 7 describes these anti-bilingual education laws). However, while it is true that Hispanic students have the highest high school dropout rate among the race/ethnicity categories in the U.S. (see Table 1.1), this is not because they have received bilingual instruction. In fact, many of these students have never had bilingual education.

In her book, *Learning and not learning English: Latino students in American schools*, Guadalupe Valdés (2001) points out that bilingual education is an option actually open to only a small fraction of immigrant children, primarily in the first three years of elementary school (see Table 1.2—(4) transitional bilingual education). She notes that in California, for example, even before the passage of Proposition 227 (which abolished bilingual education in that state), only 409,874 students (29%) out of a total of 1,406,166 **English Learners (ELs)** were enrolled in bilingual education programs. Once Proposition 227 passed, only 8% of the state's EL students were enrolled in bilingual education

TABLE 1.1

Percentage of 16- through 24-Year-Olds Who Are Not Enrolled in School
and Have Not Earned a High School Credential, by Race/Ethnicity

Year	Total	White	Black	Hispanic	Asian/Pacific Islander	American Indian/Alaska Native
1990	12.1	9.0	13.2	32.4	4.9	16.4
2000	10.9	6.9	13.1	27.8	3.8	14.0
2008	8.0	4.8	9.9	18.3	4.4	14.6

Source: Adapted from U.S. Department of Education, National Center for Education Statistics, 2011

programs (through waivers signed by parents). Given that the vast majority of
the ELs in California are Spanish-speaking—85% of the total EL population,
according to a Migration Policy Institute report (Batalova & McHugh, 2010)—
what this means is that the majority of the Spanish-speaking ELs in California
have not received bilingual instruction. Therefore, the poor academic
performance of Hispanic students could not be due to bilingual education.
What's more, since the passage of anti-bilingual education legislation in
California, Arizona, and Massachusetts, the achievement gap between language
minority and mainstream children in those states has actually widened
(Gándara & Hopkins, 2010a).

The issues related to the academic performance of language minority students are far more complex than just what language is used for instruction. To
understand the factors that contribute to the poor educational performance of
Hispanic and other language minority students, one needs to first examine the
instructional options that are available for students who come to school speaking languages other than English. Table 1.2 shows six different program models
for educating ELs in the U.S. Among the six options, the **monolingual education**
program models (i.e., (1) **submersion**, (2) submersion with ESL pull-out, and
(3) structured immersion) are much more common than the bilingual education program models (i.e., (4) transitional bilingual education, (5) developmental bilingual education, and (6) two-way immersion). States reporting the
types of language instruction programs funded under Title III of the *No Child
Left Behind Act* overwhelmingly favor English-only instructional programs over
bilingual education programs (Viadero, 2009).

Bilingual education programs tend to be found in states with large numbers
of students from the same first language background. Since Spanish speakers
constitute 73% of all ELs in the U.S. (Batalova & McHugh, 2010) and they tend
to be concentrated in certain areas of the U.S., most of the bilingual education
programs offered in the U.S. are in Spanish and English. Of the bilingual

education program options, **transitional**, or **early-exit**, **bilingual education** programs are the most common. The goal of these programs is to provide just enough instruction in Spanish so that students can catch up to their native-English-speaking peers. Once they are deemed proficient in English (within one to three years in the program), Spanish is dropped from the curriculum and students are mainstreamed to English-only instruction. Compared to transitional bilingual education, **developmental**, or **late-exit**, **bilingual education** programs are less common in the U.S. These programs have the goal of promoting both the students' home language and English throughout most of elementary school. However, these programs are also phased out by middle school when students are mainstreamed into English-only instruction.

Of the three bilingual education models in Table 1.2, **two-way (dual) immersion** programs are perhaps the most promising in terms of developing bilingualism in language minority children. These programs recruit about half of the students from native-English-speaking homes and the other half from language minority homes. Instead of isolating language minority children in separate classrooms as do the bilingual education programs, two-way immersion programs teach literacy and subjects in English and the other language to both English speakers and ELs in the same classroom. Although two-way immersion programs offer many benefits to both the majority and minority language speaking groups (see also Chapters 4 and 8), they exist mostly in elementary schools. At the middle and high school levels, instruction in a student's primary language is rare.

The vast majority of the language minority students in the U.S. are placed in one of the monolingual education programs and are expected to be quickly mainstreamed into English-only instruction. In the submersion model, ELs are placed in mainstream instruction along with their English-speaking peers with no special help. Also known as **sink-or-swim**, this is how language minority children used to be taught in the U.S. before ESL programs were created in the 1960s. Left on their own to cope with schoolwork in an unfamiliar language, some students did learn to swim, but a lot more sank. In many elementary schools today, immigrant children are still taught all subject matter content in English but this is supplemented with some language help in the form of **ESL pull-out** classes. In ESL pull-out, children are taken out of their regular classrooms for about 30 to 45 minutes a day and given ESL instruction in a separate classroom. One obvious drawback of this model is that students have to miss classroom instruction while they are in ESL and few teachers provide students with the opportunity to make up missed classroom work.

In middle and high schools, newly arrived immigrant students face particularly tough challenges since the English used in content area subjects is

TABLE 1.2

Program Models for Language Minority Students in the U.S.

Program	Language Used in Instruction	Components	Duration	Goals
MONOLINGUAL EDUCATION MODELS				
(1) Submersion ("Sink-or-Swim")	100% English	Mainstream education; no special help with English	Throughout K–12	Assimilating ELs into English-dominant society
(2) Submersion with ESL Pull-out	90–100% in English; may or may not include home language support	Mainstream education; students pulled out for 30–45 minutes of ESL daily	As needed	Assimilating ELs; remedial English
(3) Structured Immersion (Sheltered English, Content-based ESL)	90–100% English; may or may not include home language support	Subject-matter instruction at students' level of English; students grouped for instruction	1–3 years	Assimilating ELs; quick exit to mainstream education
BILINGUAL EDUCATION MODELS				
(4) Transitional Bilingual Education (Early-Exit)	10–50% home language; 50–90% English	Initial literacy usually in home language; some subject instruction in home language; ESL and subject matter instruction at students' level of English	1–3 years; students exit as they become proficient in English	Assimilating ELs; English acquisition without falling behind academically
(5) Developmental Bilingual Education (Late-Exit)	90% home language in K–1; home language gradually decreased to 50% or less by grade 4	Initial literacy in home language; some subject instruction in home language; ESL initially and subject matter instruction at students' level of English	5–6 years	Bilingualism and biliteracy; academic achievement in English

Program	Language Used Components in Instruction		Duration	Goals
(6) Two-Way (Dual) Immersion	90/10 model: 90% home language, 10% English in early grades; 50/50 model: 50% home language, 50% English	Emergent bilinguals and native-English speakers taught literacy and subjects in both languages; peer tutoring	5–6 years	Bilingualism and biliteracy; academic achievement in English

Source: Adapted from Crawford, 2004, p. 42; García, 2009, p. 186

quite a bit more advanced than that used in the elementary school curriculum. Not only do students have to acquire English to levels comparable to those of their native-English-speaking peers, they must also meet the same grade-level standards and graduation requirements in a relatively short amount of time. Some middle and high schools place students in intensive ESL instruction (called "newcomer programs") for a semester or a year and then place them in two or three periods of ESL instruction and **sheltered instruction** (e.g., sheltered math, sheltered science, sheltered history) (Valdés, 2001). Valdés (2001) notes that in many schools, ELs are isolated in a separate world of ESL, apart from the mainstream world where "real" American schooling takes place. ELs move from one sheltered class to another with other ELs and have very few opportunities to interact with native English speakers. They also have little access to authentic English and content in the sheltered classes, which are often simplified versions of regular courses adapted for students with limited English.

Valdés (2001: 16) observes that

there is much that teachers do not know about how the English language develops in second-language learners, and there is little information available to guide them in determining when ESL students at different levels can "compete" with mainstream students. Many of them, therefore, choose to have very little to do with students who speak and write very "imperfect" English.

It is estimated that two-thirds of limited-English-speaking children are not receiving the language assistance they need in order to succeed in their academic and intellectual development (Valdés, 2001). Although there has been a lot of interest among researchers and practitioners in teaching academic English to ELs recently, most teachers have vague ideas about what academic English looks like and how it should be taught in the various subject areas (but see Chapter 7).

In addition, there are numerous other factors that contribute to the poor academic performance of Hispanic students. A Pew Hispanic Center analysis of the academic performance of EL students in five states that educate 70% of the nation's EL student population (Arizona, California, Florida, New York, and Texas) shows that ELs tend to go to schools that have low standardized test scores (Fry, 2008). The report explains that these low levels of academic performance are not solely attributable to poor achievement by EL students. These same schools report poor achievement by non-EL groups as well, and have a set of characteristics associated with poor school performance such as high student–teacher ratios, overcrowding, and many students living in poverty. The report found that when EL students are not isolated in these low-achieving schools, their gap in test score results is considerably narrower.

The Pew Hispanic Center report also found that in each of the five states, about 90% of the ELs who took the state assessments were educated in public schools in which EL students make up either a majority or a substantial minority of the student populations. In these EL-heavy schools, ELs have limited access to native English input and must learn English from other learners. Many of these students end up being "ESL-lifers," students who stay in ESL classes year after year, without ever reaching the level of proficiency in English that is necessary to exit ESL services and be mainstreamed into English-only instruction (Valdés, 2001). What schools need to do is find ways to end the isolation of immigrant students and offer courses that are designed to develop their academic English. (We shall address the topic of academic English in Chapter 7.) In sum, there are no quick, easy solutions to the problem of poor academic performance of language minority students. The challenges of educating millions of ELs in the U.S. remain *with* or *without* bilingual education (Valdés, 2001).

SUMMARY

In this chapter, I showed that bilingualism is an ordinary fact of life for the vast majority of the world's people. We saw that bilingualism is not only common in many of the historically multilingual societies of Asia and Africa, but also in the so-called "monolingual" countries where significant numbers of bilingual individuals and communities can be found. I presented five prevalent myths about bilingualism and the research evidence and facts that disprove them. Although there are more bilingual than monolingual people in the world, we saw that bilingualism is often treated as a special case and a deviation from a monolingual norm.

This monolingual view is clearly seen in how bilinguals are defined—many people think that a bilingual is two monolinguals put together in one person. But we saw that a bilingual is rarely completely fluent in two languages. Most bilinguals have different proficiencies in two languages because they learn the two languages under different circumstances and use them with different people in a variety of situations. Thus, rather than use the monolingual speaker as a yardstick against which to measure a bilingual's proficiency in each language, one should consider a bilingual as a fully competent speaker who has developed adequate competences in the two languages for his/her particular communicative needs.

The second myth was the belief that immigrants are staying in ghettos and not learning English. However, the fact is that immigrants are lining up to get into English classes that fill up all too quickly. Many immigrants are losing their mother tongues very rapidly, becoming monolingual in English in just two or three generations.

We also saw that contrary to a popular assumption that earlier is better when it comes to learning a second language, research evidence for a critical period for second language acquisition is mixed. While some studies suggest that children have an edge over adults in learning a second language, many others conclude that older learners do better. There is currently no consensus among researchers as to a specific age beyond which it becomes difficult or impossible to learn a second language to the same degree as native speakers of that language. Rather, given adequate time, effective instruction, support, and motivation, adults and older learners are quite capable of becoming bilingual. While age is not a crucial factor in second language acquisition in general, we saw that for language minority children, an earlier exposure to the societal language prevents them from establishing a firm foundation in their native languages, often resulting in subtractive bilingualism.

The fourth myth was that immigrant parents should speak in the societal language with their children to help them succeed academically. Linguistic minority parents are frequently advised by teachers, doctors, and speech therapists to stop speaking the native language at home so as not to confuse children with input from two languages. However, the view that bilingual input confuses children is not supported by empirical sociolinguistic evidence. In many multilingual societies, children grow up with two or more languages with no negative consequences to their cognitive development. Furthermore, parents are by far the most significant source of native language input for language minority children—if parents do not speak the home language to children, the children cannot normally learn it elsewhere. Significant costs are incurred when parents and children cannot communicate due to a language barrier. Therefore, parents should be encouraged to interact with their children in the language they command.

Finally, we saw that bilingual education is often wrongly blamed for the poor academic performance of language minority children. Contrary to the popular assumption that bilingual education leads to school failure of language minority students by preventing them from learning English, we found that most immigrant children in fact never receive bilingual education. The vast majority of language minority students in the U.S. are placed in monolingual education programs and are expected to be mainstreamed quickly. We saw that immigrant students tend to be concentrated in low-performing schools in poor neighborhoods. In these schools, not only do ELs perform poorly, but mainstream English-speaking populations also do badly. When immigrant students are not isolated in these low-achieving schools, they tend to perform considerably better. Thus, rather than blame language minority children's poor achievement on bilingual education, what schools need to do is to find ways to end the isolation of ELs and offer courses that are designed to teach them academic English.

The points discussed in this chapter will be explored further in the rest of the book. But first, in the next chapter, I turn to a description of how bilingualism is manifested in schools and society in a globalized world.

FURTHER READING

- Grosjean, F. (2010). *Bilingual: Life and reality.* Cambridge, MA: Harvard University Press.—François Grosjean, a leading authority in bilingualism, demystifies bilingualism in this highly readable book.
- Valdés, G. (2001). *Learning and not learning English: Latino students in American schools.* New York: Teachers College Press.—Focusing on the lives of four Mexican children in an American middle school, Guadalupe Valdés examines both the policy and the instructional dilemmas surrounding language minority education in this compelling book.

STUDY QUESTIONS AND ACTIVITIES

1. Do you consider yourself a bilingual? If so, what criteria did you use to determine that? How would you rate the level of your speaking, listening, reading, and writing skills in each language? When do you use each language and with whom? Has your bilingual ability changed over time? If you do not consider yourself a bilingual, have you studied another language? How would you rate your proficiency in that language? What would it take for you to consider yourself bilingual in that language?
2. Why is it rare for bilinguals to be equally or completely fluent in two languages? Where does the notion of the "ideal" or "full" bilingual come from and how does it affect our perception of bilingual individuals? Is it fair to

compare a bilingual's proficiency in either language to that of monolinguals? Why or why not?

3. What is a deficit-based view of bilingualism? Why should educators be wary of labeling someone as "semilingual"?

4. Why is it harmful to advise language minority parents to speak the societal language with their children at home? What costs are incurred when parents and children cannot talk to each other due to a language barrier?

5. Some people claim that bilingual education results in academic failure for immigrant students. Do you agree? What non-linguistic factors might contribute to the poor academic performance of language minority children?

2

Bilingualism in a Globalized World

As of now, English is, by all established criteria, still a *foreign* language in most of the countries of Latin America, but it is spreading like wildfire. This is so even in countries like Cuba which has had a difficult time in its relations with its mighty neighbor, the United States of America.

—Kanavillil Rajagopalan (2010: 175)

INTRODUCTION

In this chapter, I discuss how bilingualism is evidenced in schools and society in a globalized world. Technological advances of the last few decades have enabled great numbers of individuals and communities to come in contact with one another over great distances. Since this contact increasingly involves people communicating and accessing information across national and linguistic borders, the need for bilingualism and bilingual literacy has become greater than before. For bilingualism researchers and language professionals, globalization presents both exciting opportunities and new challenges. In this chapter I discuss some of these opportunities and challenges. We will see that while the forces of globalization have produced a thoroughly inter-connected world, the same forces are threatening the existence of local cultures, identities, and languages. We will also see that language is increasingly seen as a commodity, a cultural capital that is required for success in the new world order.

I will then describe the extent of the global spread of English as a lingua franca. No other language in human history has had the level of popularity and widespread usage that English has today. English is by far the most popular second language of choice and is a major driving force behind new occurrences of bilingualism in the world. It is used by more non-native speakers than native speakers, and is at the heart of an interconnected world. We will see what local varieties of English look like and how they interact with other languages with which they come into contact. We will then look at four global flows that have particular significance to our study of bilingualism in the globalized era: (1) transnational migration, (2) popular music, (3) advertising, and (4) the Internet.

OPPORTUNITIES AND CHALLENGES OF GLOBALIZATION

In his highly popular book, *The world is flat: A brief history of the twenty-first century*, Tom Friedman (2005) argues that extraordinary advances in modern technology have leveled the playing field for huge numbers of people in the world by providing unparalleled access to a global market and information network. Commercial installation of transoceanic fiber-optic cables has enabled people from distant corners of the globe to communicate with one another far more cheaply and easily than before. The Internet has made available information that was once controlled by small groups of people to billions of ordinary citizens. Anyone with Internet access can now search the entire world for new knowledge and be instantly updated on events as they unfold in different parts of the globe. In addition, air travel has given unprecedented mobility to millions of people to pursue dreams in faraway places, and container ships deliver an abundance of goods and products to every corner of the planet. The astounding ease with which people, ideas, and things move in many directions is a defining feature of a globalized world. As Appadurai (2001: 5) aptly observes, "This is a world of flows."

Many people foresee that the twenty-first century will be an online century and predominantly an English one (Nihalani, 2010). Market integration and flows of media and communication across national borders generate a robust demand for a lingua franca, and this demand is filled by a small number of languages, most notably English (Crystal, 2003). Currently, more than 80% of Internet communication is in only ten languages (see Table 2.1, p. 43). English is still the number one language on the Internet but it is followed closely by Chinese in terms of number of users. Crystal (2006) contends that the Internet is not only a technological revolution but also a social one that is fundamentally altering the way people communicate. He argues that Netspeak, or Internet language, is creating extraordinary opportunities for the expansion and enrichment of human communication.

Although globalization and the rise of the Internet offer the world's inhabitants unprecedented opportunities for creativity and collaboration, it also presents extraordinary challenges to local cultures, languages, and dialects. For example, thousands of languages in the world are threatened by the phenomenal rise of global English and other numerically powerful languages like

Chinese, Arabic, and Spanish (Nettle & Romaine, 2000; see also Chapter 3). It has been estimated that more than half of the world's 6,000 to 7,000 languages will disappear in the next century (Harrison, 2007, 2010). The world's small languages, many with a few thousand speakers or less, are quickly losing speakers as the younger generation see no value in learning and maintaining them. The situation is extremely dire for 473 of the world's 6,909 languages listed in the *Ethnologue* (Lewis, 2009) which are classified as "nearly extinct," a category reserved for languages for which "only a few elderly speakers are still living." Once the few remaining speakers pass away, these languages will forever disappear from the face of the earth barring any serious attempts to revitalize them.

OUT OF THE MOUTHS OF BILINGUALS 2.1

Preserving the Nipmuc Language

"When I was young, I didn't hear the language at all until, I think it was when I was around 10 or 11, when I started going to powwows. . . Oh, it was beautiful, I was just so amazed by it, and it sounded so beautiful to me, and I wish I could talk like that. Of course I had no idea what it meant when I heard it."

David White, a Nipmuc language teacher, interviewed in Rath (2009)

What is lost when a language dies? *The Economist* (2008, February 7) ran an obituary of Marie Smith, the last speaker of Eyak (a Native American language spoken in Alaska) who died on January 21, 2008 at the age of 89. The following is an excerpt from the obituary:

As the spoken language died, so did the stories of tricky Creator-Raven and the magical loon, of giant animals and tiny homunculi with fish-spears no bigger than a matchstick. People forgot why "hat" was the same word as "hammer," or why the word for a leaf, *kultahl*, was also the word for a feather, as though deciduous trees and birds shared one organic life. They lost the sense that lumped apples, beads and pills together as round, foreign, possibly deceiving things. They neglected the taboo that kept fish and animals separate, and would not let fish-skin and animal hide be sewn in the same coat; and they could not remember exactly why they built little wooden huts over gravestones, as if to give more comfortable shelter to the dead.

As this excerpt poignantly illustrates, when a language dies, the culture and knowledge contained in it die as well (Harrison, 2007). The imminent extinction of the majority of the world's languages is a tragic loss to humanity because the stories of their speakers and their ways of living, thinking, and being will vanish forever. Fortunately for Eyak, its structural characteristics are compiled in a grammar and a dictionary by a linguist who took interest in the language and worked with Ms. Smith. When her last surviving older sister died in the 1990s, Ms. Smith became an activist campaigning to preserve the Eyak culture and language. But since she no longer had anyone to speak the language with, "Eyak became a language for talking to herself, or to God."

As with Ms. Smith and Eyak, language is intricately linked to people's sense of who they are. This is why language preservation often goes hand in hand with efforts to assert local identities. However, even the notion that language is a marker of ethnic identities is being challenged by globalization. Heller (2003) contends that in Francophone Canada, there is a shift from understanding language as being primarily an inalienable marker of ethnic and national identity, to understanding language as a marketable "commodity," a measurable skill. Language is increasingly considered as a skill to be acquired by people who are wise enough to invest in it, and those without this skill fear being left behind in a "flat world" (Friedman, 2005). This is why parents the world over are eager to give their children the gift of a **foreign language**. More and more parents are investing in English programs and tutors for their children, and the more affluent ones are also sending their school-age children abroad to be educated in English-speaking countries (more on this later in this chapter). These families make significant personal and financial sacrifices in order to enable their children to acquire what they believe will significantly improve their future chances of success.

In a world where language is treated as a desirable commodity, educational institutions play a significant role in increasing the rate of bilingualism. But even in the field of language education, conventional views of language learning and literacy are challenged by globalization. For example, the often-made distinction between English as a Second Language (ESL) and **English as a Foreign Language (EFL)** is blurred for an increasing number of **transnational migrants** who cross and re-cross national boundaries.

As Kanno (2003) shows in her study, a Japanese adolescent in North America returning to Japan goes from learning English in a classroom with immigrant children, to learning English in Japan with Japanese students who have little opportunity to hear and practice the language outside the classroom. His status changes from being an ethnic/linguistic minority in North America to an ethnic/linguistic majority in Japan. As a linguistic minority, he was expected to learn the majority language and his Japanese language skills were not considered very important. In Japan where English skills are a highly prized asset, he may enjoy an elevated social status as a Japanese-English bilingual but may also feel that his knowledge of Japanese language and culture is constantly questioned by people who may think he is not fully Japanese. As he moves from one country to another, he must continually negotiate his hybrid identities as a bilingual and bicultural person (Kanno, 2003). For language teachers and policymakers then, understanding this reality is crucial in their work with students and families in a globalized world.

Now I will turn to a discussion of English as a lingua franca.

GLOBAL SPREAD OF ENGLISH

Graddol (2006) predicts that in 10 to 15 years, there will be as many as two billion people across the world learning English. He also predicts that, with the language spreading at a breathtaking speed, English will soon cease to be a foreign language in many of these countries and start to develop its own local characteristics. What does it mean for English to develop its own local characteristics? Localized varieties of English result from English coming in contact with other languages, and differ from British or American English in phonology, vocabulary, syntax, and usage. For instance, according to Gargesh (2006), the following are some features of English spoken in India:

Phonology: The vowels /e/ and /o/ as in *face* and *goat* are pronounced as monophthongs, not diphthongs, as in standard British or American English.

Vocabulary: Indian English uses innovations such as *finger chips* 'French fries', *full-boiled* and *half-boiled eggs* 'hard-' and 'soft-boiled eggs'.

Syntax: In Indian English, there is often a lack of subject–auxiliary inversion in questions, e.g., *What you would like to read? When you would like to come?* Also widespread is the use of *isn't it* or *no* in tag questions, e.g., *You went there yesterday, isn't it? You went there yesterday, no?*

Usage: When you want to know anything you don't say: "Please let me know." Instead you say: *Please enlighten us.* Politeness in Indian society is highly conventionalized and is part of the conversational style of Indian English. The strategy of maintaining a positive face can be seen in the example: *What is your good name, please?* A similar strategy is exhibited through insistence when offering: *Take only this much, just this much* and *Have some more, have some more.* A request in American English such as *Won't you have more?* would sound negative.

Research on the different varieties of English spoken in the world has led to various typologies based on the users and uses of the language. One such typology, originally proposed by Kachru (1985), divides the world's English speakers into three groups known as the "three concentric circles of English" (see Figure 2.1). The "Inner Circle" represents countries where English is spoken as a native language by the majority of the population (e.g., U.K., U.S., New Zealand, Australia, Canada).

The "Outer Circle" represents countries where English is spoken as a second or additional language by multilingual speakers who use a localized variety of English (e.g., Indian English, Singaporean English) along with other languages found in those countries. In most of the Outer Circle countries, English has official status in the government's language policies. For example, English is recognized as a national language along with Hindi in multilingual India where more than 200 languages are spoken. In Singapore, English is one of four **official languages** (the other three are Mandarin Chinese, Malay, and Tamil). In many countries in post-colonial Africa, English is recognized as one of the state languages and plays an important role in day-to-day social interaction (e.g., Nigeria, Zambia).

Finally, the rest of the world constitutes the "Expanding Circle" where English is learned as a foreign language (e.g., China, Russia, Brazil, Cuban). English has no official status in these countries and does not normally figure in the day-to-day interaction of the populace. However, it is increasingly valued as a medium of international communication and taught in schools.

FIGURE 2.1 The Three Concentric Circles of English

Source: Adapted from Kachru, 1985

A significant portion of the literature on **World Englishes** deals with the politics of colonization and the linguistic ecology of the former British colonies in the Outer Circle. As Omoniyi & Saxena (2010) argue, those accounts of the spread of English fall within a realm of "sociolinguistics of colonization" and represent disparities in power between the colonizers and the colonized. According to this approach, different varieties of English can be placed in a hierarchy with the native speaker Inner Circle varieties at the top. The Inner Circle varieties set standards for usage of English which are adopted to varying degrees by speakers in the Outer and Expanding Circles.

In contrast, "sociolinguistics of globalization" has prompted scholars of World Englishes to examine how globalization operates within a wider, more complex network of relationships of power and capital distribution among the three circles (Omoniyi & Saxena, 2010). This latter approach recognizes the multi-directional contributions of each circle to the other circles. For example, Bhatia & Ritchie (2006a) propose a model in which the three circles interact with one another through language mixing (Figure 2.2). This model takes into account the crisscrossing flow of linguistic contributions among the three circles without elevating the status of one over the others.

Bhatia & Ritchie's (2006a) model captures the fact that Expanding Circle speakers import Inner Circle English, nativize it (i.e., repackage it using their local language phonology and syntax), and export the resulting product back to Inner and Outer Circle countries. For instance, the word *karaoke*, which represents a mixture of Japanese and English, is made up of two parts: *kara*, a Japanese word meaning "empty," and *oke*, a truncation of the Japanese adaptation of the English word "orchestra" (**okesutora**). This Japanese adaptation of

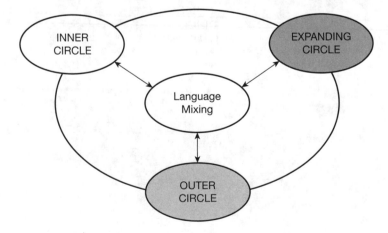

FIGURE 2.2 Global English Typology

Source: Bhatia & Ritchie, 2006a. Reproduced by permission of Blackwell Publishing

English has in turn been appropriated by Inner Circle English speakers. For example, many Americans apply American English phonology to Japanese [karaoke] and pronounce it as [kerioki]. Product names like *Pokémon*, highly popular with children in many countries, provide another example. *Pokémon* (literally "pocket monster") is a contraction of Japanese phonological adaptations of two English words, pocket (**poke**tto) and monster (**mon**suta). Both *karaoke* and *Pokémon* have become well established in Inner and Outer Circle vocabulary.

As we will see in the following sections, Bhatia & Ritchie's (2006a) model of mutually feeding relationships among the three circles (Figure 2.2) is a useful tool in our understanding of the linguistic and cultural flows of the globalized world.

GLOBAL FLOW #1: TRANSNATIONAL MIGRATION— PEOPLE IN SEARCH OF A BETTER LIFE

One of the prominent characteristics of globalization is significant shifts in population made possible through advances in transportation technology. More and more people are moving from one country to another in search of a better life. The International Organization for Migration (2011) reports that the total number of international migrants has increased over the last ten years from an estimated 150 million in 2000 to 214 million persons (3.1% of the world population) today. This figure includes immigrants, migrant workers, refugees, asylum seekers, business and expatriate workers, international students, and even tourists. At present, there are 42.3 million refugees and internationally displaced persons (International Organization for Migration, 2011).

A large body of literature discusses issues related to language shift and maintenance among immigrants and their progeny as they settle down in a new country (e.g., Haugen, 1989; Shin, 2005; Taft & Cahill, 1989; Young & Tran, 1999). While traditional immigrants—those who leave their country of origin for a new country and stay there—are still a significant part of movement of people around the world, international migration in the globalized era is increasingly characterized by transnationalism, or the ability to go back and forth to the country of origin (García, 2009; Lo & Park, 2012; Yi, 2009). Transnational migrants present a different challenge to bilingualism scholars because, unlike traditional immigrants who more or less adopt the language of their host country and lose their native languages in the process, transmigrants' back-and-forth movement between countries requires the development and maintenance of both languages.

Transmigration is motivated by a variety of economic, political, and educational factors in both the host and home countries. To illustrate a recent case,

I reproduce below a vignette from a research proposal written by one of my M.A. TESOL students, Angela Lima:

> Earlier this year at our friends' son's birthday party, eight-year-old Luzmaría sat down next to me and said in perfect American English, "Guess what, Angela, we're going back to Guatemala before Christmas!" I thought to myself, "back?" because I knew she had never been there. I asked in reply, "Is your dad taking you for Christmas to see your family?" Luzmaría answered, "Yeah, and with my mom, and we're staying there forever."

Angela notes that Luzmaría was born in the U.S. to a Guatemalan father who is a legal permanent resident of the U.S. and a Guatemalan mother who has no legal status. The couple has made their home in the U.S. for more than 15 years. Recently, Luzmaría's father's business did poorly and the family lost their house in Maryland. The current recession in the U.S. and rising anti-immigrant sentiments are driving Luzmaría's family as well as multitudes of others in similar situations to return to their country of origin. This is forcing the children, many of whom are U.S. citizens and are growing up in the U.S., to "go back" to countries in which they have never lived or have only spent minimal time as youngsters. These children are educated in U.S. schools, identify culturally with Americans in English, and have varying degrees of proficiencies in their parents' native language. Once in Guatemala, however, Luzmaría will be expected to interact with others in Spanish, and may or may not receive help with accessing the school curriculum in Spanish. It is not clear whether there will be a Spanish as a Second Language class at her school and how understanding her teachers and peers will be of her insufficient command of Spanish.

Many returnees experience difficulties as they adjust to their new surroundings. King & Ganuza (2005) investigated the language and educational situation of Chilean transmigrants in Sweden whose families fled tyranny in Chile under Pinochet from the early 1970s to the late 1980s. They show that transmigration in both directions result in social and educational difficulties for the adolescents. In Sweden, Chileans tended to be assigned to apartments in segregated suburbs with other immigrant groups, and thus most have had limited contact with mainstream Swedish society. Parents who return to Chile typically struggle with unemployment, low wages, and insufficient housing, as well as discrimination for being *retornados*.

Children generally do not receive any special support from the school system, and struggle with feelings of insecurity and fear. King & Ganuza (2005) note that the educational integration of *retornados* is further complicated by the fact that they have twice been linguistic minorities forced to learn a language under stressful conditions (first learning Swedish during exile, and then re-learning or improving their Spanish upon return to Chile). Similarly, the children of Mexican transnationals in Martinez-León & Smith's (2003) study face a number of challenges including a shortage of linguistically qualified teachers, lack of materials, and pejorative attitudes toward the language varieties spoken by *retornados*.

Orellana, Thorne, Chee, & Lam (2001) investigated three different transnational communities in California: (1) Mexican and Central American migrants in Los Angeles, (2) Yemeni families who live in Oakland, and (3) "parachute kids" who have migrated from Korea to attend school in the U.S. The authors report that chain migration—which involves one or more adults migrating first and gradually sending for other family members—is a common pattern for Mexican and Central American migrants in Los Angeles, and for Yemeni migrants in Oakland. These families often make arrangements for children to stay with relatives in the home country to avoid the uncertainties of life during the transition. Orellana et al. (2001) note that even when the children settle in the U.S., the Central American, Mexican, and Yemeni parents keep open the option of "sending their children back home" in order to avoid problems, especially during the teenage years. All of the families maintain active ties to their homeland by traveling back and forth, and stay connected with family and friends by communicating via phone or email and sending and receiving video images.

Aside from family migration, individuals who have been internationally adopted are going back and forth between their birth country and adoptive country. In her study of transnational adoptees, Volkman (2005) notes that what used to be a unidirectional movement of children from poor countries to more affluent ones has now become a crisscrossing flow of adoptees revisiting the countries of their birth. Volkman (2005: 2) contends that these returning adoptees are striking instances of larger transnational processes and that

> travel in its many forms, the rise of the internet and the global cyber-spatial communities it produces, and efforts to create international legal frameworks all produce new forms of family and new articulations of identity that may not coincide easily with notions of the nation.

Educational Migration

In recent years, an increasing number of families have gone abroad to help their school-aged children gain international education credentials and to provide them with an opportunity to learn English as a global language. This phenomenon, called "early study abroad," has been very popular among middle-class Asian families who use the overseas experiences and linguistic capital gained through transnational migration for their class maintenance and upward mobility (Park & Bae, 2009).

One of the transmigrant groups in Orellana et al.'s (2001) study is the Korean "parachute kids," school-age children who continue to reside in the U.S. either on their own or with a "homestay" family following their parents' return to Korea. The parents migrate chiefly for the purpose of educating their children in the U.S. and return to Korea as soon as the children are placed in their new living arrangement (the name "parachute kids" comes from the way the parents seem to fly over the destination and drop off the children without actually landing). These families hope to use the knowledge and networks their children acquire in the U.S. as entry into the country and to broaden their economic fields of operation (Orellana et al., 2001). In addition, as Orellana et al. (2001) point out, having children attend school in the U.S. also increases the children's chances of studying at U.S. colleges and universities and avoids the intense competition for a limited number of slots in top Korean universities.

Whereas "parachute kids" usually live and study in the host country without their parents, some children migrate and live with their mothers in the host country while the fathers stay behind. Huang & Yeoh (2005) show that educational migration of children from China to Singapore takes the form of school-age children (between the ages of seven and 18) accompanied by their mothers during part or all of the course of their study. These mothers—popularly referred to in Singapore as "study mothers"—not only have to negotiate their transnational family situations having left spouse and other family members behind, but also must maintain their lives as *de facto* single parents in Singapore. A similar pattern is found with the Korean "*kirogi*" mothers who must negotiate their new role as sole parents overseas (Lee, 2010). (*Kirogi*, which means "wild goose" in Korean, refers to the bird's migratory behavior.) Education in English and the accumulation of cultural capital are key factors which drive these families to endure prolonged separation (Waters, 2005).

As transnational families operate in multilingual spaces, their experiences are influenced by competing language ideologies. In their study of Korean early study abroad students and families in Singapore, Park & Bae (2009) showed that in Korean society, dominant ideologies of English co-exist with new ideologies that attribute great capital value to Chinese. Global English is on the rise, but so is global Chinese, and an increasing number of Koreans consider Singapore's multilingual environment and policies to be conducive to developing both their English and Chinese skills. In addition, while most Korean families regard Inner Circle varieties of English (e.g., American English) to be most desirable, their being situated in Singapore led them to also value local varieties of English (Singlish, or Singaporean English) in their interactions with Singaporeans. For example, Park & Bae note that one of the students they interviewed, Jiyeong, who was attending a local primary school, expressed that not using Singlish in interaction with local students carried significant risks in her interaction with Singaporeans (2009: 374):

Bae: Do you feel Singlish affects you a lot?

Jiyeong: When I speak with local kids I use Singlish. And when I speak with an American I use an American pronunciation.

Bae: So you're almost like a Singaporean, then?

Jiyeong: When I use an American pronunciation, the kids sometimes don't understand me and it's a bit awkward. If I try to sound elaborate [*baleum gullimyeon* (lit: "roll one's tongue")] they think I'm being pretentious.

Bae: So you use Singlish with Singaporean kids. Don't you get confused?

Jiyeong: At first I used to speak American style. But now I use Singlish, and I taught them some Korean so now they like it.

As seen in this excerpt, transnationals' language practices are shaped by both global ideologies and local circumstances. That Jiyeong uses a localized variety of English to interact with Singaporeans (and even teaches them Korean) while holding on to dominant ideologies of Inner Circle English is a good example of the kind of linguistic and cultural adaptations made by transnationals as they negotiate their multilingual identities.

Next, I turn to a discussion of bilingualism in popular music.

GLOBAL FLOW #2: POPULAR MUSIC— CULTURAL HYBRIDIZATION

In a globalized world, popular music flows easily across national boundaries. Because English is the dominant language in popular music today, music is an aspect of the mass media that provides motivation for learning English (McKay & Bokhorst-Heng, 2008). According to Pennycook (2007), popular music is a clear illustration of *transcultural flows* where global and local languages mix to create new language and art forms. He argues that English is "a translocal language, a language of fluidity and fixity that moves across, while becoming embedded in, the materiality of localities and social relations" (2007: 6). In many countries, exposure to popular songs in English has led to plenty of language mixing in locally produced pop music.

As Kachru (2006) points out in her study of Hindi popular songs, such mixing can serve various purposes, such as providing social commentary or achieving satirical and humorous effects. For example, in the following line from a song analyzed by Kachru (2006: 230), the word *funda* can represent both an abbreviation of the English word *fundamental* and the anglicized pronunciation of the Hindi word *phandā*, "a noose, lasso, knot":

Pyaar Ka *Funda Hit* Huaa Apnaa Chakkar *Fit* Huaa
("The lasso of love found its mark self's plan worked")

Kachru (2006) explains that in addition to serving the needs of rhyme and connecting the word *funda* with the fundamental philosophy of life that the song mentions, using *funda* in the song also exploits this double meaning of the word to add to the satirical effect. She argues that this type of bilingual word play resonates with the listeners because there are many expressions in both Hindi and English that compare being in love with being caught in a net or snare.

Lee's (2004) study of South Korean popular music, or K-Pop, shows that **code-mixing** is used by Korean youth to assert their identity, challenge dominant representations of authority, and reject older generations' conservatism. She argues that while the English used in K-Pop represents self-indulgent attitudes, Korean lyrics within the same song represent more reserved and conformist views. She contends that mixing the two languages symbolizes Korean youth's attempt to define their identities in a world characterized by tension between global and local ideologies. Similarly, Moody (2006) asserts that the use of English in Japanese popular music, or J-Pop, challenges and redefines Japanese ethnolinguistic identity. He argues that the J-Pop mode of mixing Japanese and Western forms and content blurs ethnic identity boundaries and challenges the belief that Japanese is unique.

While mixing English with local languages is a prominent feature of popular music in many countries, globalization is not only about the transmission of Western cultures and ideals to non-Western countries. In other words, it is not a one-way flow. For example, Iwabuchi (2002) contends that contrary to the popular belief that globalization is the worldwide spread of Western—particularly American—popular culture, Japan's "localizing" strategy of repackaging Western popular culture for Asian consumption has resulted in a broad adoption of Japanese popular culture throughout East and Southeast Asia. Similarly, Ryoo (2009) points out that South Korea is now a brisk exporter of music, TV programming, and films to the Asia-Pacific region. He explains that K-Pop, which is itself heavily influenced by Western culture and English mixing, is preferred over Western music throughout Asia because it contains Asian values and sentiments while being just Westernized enough to mediate information from the West to Asia.

This pan-Asian movement is now spreading to the U.S., which Iwabuchi (2002) terms as "trans-Asian cultural traffic." Korean Americans and Korean students studying abroad in the U.S. play an important role in spreading Korean pop culture in the U.S. (Nakagawa, 2010). For some Korean Americans, consumption of Korean pop culture is motivated by their search for an identity and a sense of belonging as an ethnic and racial minority in the U.S. The physical and psychological distance between Korea and Korean Americans is greatly reduced by the widespread use of the Internet, satellite, and cable technologies that enable pop culture to flow easily in both directions (Nakagawa,

2010). What we witness then is a two-way traffic of transcultural flows of Korean artists importing and localizing American pop music, which is then exported back to the U.S.

GLOBAL FLOW #3: ADVERTISING—SELLING GOODS AND SERVICES IN MORE THAN ONE LANGUAGE

Bilingualism sells. Throughout the world, marketers promote products and services through bilingual advertisements to target customers who are bilingual. "Glocalization" is a term used to refer to the modification of a global product to meet local needs and norms, and make it more marketable in various parts of the globe (Robertson, 1995). Representing both a hybrid entity and tension between the global and the local, glocalization is a major theme in bilingual advertising. Advertisers that speak to the lived experiences of an increasing number of bilingual people in the world have a better chance of selling their products than those who ignore this reality. The Latino population in the U.S. presents a great case study for bilingual advertising (García, 2008b). In the U.S., Latinos account for about 15% of the total population (44 million) and are the fastest-growing segment of the population. The Latino group as a whole has a spending power of $1.2 trillion and marketers are increasingly targeting the nearly four million Latinos who have annual incomes over $75,000 (Lafuente, 2008; see also Figure 2.3).

Advertisers are keen to take advantage of the bilingual and bicultural backgrounds of the U.S. Hispanic market. For example, in 2006, Toyota Motor Corporation launched a bilingual Spanish-English TV commercial during Super Bowl. In the 30-second ad, a Latino father drives his young son in their hybrid Toyota Camry. The boy asks his father, "Papá, why do we have a hybrid?" to which the father responds, "For your future . . . . It uses both [gas and electric power]," explaining the car's hybrid technology. The child then observes aloud, "Like you, with English and Spanish!" and the father chuckles and agrees, "Sí." By drawing a parallel between the hybrid use of Spanish and English by U.S. Latinos and the car's hybrid technology, this commercial is a nod in recognition of the purchasing power of this increasingly affluent segment of the U.S. population. Toyota decided to launch this bilingual ad because it is the most popular automaker among U.S. Hispanics and the Super Bowl is highly popular with Hispanic viewers—a quarter of all Latinos over the age of 18 watch the game (Puente, 2006).

In addition to TV advertising, marketers are increasingly tapping the Internet to appeal to the bilingual/bicultural lifestyle of a growing number of young Latinos with programs such as Dr. Pepper's Vida23 ("Life23"—23 refers to the number of flavors in Dr. Pepper) and 7UP's Sevenisima. Vida23 campaign centers around songs performed by musician CuCu Diamantes in

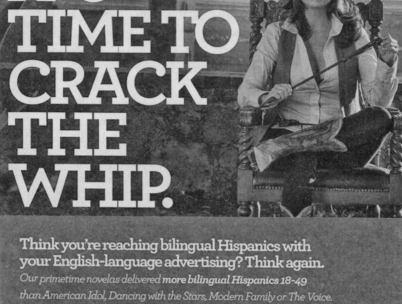

FIGURE 2.3 Univision's Call for Businesses to Advertise Bilingually in Spanish and English. Reproduced by permission of Univision.

Spanish and English, and users can download the songs and create their own mixes on the company's website (http://www.drpepper.com/promotions/vida23/).

Marketers also use traditional print advertising to reach Latino audiences in Spanish and English. Koslow, Shamdasani, & Touchstone (1994) examined 367 Hispanic consumers' responses to varying degrees of Spanish language usage in print advertising. They found that Spanish language advertising increased Hispanic consumers' perception of advertiser sensitivity to their culture, which enhanced their affect toward the advertisements. However, they found that advertising exclusively in Spanish had the adverse effect of intensifying the participants' insecurities about language usage. Many U.S. Latinos see themselves as both Latino and American, and the use of Spanish-only advertisements are seen as an inability of the marketers to recognize their multiple identities. The authors conclude that advertisers targeting U.S. Latinos should use some mixture of Spanish and English.

Although an important function of bilingual advertising is reaching people who speak two or more languages, bilingual advertising in many countries is directed at those who do not have a working knowledge of one of the targeted languages. For example, people who have little or no proficiency in English may purchase a product that is advertised in English because they equate English with Western values and high quality. Sprinkling an ad with a few words from a foreign language often gives the product a feel of sophistication and prestige. The mere presence of a different language (an unfamiliar script definitely adds to the coolness factor) acts as a hook to lure the viewer to examine the ad more carefully.

Baumgardner (2006) provides numerous examples of the use of English as an attention-getting device in Mexican newspaper and magazine advertising. For example, he shows English juxtaposed with Spanish in a newspaper advertisement by Hidromax, seller of swimming pools and spas, which uses the English phrase, "The pools of the future!" followed by the Spanish phrase, ". . . algo nuevo bajo el sol" (. . . something new under the sun). He states that code-mixed advertisements like this that incorporate an English word, phrase, or sentence in otherwise Spanish text abound in Mexican print media.

Baumgardner points out that English words used in such advertisements are often already established **borrowings** in Mexican Spanish. For example, Japanese carmaker Nissan uses the common compound "full-size" in its ad for Nissan Titan. *Full-size*, like many other English borrowings associated with the car (*cab forward, camper, custom, hot rod, overdrive*), is an established English borrowing recognized by many Mexicans without English proficiency. However, many other ads use English words that are not established borrowings. For example, he shows that an ad for Pure shampoo is in Spanish except for the following: ". . . el único shampoo 2 en 1 que no causa *build-up*" (the only two-in-one shampoo that does not cause build-up). *Build-up* is not an established English borrowing in Mexican Spanish. Baumgardner observes that Mexicans perceive products using English slogans, labels, and names as more reliable or of superior quality regardless of their literal comprehension.

Similar conclusions are drawn from studies of bilingual advertising in other countries. In her analysis of print ads, product labels, and TV commercials in

Russia, Ustinova (2006) shows that language mixing is a dominant feature in Russian advertisements. She states that the strategy of Russian TV commercials is predominantly a "think and act both global and local at the same time" approach, and that more than 75% of the commercials she analyzed integrate two or more languages with Russian-English mixing being the most common. She reports that there is a preference for using English names and the Roman script for a variety of products, such as electronic appliances, cars, personal care, laundry, and household products. She explains that there is a broad perception among Russians that English signals novelty, prestige, and high quality products. Similarly, in a study of Korean advertising, Jamie Shinhee Lee (2006) shows that mixing English with Korean expresses modernity and globalization in contemporary South Korea. She contends that English mixing in South Korean TV commercials indicates younger generations' modern identities, whereas the absence of English signifies older generations' traditional identities.

Much of the English that is used in advertising in Expanding Circle countries is not based on Standard English used in Inner Circle countries. In fact, the Internet site, www.engrish.com, shows many examples of bad, mangled English found in product labels, restaurant menus, and store signs in countries like Japan, China, and Korea (see also Figures 2.4 and 2.5). As Dougill (2008: 21) points out, many of these are non-native user errors in functional English: "'No smrking' says one public notice in China. 'Please slip carefully', says another while yet another stipulates, 'No entrance to stranglers.'"

FIGURE 2.4 "Want Some Dilicious Thai Food?"

FIGURE 2.5 A Warning Sign on a Norwegian Car Ferry

The point is not whether the uses represent accurate or standard language. In fact, linguistic accuracy is irrelevant to the consumers of these products. The mere use of a foreign language in speech and writing signals stylishness, glamour, and novelty. As Baumgardner (2006: 257) puts it, the use of English in a shop name "adds a certain *je ne sais quoi* to the shop's aura even when clients do not necessarily understand the meaning of the name." Bhatia & Ritchie (2006a) observe that print advertising in Japan exhibits a strong tendency to mix Japanese with foreign languages, particularly with English. Since the incidence of bilingualism with English is very low even among the youth, the message of the English text is often incomprehensible. In fact, Dougill (2008: 19) observes that English is never even read. He argues that it is purely decorative:

> The peculiarities of Japanese English (called Janglish or Engrish by some) continue to adorn the country's buildings, goods, and items of clothing. 'Funny bunny cute life,' says a piece of writing paper. "No human, go ape," shouts a carrier bag. "Please look at my weather cock," requests a pencil case. "Quench your thirst with perspiration," suggests a drink can. "I hope to play along with the heartiest gadgetry manifesting my destiny," claims a pompous piece of stereo equipment . . . English is the gateway

to dreams and faraway places. In a word, it's *chic*. As a result, newly built shops boast "Since 2007," noticeboards say "Recycle yourself," and bullet trains have "Ambitious Japan" written on them. The look is the thing.

GLOBAL FLOW #4: THE INTERNET— THE GREAT FLATTENING FORCE

As perhaps the greatest flattening force in a globalized world, the Internet has dramatically increased people's contact with speakers of other languages. As García (2009: 29) explains, human communication in the twenty-first century is characterized by discourses that function simultaneously in space and time:

> What is different today from the ways in which people used language in the nineteenth and twentieth century is that we can simultaneously and collaboratively engage in many different language practices at the same time, as happens in electronic instant messaging and chatting. And in so doing, there is a measure of "agency" that did not exist prior to the technological revolution. That is, speakers are now free to choose a broader range of language practices than those offered by the immediate community and the school; and they can use them in ways that are not reflected in more institutionalized language practices of schools and official publications.

In today's multilingual, global world, people are communicating on the Internet not only in its established lingua franca, English, but also in a multitude of other languages (Danet & Herring, 2007). Since the Internet began expanding globally in the 1990s, the number of non-English-speaking users has grown to 1,430 million, or roughly three-quarters of all Internet users (Miniwatts Marketing Group, 2010). Although English continues to be used most often on the web (27% of total Internet use in the world in 2010, according to Miniwatts Marketing Group), Chinese follows closely behind (23% of total worldwide Internet use in 2010). Table 2.1 displays the top ten languages used on the web in terms of number of users.

As can be seen in Table 2.1, between 2000 and 2010, the greatest language growth on the Internet was experienced by Arabic (2,501%), followed by Russian (1,826%), Chinese (1,277%), Portuguese (990%), and Spanish (743%). English saw only a 281% growth in the last decade (Miniwatts Marketing Group, 2010). What is striking about this table is that with just ten languages, 82% of the two billion Internet users in the world can be reached. We should note however that although Table 2.1 gives some idea of the size of the world's biggest languages and Internet penetration in various countries, it assigns only

TABLE 2.1

Internet World Users by Language

Language	Millions of Users	As Proportion of Total Internet Users	Growth from 2000 to 2010
English	537	27%	281%
Chinese	445	23%	1,277%
Spanish	153	8%	743%
Japanese	99	5%	111%
Portuguese	83	4%	990%
German	75	4%	173%
Arabic	65	3%	2,501%
French	60	3%	398%
Russian	60	3%	1,826%
Korean	39	2%	107%
Top 10 languages	*1,616*	*82%*	*421%*
Rest of the languages	*351*	*18%*	*589%*
World Total	*1,967*	*100%*	*445%*

Source: Adapted from Miniwatts Marketing Group, 2010

one language per person and thus does not capture the bi- or multilinguality of many people in the world.

Nor does Table 2.1 capture the prevalence of language mixing found in Internet texts. In his analysis of Chinese Internet Language (CIL) found in Bulletin Board Systems, chatrooms, Internet novels, personal emails, and Internet news and advertisements, Gao (2006) shows that English heavily influences CIL at the lexical, sentential, and discursive levels. For example, Gao (2006: 302) shows the following examples of Chinese-English mixing posted in online Bulletin Board Systems:

(a) X   gei   ren   yi   zhong   qinqie   de   feel
    X   give   person   one   type   cordial   Particle
    "X gives you a cordial feeling."

(b) Let's Show   *Huanying*   renhe   *dui*   *huaju*
                  welcome   any   concerning   stage play
    you xingqu   *de*   *tongxue!*
    have interest   Particle classmate
    "Let's put on a show! Any student who is interested in drama is welcome!"

Gao (2006) notes that even when there is no overt language mixing, the influence of English can be seen in Englishized Chinese words and grammar.

For example, he shows that many Chinese terms used in Internet communication have been borrowed from English, such as the word *mao* ("modem"), *Shichuang* ("Windows"), and *yimeier* ("email"). Furthermore, Chinese Internet users have modeled on English to create new expressions, such as the abbreviations *PP* ("beautiful," from *piaopiao* in Chinese), *jj* ("elder sister," from *jiejie* in Chinese), *DD* ("younger brother," from *didi* in Chinese), and *TMD* ("goddamn," from *tamadi* in Chinese).

At the level of syntax, Gao (2006) notes that Englishized Chinese sentences display English grammar. For example, in (c) below, the prepositional phrase *zai jia li* ("at home") was moved from before the verb phrase *chi wufan* ("to have lunch") to after it, reflecting an English word order. In (d), the time phrase *mingnian* ("next year") was moved from before the verb phrase *qu meiguo* ("to go to the US") to after it, also reflecting an English word order.

(c) Wo   chi   wufan   zai   jia   li
     I   eat   lunch   Preposition   home   inside
     "I'll have lunch at home."

(d) Wo   qu   Meiguo   mingnian
     I   go   US   following year
     "I am going to the US the next year."

Gao (2006) contends that Chinese Internet Language (CIL) has potential to change the ways in which Standard Chinese is spoken and written. Although not all components of CIL will turn into part of the conventionalized Chinese language, Gao (2006) argues that some electronic expressions are more likely to be accepted than others by Chinese speakers. This argument has significant implications for traditional concepts of language contact which results from colonization and emigration (Weinreich, 1963). In an era of globalization, theories of language contact and change must take into account communications in both physical and virtual spaces.

Code-mixing is a prominent feature of Internet language involving other languages. Warschauer, El Said, & Zohry (2002) found that while English is the dominant language used online among early Internet adopters in Egypt, a written form of Romanized Egyptian Arabic is also widely used in informal communication by this group. The authors argue that the participants' use of English does not signify an embrace of Western culture or an abandonment of Egyptian identity. On the contrary, the use of English reflects the participants' ability to absorb the best from a broad array of cultures and make it their own. The participants used their own local language, Egyptian Arabic, as a vehicle to express their most personal thoughts and feelings while they used English for more formal communication. This is a prime example of how Internet communication in the twenty-first century involves both the homogenizing tendencies of the global and the particularizing tendencies of the local (Robertson, 1995).

CONCLUSION

In this chapter, we have seen ways in which bilingualism is manifested in schools and society in a globalized world. We have seen that while globalization has leveled the playing field for great numbers of people by opening up access to international markets and information networks, its universalizing tendencies are also perceived to be harmful to local languages, cultures, and identities. We have seen that English is a powerful lingua franca whose popularity and widespread usage have been unmatched in human history. It is taught in schools in many countries around the world as a compulsory subject along with mathematics and literacy in the societal language, and is considered a basic skill without which one cannot cope in a flat world. It is by far the most popular language of the Internet, scientific journals, and popular culture, and is used to reach customers who are not even proficient in it. In short, English is a language that is both coveted and feared for its phenomenal and far-reaching impact in a global world.

However, English may not remain as the only global language of the twenty-first century. Lo Bianco (2009) points out that China's economic success has stimulated interest in learning Chinese throughout the world. Lo Bianco (2009: 294) adds that

> the expansion of Chinese as a foreign language is set to continue for a considerable period, highlighting a long-established pattern in which approximately a decade of economic and political success by a new power produces an elevated demand for study of its language.

As economic and political power shifts from the affluent countries in the West to China, India, and other developing countries, we are likely to see a rise in power of other lingua francas such as Chinese, Hindi, Arabic, and Spanish (García, 2008a; Graddol, 1997). Thus, instead of English solely dominating the global linguistic landscape, a small number of numerically powerful languages will increasingly share power and influence with English.

Furthermore, as power shifts from developed countries (the traditionally immigrant-receiving countries) to the emerging economies (the traditionally immigrant-sending countries), we are likely to see greater rates of return migration. Return migration is motivated not only by improved economic conditions back home but also by increased anti-immigrant measures adopted by host countries whose citizens feel threatened by forces of globalization and rising unemployment brought by a global recession.

In an article titled "Adios Arizona," *The Economist* (2010, November 27) reports that about 100,000 Hispanics, mostly of Mexican descent, have left Arizona for Mexico or for other states because of SB 1070, a controversial law passed in Arizona in April 2010 with the goal of identifying, prosecuting, and deporting illegal immigrants. This mass exodus translates to a lot of turmoil for the individuals and families involved, and for Arizona's economy. Anti-immigrant sentiments are on the rise in Europe as well. *The Economist* (2010, November 13) reports that many Turkish families in Germany (home to about 12 million immigrants) are seriously thinking about going back to Turkey. The reintegration of returnees and their children has all sorts of social and educational ramifications for receiving societies and is likely to be a salient issue in the coming decades.

Finally, I end this chapter with an excerpt from David Harrison's (2010) book, *The last speakers: The quest to save the world's most endangered languages*, which provides a glimmer of hope to those trying to preserve the world's dying languages. Harrison explains that the information revolution and the widespread availability of online technologies, often seen as a menace to linguistic and cultural diversity, are actually helping determined individuals and communities to promote endangered languages. He is encouraged to see people taking advantage of the very technology that has imperiled the existence of small languages to reclaim them:

> Although many small tongues will cease to be spoken and the knowledge they contain erased, the situation is not all dire. I see hope in a vibrant global movement to reclaim and enliven small tongues. A determined push-back against the steamroller of globalization is happening right now. I hear it in Mohawk-language kindergartens, Navajo pop music, and Ojibwe Facebook postings. These familiar media present new and powerful platforms for many of the world's smallest languages. Their speakers, also wired global citizens, cleverly apply new media to sustain ancient words. Rather than viewing technology and globalization as threats, they dive into the information sea, using it to buoy their languages to new heights.
>
> (Harrison, 2010: 17–18)

The globalized era is an exciting time for bilingualism scholars and language professionals. As Harrison aptly points out, rather than viewing technology and globalization as threats, the more we understand and work with them, the more everyone benefits.

FURTHER READING

- *English Today*—A journal published four times a year by Cambridge University Press, *English Today* features short, highly readable articles on the status of different varieties of English across the world.
- Crystal, D. (2006). *Language and the Internet* (2nd ed.). Cambridge: Cambridge University Press.—David Crystal, a renowned linguist and a leading authority on language, shows that discourse on the Internet enriches the existing varieties of English and extends our range of expression.
- Crystal, D. (2009). *Txtng: The gr8 db8*. Oxford: Oxford University Press. —This book by David Crystal looks at every aspect of the phenomenon of text-messaging and considers its impact on language, literacy, and society.

STUDY QUESTIONS AND ACTIVITIES

1. How has the Internet changed the way people communicate? What are some similarities and differences between online communication and face-to-face conversation? How are emotions (e.g., happiness, anger, annoyance, surprise, puzzlement) expressed face-to-face and online?
2. Interview someone who speaks a localized variety of English (e.g., Nigerian English, Indian English, Jamaican English). When did that person learn English and under what circumstances? What other language(s) or dialect(s) does he/she speak? Ask him/her to give you examples of how that variety differs from Standard English (e.g., American, Canadian, British, etc.) in terms of pronunciation, vocabulary, grammar, and usage.
3. Analyze a bilingual song or a poem. What is the song (or poem) about and how does language mixing serve the artist's purpose? Why do you think the writer decided to use two languages? What are the benefits and disadvantages of writing in two languages? Provide a transcript of the song (or poem) with translations in English.
4. What role do educators and language professionals (e.g., teachers, linguists, materials writers) play in preserving linguistic diversity in the world?

The Politics of Bilingualism

To say that a language is dead is like saying a person is dead. It could be no other way—for languages have no existence without people. A language dies when nobody speaks it anymore.

—David Crystal (2000: 1)

INTRODUCTION

In this chapter, we explore the politics behind people's language choices in a bilingual community. I will first describe the extent of language diversity in the world and factors that give rise to bilingual societies. Key sociolinguistic concepts such as **diglossia**, language shift, and **language maintenance** will be discussed, along with the different societal circumstances under which people become bilingual. I will look at a few of the world's multilingual countries and consider the ideological motivations behind national language policies. I will show how individual language choices are influenced by societal power structures and how bilingualism frequently serves as a precursor to monolingualism for language minority populations.

Societal bilingualism is often a result of contact between two or more language groups that do not have the same numerical, economic, and political power (Grosjean, 1982). Linguistic prestige is not so much a reflection of an inherent beauty in individual languages but rather the perceived power of those who speak them. Far from being simply a communicative device, language is a means to seize and hold onto power. In a world where large numbers of people must compete for access to limited resources, mastery of the societal language is considered a ticket to upward social mobility. As we will see in this chapter, people who are in positions of authority will try to maintain their status by using their language as a barrier to social advancement for others while those in weaker positions will try to break through that barrier by learning that language.

Set against powerful societal languages that symbolize the finer things in life, many minority languages are struggling to survive. Rather than becoming bilingual, minority language speakers are switching completely to the societal language. In some cases, open discrimination and persecution of certain minority groups drive entire communities to abandon their native languages. I will discuss the role of national policies in deciding the language of education for the masses and dissuading some people from passing on their languages to their children. Learning a second language is often a matter of choice and individual preference for social majorities but a matter of survival for minority populations. We will see what **language death** means for the study of human history and thought and why preventing it should be everyone's business, not just that of people whose languages are dying. I first begin with a definition of language.

WHAT IS A LANGUAGE? WHAT IS A DIALECT?

In order to understand the extent of linguistic diversity in the world today, we must first define language. Linguists often use the degree of "mutual intelligibility" between two speech varieties to decide whether they are separate **languages** or **dialects** of the same language. For instance, an English speaker and a Chinese speaker cannot communicate with each other without an interpreter. English and Chinese are totally unrelated to each other and mutually unintelligible. They are two different languages.

However, a Southern American English speaker has little or no difficulty in communicating with, say, an English speaker from Michigan. The Southern and Midwestern varieties of American English do differ in terms of phonology (e.g., a Southern American English speaker may pronounce the words "pin" and "pen" the same way as "pin" whereas a Michigander would say them differently), vocabulary (e.g., a soft drink may be called "soda pop" in Michigan but "Coke" in the South), and grammar (e.g., double modals are possible in Southern American English as in "I *might could* build a house" but not acceptable in Michigan English) (see also Charity Hudley & Mallinson, 2011). But these differences are not significant enough to cause major problems in communication. These two varieties are mutually intelligible and are considered dialects of American English. Dialects may thus be defined as mutually intelligible forms of a language that differ in systematic ways from each other.

However, it is not always easy to decide whether the systematic differences between two speech varieties reflect two dialects or two different languages. Definitions of languages and dialects are influenced not only by degrees of mutual intelligibility, but also by non-linguistic factors such as culture, ethnic and national identity, and religion. For instance, two mutually intelligible speech varieties (i.e., "dialects" according to a linguistic definition) may be called different languages. Swedish and Norwegian are mutually intelligible to a large extent but are considered separate languages since they are the official languages of Sweden and Norway and thus markers of national identity.

Similarly, Hindi and Urdu are mutually intelligible to a large extent and are sometimes collectively referred to as Hindustani. But there are political and religious motivations for considering these as separate languages. Hindi is the official language of India while Urdu is the official language of Pakistan and one of the officially recognized regional languages in India. The India–Pakistan border is one of the most intensely contested and politically volatile regions in the world, and rivalry between Hindi and Urdu speakers is fueled in part by religious differences. Though mutually intelligible, a distinguishing feature of Hindi and Urdu is the different writing systems—while Hindi is written in the Devanagari script, Urdu is written in the Perso-Arabic script (see Figures 3.1 and 3.2). There is also a difference in literary affiliation—Urdu borrows its technical and learned vocabulary from Persian and Arabic, whereas Hindi borrows the same kinds of terms from Sanskrit (Bhatia & Ritchie, 2006b).

Conversely, mutually unintelligible varieties (i.e., "languages" using a purely linguistic definition) may be called dialects of the same language. This is true in the case of Chinese. Broadly, Chinese has seven "dialect" groups—Putonghua (Mandarin), Wu, Xiang, Gan, Hakka, Yue (Cantonese), and Min—all of which have distinctive tonal systems and are widely believed to have evolved from the same language system (Li & Lee, 2006). But there is considerable variation within each of the major dialects in terms of phonology, vocabulary, and syntax. So much so that

> the Chinese dialects are more appropriately seen as members of a language family akin to Romance languages . . . intelligibility in some cases may be more problematic than in communication between say, a Spanish and an Italian national, each speaking their native language.
>
> (Li & Lee, 2006: 744)

Despite the lack of mutual intelligibility, there is a widely held view that the different dialect groups in China share a common linguistic and cultural heritage, and this perception is widely credited to a common logographic writing system (Li & Lee, 2006). Unlike an alphabetic writing system which represents the sounds of a spoken language, a logographic writing system represents ideas and is independent of the phonetic pronunciations of the individual dialects. Thus a logographic writing system facilitates communication among speakers of different Chinese dialects whose pronunciations can be worlds apart. For example, the phrase "Happy Birthday" is written in Chinese as a 生日快樂" (the

गोबर ने और कुछ न कहा। लाठी कन्धे पर रखी और चल दिया। होरी उसे
जाते देखता हुआ अपना कलेजा ठंढा करता रहा। अब लड़के की सगाई में देर न करनी
चाहिए। सत्रहवाँ लग गया; मगर करें कैसे? कहीं पैसे के भी दरसन हों। जब से तीनों
भाइयों में अलगौझा हो गया, घर की साख जाती रही। महतो लड़का देखने आते हैं,
पर घर की दशा देखकर मुँह फीका करके चले जाते हैं। दो-एक राजी भी हुए, तो रुपए
माँगते हैं। दो-तीन सौ लड़की का दाम चुकाये और इतना ही ऊपर से खर्च करे, तब
जाकर व्याह हो। कहाँ से आवें इतने रुपए। रास खलिहान में तुल जाती है। खाने-भर
को भी नहीं बचता। व्याह कहाँ से हो? और अब तो सोना ब्याहने योग्य हो गयी।
लड़के का व्याह न हुआ, न सही। लड़की का व्याह न हुआ, तो सारी बिरादरी में हँसी
होगी।

Gobar said nothing more. He put his staff on his shoulder and walked
away. Hori looked with pride at the receding figure of his son. He was
growing into a fine young man. Time he married. But Hori had no money
for the marriage. With the division in the family they had fallen on evil
days. People did come to see Gobar and approved of him. But when they
saw the family down and out, they washed their hands of the idea. Those
who agreed pitched the demand for bride money so high that Hori was
helpless. He had to marry off Sona too. It was bad enough if a son did
not marry, but for a grown-up girl to remain unmarried was sacrilege.
How could he look his friends in the face with an unmarried girl in the
house?

PREMCHAND, *Godan*

FIGURE 3.1 Hindi

four characters mean "birth," "day," "fast," and "happy" respectively) but is
pronounced quite differently as "shēng rì kuài lè" in Mandarin, "sàang yaht faai
lohk" in Cantonese, and "sang niq khuâ loq" in Shanghainese (Wu).

Since a common writing system unites the Chinese people from different
parts of the country, one may think that all that the Chinese have to do is to
simply write to each other back and forth to communicate. However, because
standard written Chinese is modeled on Northern Mandarin, the degree to
which speakers of Southern dialects are able to write the way they speak is
much lower than that by Mandarin speakers. Since the founding of the People's
Republic of China (PRC) in 1949, the Chinese government has promoted
Putonghua (Mandarin), based on the Beijing dialect, as the national lingua
franca, particularly in the domains of education and the media. Li & Lee (2006)
observe that this helps explain the lower rate of educational achievement

ستاروں سے آگے جہاں اَور بھی ہیں   ابھی عشق کے امتحاں اَور بھی ہیں

تہی زِندگی سے نہیں یہ فضائیں   یہاں سینکڑوں کارواں اَور بھی ہیں

قناعت نہ کر عالمِ رنگ و بُو پر   چمن اَور بھی آشیاں اَور بھی ہیں

اگر کھو گیا اِک نشیمن تو کیا غم   مقاماتِ آہ و فغاں اَور بھی ہیں

تُو شاہیں ہے پرواز ہے کام تیرا   ترے سامنے آسماں اَور بھی ہیں

اِسی روز و شب میں اُلجھ کر نہ رہ جا   کہ تیرے زمان و مکاں اَور بھی ہیں

Beyond the stars there are still other worlds;
There are other fields to test man's indomitable spirit.

Not devoid of life are those open spaces of heaven;
There are hundreds of other caravans in them as well.

Do not remain contented with this sensible world;
Beyond it there are other gardens and nests as well.

If thou hast lost one nest, what then?
There are other places for sighing and wailing as well.

Thou art an eagle; thy business is to soar in the empyrean;
Thou hast other skies in which thou canst range as well.

Be not entangled in this world of days and nights;
Thou hast another time and space as well.

MUHAMMAD IQBAL, *Bal-e-Jibril*

FIGURE 3.2 Urdu

Source: Katzner, 2002. Reproduced by permission of Taylor and Francis Group, LLC, a division of Informa plc.

among non-Mandarin speakers. The Chinese government's promotion of Putonghua as a national language privileges Putonghua speakers while putting other dialect groups at a disadvantage. I will return to issues related to national language policies later in this chapter.

LANGUAGE DIVERSITY IN THE WORLD

Despite the complexities in distinguishing between languages and dialects, a survey of the languages spoken in the world today reveals a huge disparity in language sizes as measured by the number of speakers. *The Ethnologue* reports that while 389 (or about 6%) of the world's 6,909 known living languages have more than a million speakers each and account for 94% of the world's population, the remaining 94% (or 6,520 languages) are spoken by only 6% of the world's people (Lewis, 2009). Over 40% of the world's population are covered by just nine languages, each with more than 100 million speakers (see Table 3.1). In contrast, the great majority of languages are spoken by far fewer people—55% (or 3,801) of the world's languages have less than 10,000 speakers each, and 26% (or 1,787 languages) have less than 1,000 speakers each.

Figure 3.3 shows a map of the world with each dot representing the geographic center of the 6,909 living languages in *The Ethnologue* database. Notice the highly uneven distribution of languages with some areas of the world dotted heavily and others more sparsely. One of the intensely dotted areas, the island of New Guinea, which the nation of Papua New Guinea shares with the Indonesian state of Irian Jaya, is home to just 0.1% of the world's population,

TABLE 3.1

Top Nine Languages in the World in Terms of Number of Native Speakers

Rank	Language	# of Speakers (in Millions)	% of World's Population
1	Chinese (Mandarin)	845	14.2
2	Spanish	329	5.5
3	English	328	5.5
4	Arabic	221	3.7
5	Hindi	182	3.1
6	Bengali	181	3.0
7	Portuguese	178	3.0
8	Russian	144	2.4
9	Japanese	122	2.0
Top 9 Total		*2,530*	*42.4*

Source: Adapted from Lewis, 2009

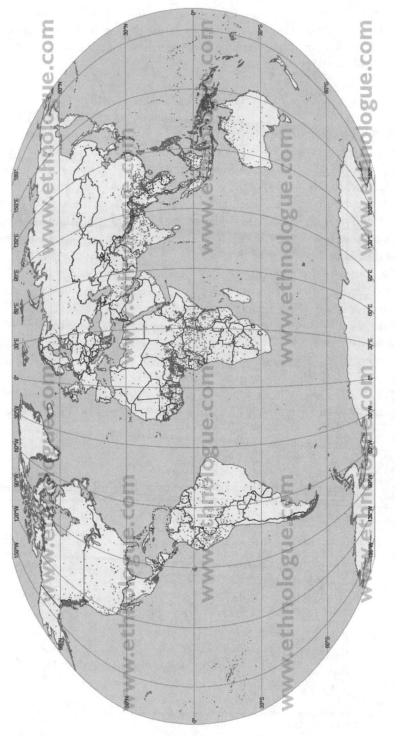

FIGURE 3.3 Languages of the World (Each Dot Represents the Geographic Center of a Language.)

Source: Lewis, 2009

yet its residents speak 1,100 languages, or one-sixth of all the world's languages. More than 100 languages are spoken on the tiny archipelago of Vanuatu, home to about 190,000 people in the South Pacific Ocean near Australia. According to *The Ethnologue*, Europe is the least linguistically diverse continent with only 3.4% of the world's languages. Asia, Africa, and the Pacific are the most linguistically diverse, with 33.6%, 30.5%, and 18.1% of the world's languages respectively.

But linguistic diversity is decreasing rapidly around the globe. Nettle & Romaine (2000) estimate that about half of the known languages of the world have vanished in the last 500 years, and that at least half of the more than 6,000 languages spoken today will become extinct over the next century. As illustrated in Figure 3.4, many of the small languages are disappearing due to the spread of giant languages like Chinese, Spanish, English, Arabic, and Hindi, which, Skutnabb-Kangas (2000) explains, are "killer languages." It's not that languages themselves can kill other languages, but as Skutnabb-Kangas (2000: 46) argues, "the speakers of these powerful languages have arrogated to themselves and to their languages more structural power and (material) resources than their numbers would justify, at the cost of speakers of other languages." Language death is ultimately about speakers of weaker languages ceasing to use

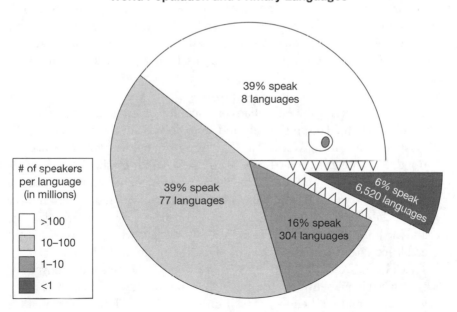

FIGURE 3.4 "Killer Languages"

Source: Sarah J. Shin; adapted from Lewis, 2009

their own languages altogether (either by choice or by force) and shifting to more powerful languages.

Why should anyone care that languages are dying? Crystal (2000) contends that the loss of any language is everyone's loss because languages contain millennia of accumulated human knowledge that cannot be replaced once gone. Harrison (2010: 10) explains:

> We imagine eureka moments taking place in modern laboratories or in classical civilizations. But key insights of biology, pharmacology, genetics, and navigation arose and persisted solely by word of mouth, in small unwritten tongues. This web of knowledge contains feats of human inge-nuity—epics, myths, rituals—that celebrate and interpret our existence ... The fate of languages is interlinked with that of species, as they undergo parallel extinctions. Scientific knowledge is comparable for both domains, with an estimated 80 percent of plant and animal species unknown to science and 80 percent of languages yet to be documented. But species and ecosystems unknown to science are well known to local people, whose languages encode not only names for things but also complex interrelations among them. Packaged in ways that resist direct translation, this knowledge dissipates when people shift to speaking global tongues.

Similarly, Nettle & Romaine (2000) argue that language survival and preservation of environmental resources go hand in hand. They point out that knowledge contained in indigenous languages has much to contribute to scientific theories by uncovering potentially very useful perspectives on a variety of ecological problems:

> Through wandering the Australian continent for generations, Aboriginal people knew the land intimately and were able to survive in relatively harsh terrain. During World War II an American fighter plane returned from New Guinea into northern Australia, where it crashed. The four survivors had no compasses or navigational equipment, but proceeded to set out to try to find help. Three starved to death, with food all around them. Unlike the Aborigines, the Americans had no idea what was edible and inedible. Many of the trees and vines have parts which can be made edible if treated in certain ways. One plant, for instance, yields *mirang*, or "black bean." After the beans have been gathered, the nuts are removed and placed in piles inside ovens dug in the ground. They are then covered with leaves and sand and a fire is lit on top of them. They are steamed inside in a matter of hours or for whole days. When they are taken out of the oven, they are sliced up with a knife made from snail shell and put

into dilly bags in a running stream for a couple of days. Then they are ready to be eaten. If the beans are not sliced fine enough, they remain bitter. None of this knowledge is written down but is passed on orally from generation to generation . . . little serious effort has been made to tap this indigenous knowledge about local ecosystems.

                                                              (Nettle & Romaine, 2000: 70–71)

What is sad about this story is that before this sort of knowledge (which took generations to fine-tune) could be documented, languages are becoming extinct. Nettle & Romaine (2000: 14) aptly point out, "As a uniquely human invention, language is what has made everything possible for us as a species: our cultures, our technology, our art, music, and much more. In our languages lies a rich source of the accumulated wisdom of all humans." Readers interested in detailed accounts of the world's endangered languages and what can be done about them are referred to some excellent books on the topic listed at the end of this chapter. But the imminent mass extinction of the majority of the world's languages is a human tragedy. What is probably more tragic is that most people do not even know (or care about) what we stand to lose when languages die.

I will now turn to the sociopolitical forces that threaten small languages and peoples, and how some groups have defended their languages despite the pressures. But first, I describe diglossia, a central concept in our understanding of the power dynamics in multilingual societies.

DIGLOSSIA

The term bilingualism is typically used to describe the use of two or more languages by an individual. When the focus shifts to how multiple languages are used in a given society, linguists use the term diglossia. A bilingual community is unlikely to use two languages for exactly the same purpose—each language serves a specialized function and plays a certain role. One language is usually used in informal interactions in the home and in the community (referred to as the "Low (L) variety") and another is used in more formal, prestigious domains such as government, media, and education (referred to as the "High (H) variety") (see Ferguson, 1959; Fishman, 1967). A speech community is diglossic when specific language situations call for the use of one language or the other.

Ferguson (1959) first described diglossia in terms of two dialects serving different functions in a given society. He provides the example of Switzerland where Swiss German (Schweizerdeutsch) is widely used in the home and community as the Low variety, and Standard High German (Hochdeutsch) is used in school, government, and businesses as the High variety. Swiss German is the spoken everyday language whereas Standard High German is the language of formal settings and written communication. Egypt provides another example, with Classical Arabic serving as the High variety, and Colloquial Arabic as the Low variety. Using Colloquial Arabic to write a formal letter would be considered highly inappropriate. Similarly, a person speaking Modern Standard Arabic (a modern version of Classical Arabic) in informal interactions with family and friends would sound stilted and pedantic. The L variety is acquired as one's mother tongue and is used throughout life in informal interactions of the family and community. The H variety, on the other hand, is never learned at home and is related to institutions outside the home (see Table 3.2 for a typical distribution for High and Low varieties in a diglossic society).

Fishman (1967) extended Ferguson's definition of diglossia to include not only dialects, but also different languages. Thus Ferguson's (1959) original distinction between a High variety and a Low variety can be applied to a **societal language** (High variety) and a **home/community language** (Low variety) in a bilingual society. In Paraguay, Spanish is the H variety, the official language of government and education, while Guaraní, spoken by 90% of the population, is the L variety, the language of informal interaction in the home and the community. In Ecuador, Spanish is the H variety and Quechua the L variety. In many post-colonial countries such as Paraguay and Ecuador, the language of the former colonizers serves as the H variety even after independence.

According to Fishman, individual bilingualism deals with language choice that is more or less flexible whereas diglossia depends on more rigid, functional distribution of the two languages in various situations. However, boundaries

TABLE 3.2

A Typical Distribution for High and Low Varieties in Diglossia

Context	High Variety	Low Variety
Conversation with family and friends		✓
Social interaction in the community		✓
Storytelling		✓
Oral language teachers use to teach pupils in the classroom		✓
Academic textbooks	✓	
Political speeches	✓	
Religious texts and sermons	✓	
Letter writing	✓	
TV news broadcast	✓	

between two languages are not so clear cut in many bilingual societies, and it is not always possible to predict with certainty which language will be used in a particular situation. For example, Romaine (2006) notes that in Quechua-speaking parts of Peru, the indigenous language, Quechua, is used as the language in the home and community (the L variety), whereas Spanish is used for everything outside those domains (the H variety). But students who talk with one another in Quechua outside the school often do so inside the school even though school is not considered part of the home/community. Similarly, a mother sitting in front of her home may address the school director in Quechua even though she would normally use Spanish (the H variety) to address him at school.

What complicates matters further is that in some multilingual societies, there are not two, but three, four, or more languages and dialects in a triglossic or even polyglossic relationship (Morocco and Singapore are two such countries, which I will describe later in this chapter). Moreover, bilingual speech in diglossic communities is frequently characterized by code-switching—the spontaneous mixing of two languages within the same conversation. I will describe code-switching in detail in Chapter 6. But in the following, I turn to the societal circumstances under which people become bilingual.

OUT OF THE MOUTHS OF BILINGUALS 3.1

Private Language, Public Language

"Speaking Italian at home was fine, but in public it felt awkward, uncomfortable. I had a private and a public life, defined by language use. I loved my family, my grandmothers, my home, and the good times we enjoyed together. At home, I felt happy, gregarious, secure, a big talker (nicknamed *chiacchiarone* = chatterbox). But, in public, I tended to be shy, timid, quiet, reserved, very polite."

(Fantini, 2009: 244)

WHAT GIVES RISE TO BILINGUAL SOCIETIES?

There are over 6,000 languages in the world today and only about 190 countries, which indicates how common bilingualism (or multilingualism) must be in the world's nations. No matter where we go in the world, we are likely to find distinct linguistic groups within national borders. Communication between different groups involves either one group learning the language of another group, or both groups learning a third language for between-group communication. Rarely will two different groups living side by side learn each other's language with equal eagerness. This is because in any contact situation, one group always has more resources, people, or political influence than the other. Since the more powerful group controls the affairs of the state, it has little incentive to learn the other group's language. Most likely, the more powerful group will make their language the official language of the government, education, and the media, which increases their social and educational advantage. All other groups whose languages are not endorsed by the state are relegated to a minority status.

Dorian (2006) notes that there are two main types of **language minorities**. The first type involves minorities who migrate into an area where another group and their language are dominant. The second type represents indigenous populations, around which a modern nation-state came into being through a process of military conquest or political reorganization. The label "minority" is often simply a euphemism for non-elite or subordinate groups, whether they constitute a numerical majority or minority compared to some politically dominant group (Romaine, 2006). The relative status of minority languages varies widely—some countries support their linguistic minorities while others neglect or repress them. As we will see, the official bi-/multilingual policies of countries like Switzerland, Canada, and Belgium protect the language rights of the minorities in those countries. But in most places, minority languages have no legal status and speakers of those languages must either learn the official language or rely on bilingual interpreters if they want to participate in political, legal, and educational activities of the mainstream society.

Let us now turn to language maintenance and language shift, major concepts in our understanding of the bilingualism of linguistic minority groups.

LANGUAGE MAINTENANCE AND SHIFT

Language shift refers to the process whereby a speech community switches to another language. When a linguistic community ceases to use its original language, language death is said to occur. Language maintenance refers to the protection and promotion of the native language of a speech community, particularly among linguistic minorities. It is perfectly possible for minority groups to be bilingual, that is, they can learn the societal language while maintaining their mother tongues. In such cases, the two languages will be in a diglossic relationship—the societal language is used for formal purposes in the larger society while the native language is used for social interaction in the home and the co-ethnic community. But what happens more frequently is that minority populations are either linguistically assimilated into mainstream society by force, or voluntarily give up their languages.

Forced cultural assimilation of indigenous populations has been a common practice in many parts of the world. Cummins (1996) notes that prior to the 1970s, it was extremely common for teachers to reprimand language minority students for speaking their home language in the school. In the U.S., Native American children have been taken from their families, sent to boarding schools in faraway places and punished when caught speaking their native languages. In Swedish state schools in the late nineteenth century and first half of the twentieth century, Finnish and Sami, the minority and indigenous languages, were forbidden not only during classroom instruction but also during the breaks (Skutnabb-Kangas, 2000). All too often, the message communicated to students is that they must no longer identify with their native language and culture, which are deemed objectionable in the school and society.

As perhaps the single most powerful socializing institution in children's lives, the school passes on cultural knowledge and practices to its students and assimilates linguistic minority populations into mainstream society. Language socialization at school takes place openly, as teachers instruct students on what to say and how to say things, as well as subtly in teachers' interaction with students (Heath, 1983). Once language minority children enter school, they quickly realize that the language they speak with their family members has no appreciable value in school and that they need to learn the school language to be accepted by their teachers and peers (Wong Fillmore, 1991).

The school endorses mainstream, middle-class values, and children who do not come to school with the kind of linguistic and cultural background supported in the schools are likely to experience conflict (Romaine, 1995: 242). Children are, therefore, motivated to learn the language of school, while, at the same time, discontinue using their mother tongues. This motivation is often the initial driving force in language shift in the family, as children start speaking the majority language to their parents and siblings at home. As the children learn and use the majority language at home, the parents also switch over to it at least in speaking with the children.

But parents may also consciously decide not to teach their native languages to their children. The belief that the majority language is more prestigious and socially beneficial than the minority language is a powerful deterrent to home language maintenance. No parent who has been denied opportunities due to her cultural background wants her children to suffer the same fate. In a study of Xhosa-speaking families in South Africa, De Klerk (2000) showed that a significant factor in the Xhosa community's shift to English was the parents' enrollment of their children in English-medium schools. Most of the children in these English-medium schools are whites who speak English as their native language. While part of the Xhosa-speaking parents' reason for choosing

English schools was a dissatisfaction with poor conditions in the Xhosa-medium schools, the more important reason was the parents' belief that English will prepare their children for better jobs.

A large body of research has shown that pressures for language shift are significant in many language minority families and communities. Observations of different communities that come into contact with a majority language have shown that there is almost always a complete shift in language use within three generations (Fishman, 1991). Among immigrants in the U.S., the typical pattern has been that the first generation learns some English while remaining strongest in the native tongue; the second generation usually becomes bilingual with more developed literacy skills in English; and the third generation is English-dominant with little or no capability in the language of the grandparents. However, recently, more and more language minority families and communities are undergoing a complete shift in language within two generations with no intervening bilingual generation (Wiley, 2001). This obviously creates major problems as parents and children living in the same household cannot communicate with each other.

The U.S. has often been described as a "language graveyard" because of its history of receiving millions of immigrants and extinguishing their mother tongues within a few generations (Portes & Rumbaut, 2006). Based on the findings from *Children of Immigrants Longitudinal Study*, a survey that followed 5,000 1.5- and second-generation youth who arrived in the U.S. prior to adolescence, as well as U.S.-born children of immigrants, Rumbaut (2009) concludes that even Spanish (the language spoken by the biggest linguistic minority group in the U.S.) does not challenge this unsavory reputation. Even though Spanish speakers in the U.S. tend to retain their mother tongue better than do other immigrant groups—due in part to their large numbers and geographic concentration in certain areas—their language preference shifts to English over time, usually by the third generation.

Thus the overall picture for minority languages is quite bleak, with language shift as the norm and maintenance as the exception (Dorian, 2006). But minority languages can be maintained if certain conditions are present. Summing up the research on language maintenance strategies, Crystal (2000) shows that a minority language will progress if its speakers:

1. increase their prestige within the dominant community;
2. increase their wealth relative to the dominant community;
3. increase their legitimate power in the eyes of the dominant community;
4. have a strong presence in the educational system;
5. can write their language down;
6. can make use of electronic technology.

While doing the above does not automatically guarantee the survival of small languages, Crystal argues that the primary goal of linguists (and language educators) should be to help minority language speakers increase their relative standing in society. He likens linguists' efforts to preserve languages to medical doctors preserving the physical health of patients:

> in exactly the same way as doctors only intervene with the primary aim of preserving the physiological health of patients, so linguists should only intervene with the primary aim of preserving the linguistic health of those who speak endangered languages. The concept of linguists working on such languages with no interest in the people who speak them—other than to see them as a source of data for a thesis or publication—is, or should be, as unacceptable a notion as it would be if doctors collected medical data without caring what happened subsequently to the patients.
>
> (2000: 145)

Language preservation is really about caring for the overall well-being of speakers of those languages.

Let us now look at some of the multilingual countries of the world.

INCIDENCE OF BI-/MULTILINGUALISM
IN DIFFERENT COUNTRIES

As discussed earlier, bilingualism is present to varying degrees in practically all countries of the world. This is the case whether the countries are officially bilingual or not. In discussing the incidence of bilingualism, Mackey (1967) makes a useful distinction between the official, *de jure* bilingualism of a country and the actual, *de facto* bilingualism of its people. He points out that there are actually fewer bilingual people in the officially bilingual countries than there are in the so-called monolingual countries because "bilingual countries were created not to promote bilingualism, but to guarantee the maintenance and use of two or more languages in the same nation" (1967: 11).

Officially Bi-/Multilingual Countries with Few Actual Bilinguals

A good example of an officially multilingual country that has few actual bilingual speakers is Switzerland. Switzerland has four official languages, which vary greatly in the number of speakers. (Swiss) German is spoken by 64% of the Swiss population in 19 of the country's 26 cantons while French is spoken by 20% of the population in four cantons in the western part of the country. Italian and Romansh (a language similar to Latin) are spoken by 7% and 0.5% of the population respectively (Swiss Federal Statistical Office, 2011). However, only about 6% of Swiss citizens can be considered multilingual in the country's four official languages, and English is much preferred over the other official languages as a second language (Romaine, 2006). Although all four languages are recognized by the Swiss government, they do not have the same prestige. For example, very few Swiss learn Romansh or Italian, but most speakers of Romansh and Italian learn either German or French. German and French are clearly the more dominant languages in Switzerland.

Canada has English and French as its two official languages, but the rate of individual bilingualism in the official languages varies widely among the provinces, and is typically asymmetrical. French-speaking Canadians are much more likely to be bilingual in the country's two official languages than English-speaking Canadians. In Belgium, Dutch-speaking Flemings represent about 60% of the population mostly in the north and west of the country, and French-speaking Walloons represent about 40% in the south and east. A small German-speaking minority represents less than 1% of the population. But here too, the incidence of individual bilingualism in the country's official languages is uneven—a higher percentage of Dutch-speaking Flemings speak French than French-speaking Walloons speak Dutch.

In all three countries, language differences are associated with distinguishable territories within the country. These countries are essentially collections of largely monolingual regions whose languages are protected by law. The reason these countries have chosen official bi-/multilingualism is that "they wish to recognize the linguistic identity of the groups that make up the country,

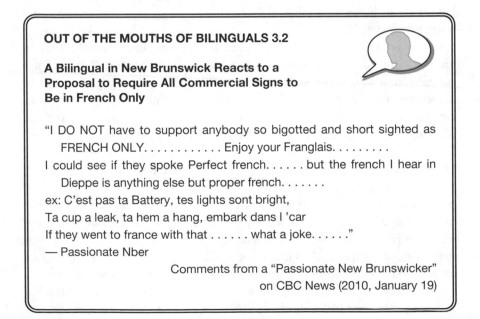

OUT OF THE MOUTHS OF BILINGUALS 3.2

A Bilingual in New Brunswick Reacts to a Proposal to Require All Commercial Signs to Be in French Only

"I DO NOT have to support anybody so bigotted and short sighted as
   FRENCH ONLY. . . . . Enjoy your Franglais. . . . .
I could see if they spoke Perfect french. . . . . . but the french I hear in
   Dieppe is anything else but proper french. . . . . . .
ex: C'est pas ta Battery, tes lights sont bright,
Ta cup a leak, ta hem a hang, embark dans I 'car
If they went to france with that . . . . . . what a joke. . . . . ."
— Passionate Nber

Comments from a "Passionate New Brunswicker"
on CBC News (2010, January 19)

and they want to help certain linguistic minorities maintain and 'defend' their language against the larger groups" (Grosjean, 1982: 19).

Officially Monolingual Countries with Many Actual Bilinguals

In contrast, there are officially monolingual countries which are in fact highly multilingual. In Ghana, for example, there are 79 different languages, and in Nigeria some five hundred. But English is the sole official language of both countries. In Niger, 21 languages are spoken, and in Senegal, 37 languages. But French is the only official language of these countries. In Mozambique, a former Portuguese colony, Portuguese is the sole medium of government-controlled national communication, and the 20 or so African languages of Mozambique do not play any role in government and education. Upon independence, many post-colonial countries chose the former colonial language to facilitate the cultural and linguistic unity of the newborn nation without favoring any one ethnic group. Since English, French, and Portuguese were no one's mother tongue, they could serve as neutral languages for administrative purposes.

But the colonial languages are not widely used by the people of these countries. In fact, less than 10% of people in lusophone Africa are able to function through Portuguese, and between 5% and 20% of those in anglophone Africa can communicate in English (Kamwangamalu, 2006). Although French is the official language in Senegal, Wolof, a lingua franca in West Africa, is spoken more extensively by the general population. French is learned and used only by a small minority. In Sierra Leone, Krio is widely used as a lingua franca in trade and social interactions among different ethnic groups, but English is the country's official language. If so few people can actually understand and use the colonial languages, why were they chosen over African languages that are more widely spoken?

Kamwangamalu (2006) points out that in Southern Africa, there are two types of bilinguals: **elite bilinguals** and **natural bilinguals**. Elite bilinguals are individuals who, in addition to their mother tongue, are highly educated in a foreign language (i.e., the colonial language). Since not everyone can afford the cost of an education in Southern Africa, elite bilinguals constitute a minority social class made up of government officials, academics, and those in higher positions in business or the civil service. In contrast, natural bilinguals are those who are fluent in two or more indigenous languages and use them as a means of communication in everyday life. In addition to their mother tongue, they acquire the other languages as a result of interethnic marriages or exposure to communities that speak different languages. While natural bilinguals constitute the majority of Southern Africa's population, it is the elite bilinguals who have the political clout.

Kamwangamalu (2006: 729) observes that the ruling elite have defended the inherited colonial policies, which promote former colonial languages at the expense of the indigenous African languages, for reasons such as "elitism and vested interests, ethnolinguistic rivalries among language groups, financial constraints, and the lack of political will." The colonial languages are status symbols in these countries and clearly the High varieties in a diglossic relationship with the African indigenous languages (the Low varieties). Since opportunity to learn the colonial language is available only to a small minority, it acts as a barrier between the political elite and the masses. The political elite is naturally interested in insisting on the use of the colonial language so it can maintain its hold on political affairs.

HOW LANGUAGE POLICY AFFECTS SOCIETAL BILINGUALISM: THREE CASES

Language is an integral part of national identity. Presented with the task of choosing the language(s) that will represent their newly independent nations, some governments have adopted drastic, sweeping policies that are far removed from actual patterns of language use by the public. These policies, driven by ideologies, put some languages on a pedestal while downplaying others. Below, I discuss the language policies of three countries—Latvia, Morocco, and Singapore—and their effects on language use.

Latvia

Following a period of Soviet occupation after World War II, Latvia regained its independence in 1991. During the Soviet period, Latvians were required to learn Russian as a second language but Russians did not have to know Latvian. After independence, the Latvian government made Latvian the only official language in an effort to shift the balance of power back to the Latvian side. Many Russians in Latvia who did not know Latvian could not become Latvian citizens because a new law required knowledge of Latvian for citizenship (Dilans, 2009). Russian, which was widely spoken during the Soviet period, is by far the largest minority language in Latvia and is understood by virtually all Latvians who started their education during the period of Soviet rule. However, the official language policy labels Russian as a "foreign" language and discourages young Latvians from learning it.

Latvia is very much a *de jure* monolingual and *de facto* bilingual society (Dilans, 2009). Although official policy prescribes Latvian monolingualism in formal education, Dilans (2009) states that there is a trend among Latvians to maintain Russian skills informally. This is because the majority of Latvians still think that Russian is an important language. While many Latvians feel that making Latvian official and de-emphasizing Russian is good for nation-building purposes, they also know the practical value of Latvian-Russian bilingualism in the region. Some also fear that the government's insistence on Latvian monolingualism will lead to the decreased overall competitiveness of the nation. The Latvian case provides an example of a mismatch between what is envisioned by the government (i.e., ideology) and what is practiced by the people.

Morocco

Another illustrative example comes from Morocco, a country that has been multilingual for centuries. There are three major language groups in Morocco: Berber, Arabic, and French. Berber, the indigenous languages of the Maghreb, has survived as the Low language in a diglossic relationship with Arabic (the High language) for 14 centuries. However, as is true in other Arabic-speaking countries, Moroccans use different varieties of Arabic, which can be placed along a continuum. At one end of the continuum is Modern Standard Arabic (MSA)—the written, standardized form used in religion, education, and government matters. At the other end is Dialectal Arabic (or Colloquial Arabic)—the spoken, non-standard form used in informal contexts. What this means is that there is another layer of diglossia in Morocco, with MSA as the High variety, and Dialectal Arabic as the Low variety.

In the early part of the twentieth century, a new High language entered the Moroccan linguistic scene. During the French Protectorate, French was clearly the High language of Moroccan society though it could not compete with Arabic in religious domains. Even today, French is still widely perceived to be the language of social success, and maintains a privileged position in domains such as commerce and finance, science and technology, and the media. This is despite the fact that the Moroccan government has implemented a drastic Arabization policy, with the goal of creating a monolingual Arabic-speaking nation (Marley, 2004). However, even after decades of implementation of the Arabization policy, French continues to be used in many important domains, and Berber speakers have become increasingly vocal in their demands for linguistic rights. Marley (2004) notes that despite the government's prescription for monolingualism in Arabic, many Moroccans see bilingualism as key to a successful future for their country.

Singapore

Singapore provides a fantastic case study of how policy can make a difference in individual language behavior. Composed of three main ethnic groups—77% Chinese, 14% Malay, and 8% Indian—Singapore has adopted a multilingual policy that gives four languages—Mandarin, Malay, Tamil, and English—official status (Bokhorst-Heng & Caleon, 2009). The government has promoted what is known as "English-knowing bilingualism"—all children must learn English plus a mother tongue through bilingual education. Singapore is simultaneously a nation and a city with only about five million people. Its leaders decided early on that knowledge of English was critical for the country's global competitiveness. But because some feared that dominance of English might undermine the cultural rootedness of its diverse ethnic groups, the government decided to promote mother tongues by integrating them into education.

But the government uses a rather peculiar definition of mother tongue, which is determined by a student's father's ethnicity (Mandarin for Chinese, Malay for Malays, and Tamil for Indians) regardless of the language actually spoken by the student at home. For instance, a child who has a Cantonese-speaking father and a Malay-speaking mother is automatically classified as ethnic Chinese and as having Mandarin as her mother tongue even though nobody speaks Mandarin at home (Gupta, 1993). What this does is privilege Mandarin speakers at the expense of speakers of other Chinese dialects.

The government's pro-Mandarin policy has resulted in a massive shift to Mandarin among the ethnic Chinese, who make up more than three-quarters of the Singaporean population. This is despite the fact that the majority of the Chinese in Singapore do not speak Mandarin as their native language. In fact, many more are speakers of Hakka, Cantonese, and Hokkien, three Chinese dialects that are mutually unintelligible with Mandarin and with one another. But the government's "Speak Mandarin" campaign, started in 1979, has been so successful that whereas only 0.1% of the country's population spoke Mandarin as a mother tongue at the time of independence, almost half (47%) of the population now use Mandarin at home (McKay & Bokhorst-Heng, 2008).

In addition to the Singaporean government's emphasis on Mandarin, there is a general preference for English as the language of prestige. Because English is positioned as the language of finance, law, government, education, and higher education, it is also seen as a language of upward social mobility. There is a predominant and near exclusive use of English in high-income homes, in contrast to low-income households which typically use their mother tongue as the dominant household language (Bokhorst-Heng & Caleon, 2009). Since 2000, the government has also started a "Speak Good English Movement" for the population in general, to make Standard English, rather than Singapore's colloquial English (Singlish), the habitual form of English. The overall result is that what used to be a highly multilingual country is now dominated by Mandarin-English bilingualism (McKay & Bokhorst-Heng, 2008; Romaine, 2006).

SUMMARY

In this chapter, I discussed the politics behind people's language choices in multilingual societies. Quite simply, bilingual societies come about as a result of contact between groups of people that speak different languages. Such contact always produces a power differential—speakers of one language have more political, economic, and social influence than those of another. We saw that linguistic prestige is not an indication of intrinsic beauty in languages but rather of the perceived status of those who speak them.

We saw power differentials at work in the concept of diglossia—the functional separation of two languages (or dialects) in a multilingual society. In a diglossic situation, one language is reserved for use in formal contexts such as school, government, and the media (i.e., the High variety) while another language is used in informal settings of the home and the ethnic community (i.e., the Low variety). What this means is that people who do not know the High variety are kept out of the activities associated with power in the societies in which they live. And since the High variety is learned only at school, education takes on a special meaning. We saw that speakers of the High variety often use that variety to wield power over speakers of a Low variety and limit other people's access to socioeconomic opportunities.

We also saw that linguistic diversity is quickly decreasing around the world, with the majority of the 6,000 or so languages spoken today predicted to be gone by the end of the twenty-first century. Many small languages are dying because their speakers are no longer using them and teaching them to their children. Official language policies of most nations favor the languages of people in power, and the burden to become bilingual falls on speakers of minority languages. In the face of powerful social and political pressures, many minority language communities are turning their backs on their mother tongues. The imminent extinction of the majority of the world's languages is a tragedy, something we should work hard to avoid.

We examined the official language policies of different countries, and saw that there is often a mismatch between policy and actual patterns of people's language use. I described officially bi-/multilingual countries, whose citizens are in fact mostly monolingual (e.g., Switzerland, Canada) and officially monolingual countries whose citizens are highly multilingual (e.g., Ghana, Nigeria, Senegal). We saw that the officially multilingual countries are essentially collections of largely monolingual regions whose languages are protected by law. I presented the monolingual policies of Latvia and Morocco, which are *de facto* bi-/multilingual countries. These policies reflect the desire of the governments of these countries to bring back power to their newly independent nations. But many people in both countries see a complete move to monolingualism as unrealistic and even harmful to their national competitiveness in the wider world.

Finally, we saw in the case of Singapore that language policy can have a profound effect on people's language use. Although the Singaporean government has promoted bilingual education in English and mother tongue for all of its citizens, the government's rather peculiar definition of mother tongue, based on a student's father's ethnicity, has privileged Mandarin over all other Chinese dialects. This has resulted in a massive shift to Mandarin among the Chinese majority who are originally speakers of other Chinese dialects such as Cantonese, Hakka, and Hokkien. One reason that the government's "Speak Mandarin" campaign has been so successful is the widely held view among the different Chinese dialect groups that Mandarin is a unifying symbol of their ethnic identity. I will address the topic of identity in Chapter 5.

FURTHER READING

- Crystal, D. (2000). *Language death.* Cambridge: Cambridge University Press.—In this very readable introduction to the world's threatened languages, David Crystal explains why the imminent extinction of thousands of languages is problematic and what can be done about it.
- Fishman, J. (1991). *Reversing language shift: Theoretical and empirical foundations for assistance to threatened languages.* Clevedon, UK: Multilingual Matters.—In this foundational text in the field of language maintenance and shift, Joshua Fishman analyzes the success and failure of language maintenance efforts based on numerous case studies from around the world.
- Harrison, K.D. (2010). *The last speakers: The quest to save the world's most endangered languages.* Washington DC: National Geographic Society.—Through his detailed accounts of the last speakers of some of the world's dying languages, Harrison makes a compelling argument for preserving endangered languages.
- Nettle, D., & Romaine, S. (2000). *Vanishing voices: The extinction of the world's languages.* Oxford: Oxford University Press.—Rich with examples and anecdotes from around the world, this book is an impassioned plea to preserve the endangered languages before it is too late.

ONLINE AND VIDEO RESOURCES

- *Do you speak American?* is a documentary that explores regional and social variation in English, including ethnic, gender, and age-related differences. It also considers bilingual varieties of American English involving Spanish and French. A viewer's guide and curriculum units for high school and college classes written by the Center for Applied Linguistics (CAL) are available free of charge at: http://www.pbs.org/speak/
- http://www.culturalsurvival.org/—Cultural Survival is an advocacy group

that partners with indigenous peoples to defend their lands, languages, and cultures.

STUDY QUESTIONS AND ACTIVITIES

1. How widespread is bilingualism in the world? How is bilingualism a language contact phenomenon? What brings about language contact in different countries? Are some forms of bilingualism more stable than others?
2. Bilingualism is considered a valuable asset in many European and African countries but is often treated as a problem in the U.S. Why might this be? What kind of bilingualism is considered desirable in the United States?
3. In the video *Do you speak American?* Robert MacNeil says, "Americans are ambivalent about language. They may think that New York and Southern accents are bad English but they can also find them charming." Do you agree that people have ambivalent attitudes toward language? In your opinion, is your own variety of English prestigious or stigmatized?
4. What is your personal experience with bilingualism? Have societal attitudes toward the languages you speak affected your language maintenance or shift?

Heritage Language Education

We desperately need competence in languages—to become "a language competent society," in Tucker's phrase (1991)—and our huge and varied heritage language resources have a definite role to play in achieving such competence.

—Joshua A. Fishman (2001: 95)

INTRODUCTION

In Chapter 1, I pointed out that nearly one in five Americans speak a language other than English at home and that many of these people are bilingual in English and their mother tongue. In this chapter, I discuss reasons for promoting the bilingualism of these individuals and how doing so makes economic and political sense for the mainstream English-speaking society. I show how the languages that are learned and used by immigrant and indigenous populations in their communities are a national asset, a resource that must be treasured and not wasted. I describe the current state of ethnic and indigenous language education in the U.S. and the benefits and challenges of developing heritage language programs. I will argue that creating a "language-competent society" requires a major change in attitude toward minority languages and that language professionals and educators play a significant role in bringing about that change. I first begin with a story of an Indian immigrant who became a soldier in the U.S. Army.

On November 10, 2010, for the first time in nearly three decades, the U.S. Army graduated a Sikh enlisted soldier who was granted a rare religious exemption to wear his turban and beard (see Schafer, 2010 for the msnbc.com article). The Sikh religion requires its male followers to keep a beard and have unshorn hair covered by a turban. Since 1984, Army policies prohibiting those items had effectively prevented Sikhs who wanted to keep their articles of faith from enlisting. But Spc. Simran Lamba was recruited under the Military Accessions Vital to the National Interest recruiting program, which enlists legal non-citizens with critical language skills, such as Lamba's knowledge of Hindi and Punjabi (Kappler, 2010). The 26-year-old Indian immigrant from New Delhi came to the U.S. for his graduate studies. After graduating from New York University with a master's degree in industrial engineering, he sought to enlist in the U.S. Army and get his citizenship. He requested a waiver from the Army to allow him to keep his articles of faith. After a ten-month review, the Army approved Lamba's request on the condition that the religious accommodations will not affect training, unit readiness or cohesion, individual readiness, morale, discipline, or safety and health. In an interview, Lamba said that his black turban, full beard, unshorn hair, and religious beliefs posed no problems during his ten weeks of training. He said, "I am proud to be a Sikh, I'm proud to be a U.S. citizen, and proud to be a U.S. Army soldier."

A cursory look at the comments posted by readers of the msnbc.com article shows that many people think this is a positive step in the right direction for the U.S. military. One writer, "nassy," states, "Thank you for becoming a citizen and for wanting to fight for our country. I am a Veteran US Navy and would have loved a chance to meet you and serve with you . . ." Another writer, "TexasSteve," says, "An awesome day for Spc. Lamba! Very glad to see the U.S. Army doing this." But a few people think that making special exceptions like this is unfair. One comment posted by "sopha-1125249" states, "I find this offensive. His religion is his right . . . but not joining our military with the same amount of requirements and expectations as all those other brave people makes me wonder where this country is going. As if the USA could not teach someone in the military this language they proclaim to need!! My son proudly serves in the United States Army . . . I guess they forgot to mention to him that he can serve and do it his way! . . . This exception is wrong!!!" Another reader, "BK-2647153," writes, "Giving this soldier a 'special waiver' because he speaks a language is just wrong. It is so easy to learn a language using the Rosetta Stone program that I am sure the Army did not need this individual . . ."

Contrary to what "sopha-1125249" and "BK-2647153" claim, however, it is not so easy for Americans to learn non-European languages like Hindi and Punjabi in a short amount of time. It requires a typical English-speaking American thousands of hours of intensive language instruction to achieve the level of advanced proficiencies required by the military. Whether the Army's accommodation of the Sikh soldier's religious practice is right or wrong, the fact is that the military's need for individuals with advanced proficiencies in foreign languages is currently not being met with American citizens, which is why the U.S. government has created special provisions to naturalize non-citizens with the required skills.

The U.S. has an unprecedented need for people with highly developed skills in foreign languages. Even before the events of September 11, 2001, congressional hearings had begun to document a shortage of professionals with the language proficiencies required to carry out a wide range of federal government activities (Brecht & Ingold, 2002). Since 2002, the United States Government Accountability Office (GAO) has issued a series of reports on two key aspects of foreign language capabilities across the federal government—(1) the use of foreign language skills and (2) the nature and impact of foreign language shortages at federal agencies, particularly those that play a central role in national security. The 2010 GAO report states that the lack of foreign language capability at some agencies, including Department of Defense and the State Department, has resulted in "backlogs in translation of intelligence documents and other information, and adversely affected agency operations and hindered U.S. military, law enforcement, intelligence, counterterrorism, and diplomatic efforts" (United States Government Accountability Office, 2010).

How can the country's foreign language needs be filled? According to *The Ethnologue*, 176 languages are spoken in different communities across the U.S. (Lewis, 2009). Although many of these languages are taught in American colleges and universities, developing high levels of linguistic and cultural proficiency needed for professional purposes requires many years and far more hours of instruction than is provided by a typical college curriculum (Brecht & Ingold, 2002). It is difficult for people to attain professional-level competence in a language that is learned for the first time in college. In less commonly taught languages like Hindi and Punjabi, university programs produce only handfuls of speakers with any proficiency at all, far short of the levels required for professional purposes. At the PreK–12 levels, the choice of foreign languages narrows drastically, with only a few languages that are taught for few hours per week as a separate subject. Relatively few American students receive long-term, articulated instruction in any foreign language in their PreK–12 education (Brecht & Ingold, 2002).

There exists, however, a largely untapped reservoir of language competence in the U.S., namely **heritage language** speakers—the millions of people from indigenous or immigrant communities who are proficient in English and also have skills in other languages that were developed at home and in their communities or in their countries of origin (Peyton, Ranard, & McGinnis, 2001). Although the range of language proficiencies possessed by heritage language speakers varies widely, individuals who have used a language regularly at home since birth typically have skills that would require nonnative speakers hundreds of hours of instruction to acquire (Brecht & Ingold, 2002). Such skills include native pronunciation and fluency, command of a wide range of grammatical structures, extensive vocabulary, and familiarity with implicit cultural norms essential to effective language use (Valdés, 2000). In order to work in professional contexts, many heritage language speakers need explicit instruction in the use of formal registers and discipline-specific vocabulary, but they usually require substantially less instructional time than do non-heritage learners.

Supporting heritage language speakers to develop in their languages, then, is a logical step in addressing the nation's critical shortage of individuals with foreign language capabilities. However, heritage language speakers are often discouraged from learning their languages, and responsibility for teaching and maintaining the minority languages falls squarely on individual immigrant and indigenous communities. Indeed, public support for heritage language programs is very rare. The prevailing attitude of the American public is that the bilingualism of immigrants is a problem and a sign of resistance to integration into the mainstream society. As the comments critical of the special religious accommodation of Spc. Lamba suggest, social integration of ethnic and racial minorities is a highly contentious issue in America. Some people feel that immigrants should give up their ways of life in order to be accepted as legitimate members of their new society.

OUT OF THE MOUTHS OF BILINGUALS 4.1

What Does It Take to Be a "Good American"?

"When my grandfather arrived in New York from Argentina in the early 20th century, he spoke Spanish, Yiddish, and Russian. My grandmother, a refugee from Poland, spoke Polish, Yiddish, and Russian. Yet they spoke to my father only in English. They used Yiddish among themselves only to exchange insults or otherwise keep my father (or, later, me and my brothers and sister) from understanding them. They were adamant that my father would speak only English and would become a 'good American.'"

(Slavin, 2003: ix)

It is not clear how many Sikhs before Spc. Lamba have served in the U.S. military, but those who have done so apparently gave up their articles of faith since Lamba was the first Sikh soldier to be granted the waiver. In fact, one comment on the msnbc.com article by "Chris-2644004" states, "I have no idea exactly how many Sikhs have served as enlistedmen in the US Army in the last 30 years, but I know of one other that deserves to be noted. I was privileged enough to have served with and been able to call another Sikh soldier, Sgt. Uday

Singh, my friend. Sgt. Singh enlisted in the US Army in September 2000 and was killed in action in Habbinayah, Iraq on December 1st, 2003."

It is ironic that while the nation has such a pressing need for citizens who can function in languages other than English, those who already possess such linguistic and cultural knowledge are pressured to lose it. A great deal of effort is invested in teaching English-speaking Americans foreign languages— languages to which they have no personal or family connection. The role of foreign language programs is rarely questioned even though these programs have had little success in producing advanced bilinguals. But programs that are designed to help immigrants maintain their languages are constantly questioned and debated, as seen in a highly publicized English-only movement that has dismantled bilingual education in states like California, Arizona, and Massachusetts (see also Chapter 7; see Table 4.1 for a side-by-side comparison of heritage language and foreign language programs).

In this chapter, I discuss this apparent paradox in American language education. We will see why a major change in attitudes toward minority languages is necessary to achieve a language competent society. I will describe heritage language development efforts in both formal school systems and community-based schools and compare the degree of effectiveness of various program options. I will discuss the importance of intergenerational transmission of heritage languages and why language minority parents should be encouraged to speak their native languages with their children at home as a first step in language maintenance efforts. I will then conclude with recommendations for educators, policymakers, and families. First, I turn to a definition of "heritage language."

TABLE 4.1

Heritage Language Education vs. Foreign Language Education

Heritage Language Education	Foreign Language Education
• Geared for language minority students	• Geared for language majority students
• Constantly questioned and debated	• Rarely questioned
• Can be highly effective in producing functional bilinguals	• Has a low rate of success in producing functional bilinguals
• Learners have cultural knowledge	• Learners have little or no cultural knowledge
• Learners have family connections to the language	• Learners have little or no family connections to the language

WHAT IS A HERITAGE LANGUAGE?

There is much debate over what constitutes a heritage language (Wiley & Valdés, 2000). In the U.S., the term has been used to refer to an immigrant, indigenous, or ancestral language that a speaker has a personal relevance and desire to (re)connect with (Wiley, 2005). It has been used synonymously with community language, native language, and mother tongue to refer to a language other than English used by immigrants and possibly their children. For pedagogical purposes, Valdés (2001: 38) defines a heritage language speaker as "someone who is raised in a home where a non-English language is spoken and who speaks or at least understands the language and is to some degree bilingual in the home language and in English." Most of the five million or so students designated as ELs in American PreK–12 schools fall into this category.

Van Deusen-Scholl (2003: 221) takes a broader view and characterizes heritage language learners as "a heterogeneous group ranging from fluent native speakers to non-speakers who may be generations removed, but who may feel culturally connected to a language." She distinguishes "heritage learners" who have achieved some degree of proficiency in the home language and/or have been raised with strong cultural connections from "learners with a heritage motivation" who "seek to reconnect with their family's heritage through language, even though the linguistic evidence of that connection may have been lost for generations" (Van Deusen-Scholl, 2003: 222). An example of a "learner with a heritage motivation" is a fifth generation Chinese American who grew up in an English-speaking home but decides to take Chinese lessons as an adult to reconnect with his family's heritage.

The term "heritage language" has gained currency in the last 15 years, particularly in the U.S., but is not without problems. Some people think that it feeds into stereotypes that minority languages belong to the "other" rather than to the mainstream society. In such thinking, children in heritage language classes are relegated to their historic pasts—their heritages and heritage languages (García, 2005). Baker and Jones (1998: 509) caution that:

> the danger of the term "heritage language" is that, relative to powerful majority languages, it points more to the past and less to the future, to traditions rather than to the contemporary. The danger is that the heritage language becomes associated with ancient cultures, past traditions and more "primitive times." This is also true of the terms "ethnic" (used in the U.S.) and "ancestral." These terms may fail to give the impression of a modern, international language that is of value in a technological society.

For these reasons, in Canada, multicultural policies aimed at inclusion of heritage language programs in mainstream educational institutions have involved a shift in terminology from "heritage language" to "international language" (Duff, 2008). **International language** used in this context refers to languages other than Canada's two official languages (i.e., English and French) and Aboriginal languages (Tavares, 2000). Duff (2008: 82) points out that the change in terminology reflects a more forward-looking global focus as opposed to one that harks back to the ethnolinguistic roots of certain sectors of the population. In Europe, the term **minority language** has been used more frequently than heritage language, and a further distinction has been made between languages of immigrant and refugee groups (immigrant minority (IM) languages) on the one hand and languages of indigenous groups (regional minority (RM) languages) on the other (DeBot & Gorter, 2005).

Different terminologies go in and out of fashion, and nomenclature often reflects the political and social climate of a country at a given time. The term "bilingual education," for instance, has been suppressed in recent years since it has become associated with academic failure of immigrant students. Crawford (2004: 35) notes that instead of the term "bilingual education," "dual language, dual immersion and two-way immersion are increasingly used as 'safer' terms for what was originally known as two-way bilingual education, in hopes that avoiding the 'B-word' will minimize opposition." However, this has caused confusion among laypersons, as "dual language" is interpreted as a synonym for any form of bilingual education (see also Chapter 8).

Regardless of what terms are used to refer to heritage languages, the fact is that these are the speech varieties of ethnic/linguistic minorities who, to varying degrees, attempt to maintain and pass down their mother tongues to future generations in an English-speaking environment. As I explained earlier, this is not an easy task given the enormous social pressures placed on minority language speakers to give up their languages. In a world of limited resources and conflicting interests, promoting the interests of minority populations is not a priority for majority populations. Heritage languages are often marginalized from mainstream discussions because the majority populations do not see them as being relevant to their own lives.

Successful cases of heritage language development almost always involve the initiative and ongoing support (financial and otherwise) of members of the heritage communities in question. They are rarely initiated and supported exclusively by the society at large. But in order for heritage communities to win broad public support for language teaching efforts, they need to be able to articulate concrete benefits of language maintenance and bilingualism not only for heritage learners but also for members of the mainstream society. One type of program that holds much promise in this regard is two-way (dual) immersion education, which promotes the bilingual development of both heritage and non-heritage speakers. I will return to two-way immersion programs later in this chapter and in Chapter 8.

But in the next section, I describe heritage and foreign language education in K–12 schools and universities.

HERITAGE LANGUAGE EDUCATION AT THE K–12 LEVEL

Wiley (2005) notes that heritage and community language education policies and practices have long received attention in the U.S., though not under the currently popular "heritage language" label. Heritage language concerns have been alive among indigenous groups in America, with a high proportion of American Indian children engaged in heritage language schooling, from pre-nursery to college institutions, under tribal control or with tribal input (McCarty & Zepeda, 1998). Many immigrant communities have also educated their young in ethnic heritage schools. Fishman (2001: 86) cites a 1902 Report of the U.S. Commissioner of Education, which stated that there were 3,984 German ethnic heritage elementary schools with 318,000 students in the U.S. in the years 1900–1901. He explains that:

> By the end of the 19th century, as public schools rapidly multiplied and spread, particularly throughout the Midwest, the number of schools that taught German and that were officially German-English bilingual public elementary schools began to equal the number of nonpublic ethnic heritage schools. The legal basis for such public elementary schools was explicitly incorporated into state education law in many states. An example is the Nebraska education law of 1913, just before the outbreak of World War I, which permitted such bilingual public schools to be established (in English plus any other language) when requests to do so were received from the parents of 50 pupils in urban areas.

The outbreak of World War I led to such a severe public backlash against foreigners (particularly Germans) that many ethnic heritage schools were closed, both voluntarily and by state directives. Fishman (2001: 86) observes that German is a prime example of how U.S. foreign policy and other national interests can affect language education.

Foreign/Heritage Language Education in Public K–12 Schools

Currently, heritage language instruction at the K–12 level is provided either in public schools in the form of foreign language or bilingual education, or in community-based weekend schools. Cummins (2005) notes that in all of these settings, the teaching of heritage languages is marginalized with respect to funding provisions, number of languages involved, and number of students who participate. According to a Center for Applied Linguistics (CAL) survey of foreign language teaching in U.S. K–12 schools (Rhodes & Pufahl, 2009), only a handful of languages are taught in foreign language classes or in bilingual/ dual language programs (see Figures 4.1 and 4.2).

As can be seen in Figures 4.1 and 4.2, Spanish is by far the most popular foreign language of choice in the U.S. both at the elementary and secondary levels. Spanish is also the language most widely spoken natively by ELs in U.S. schools—more than 75% of all ELs in American public schools are from Spanish-speaking backgrounds. However, most of the languages offered by formal K–12 school systems are taught as foreign languages—only a small percentage of the programs cater specifically to heritage populations. For instance, while 88% of the elementary schools offering foreign language programs in 2008 taught Spanish, only 7% had "Spanish for Spanish Speakers" (SpSpSpkrs) classes (Figure 4.1). The same pattern can be seen at the secondary school level—while 93% of the secondary schools offering foreign language programs in 2008 taught Spanish, only 8% had "Spanish for Spanish Speakers" (SpSpSpkrs) classes (Figure 4.2).

Within the mainstream classroom, language minority students' knowledge of their native languages has often been viewed as a hindrance to learning English and other academic content subjects. In many school districts in the U.S. teachers actively discourage students from speaking their native languages in the classroom (see also Chapter 7). As a result, many heritage speakers abandon their native languages during their formative years, only to be given a less-than-optimal chance to (re)learn it later either in secondary school or in college as a "foreign" language. Obviously, this is not a good educational practice. It would be more effective if language minority students are supported to maintain their heritage languages in the first place, than to lose it and try to learn it again later.

On the whole, foreign language teaching is not a priority in American preK–12 education. In a study of language teaching practices and policies in 19 countries, Christian, Pufahl, & Rhodes (2004/2005) found that foreign language instruction generally starts much earlier in other countries. Most of the 19 countries in the survey begin compulsory language instruction for the majority of students in the elementary grades, whereas schools in the U.S. typically do not offer foreign language classes until middle school or high school. The authors argue that what the U.S. needs is a national commitment to elementary school language teaching for all children. Given the vast linguistic diversity among the K–12 student population in the U.S., they contend that heritage language instruction should be a significant part of this commitment.

It is an unfortunate fact that foreign language education in the U.S. starts too late for most students. But recent evidence suggests that even the existing

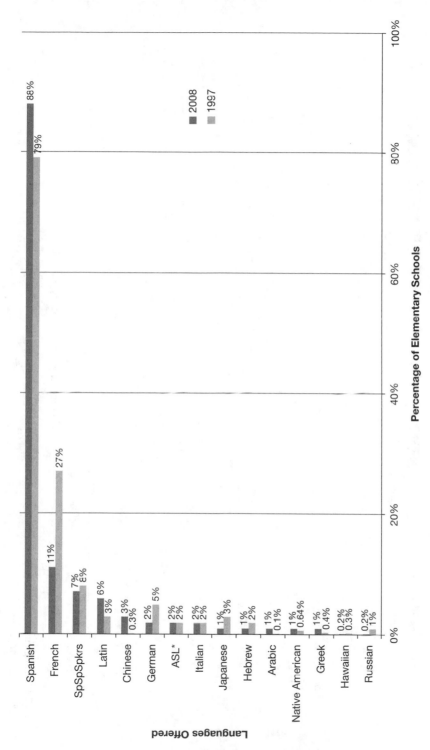

FIGURE 4.1 Languages Offered by Elementary Schools with Foreign Language Programs, 1997, 2008

*American Sign Language

Source: Rhodes & Pufahl, 2009. Reproduced by permission of Center for Applied Linguistics

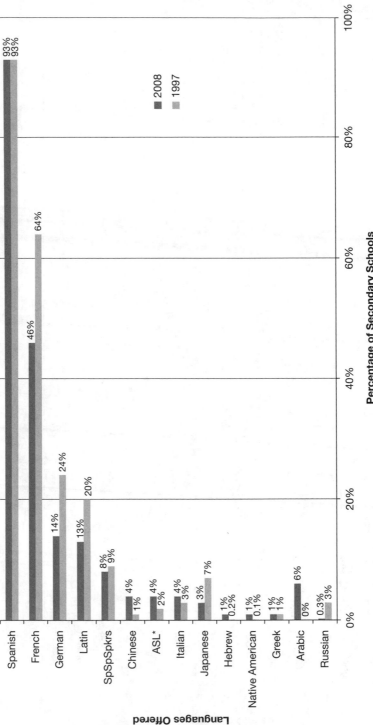

FIGURE 4.2 Languages Offered by Secondary Schools with Foreign Language Programs, 1997, 2008

*American Sign Language

Source: Rhodes & Pufahl, 2009. Reproduced by permission of Center for Applied Linguistics

language programs are threatened by an educational policy that places little emphasis on the value of knowing other languages. In the CAL survey of foreign language teaching in K–12 schools in the U.S., Rhodes & Pufahl (2009) found that the percentage of elementary and middle schools offering foreign language instruction decreased significantly from 1997 to 2008: from 31% to 25% of all elementary schools (see Figure 4.3) and from 75% to 58% of all middle schools (see Figure 4.4). The decline at the elementary level occurred mainly in public elementary schools; the percentage of private elementary schools teaching languages remained about the same.

Rhodes & Pufahl (2009) found that about a third of public elementary and secondary schools with language programs were affected by the federal *No Child Left Behind* (NCLB) legislation (Public Law 107-110). Comments from survey respondents suggested that NCLB's focus on reading and math (the two tested subjects) had drawn resources away from foreign languages which are not included in the law's testing program (Rhodes & Pufahl, 2009). NCLB requires annual testing of all students in reading and math in grades 3 through 8. These tests are "high-stakes" because schools, administrators, teachers, and students who fail to make the grade face some serious consequences.

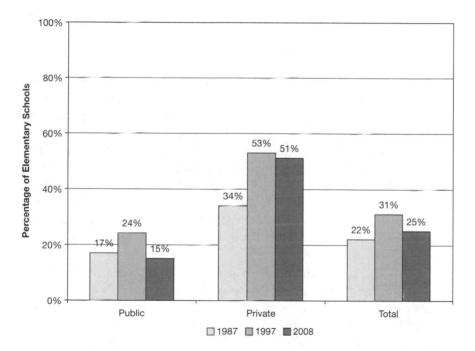

FIGURE 4.3 Elementary Schools Teaching Foreign Languages (by School Type), 1987, 1997, 2008

Source: Rhodes & Pufahl, 2009. Reproduced by permission of Center for Applied Linguistics

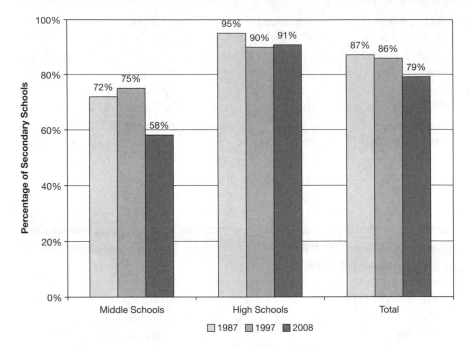

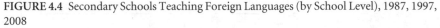

FIGURE 4.4 Secondary Schools Teaching Foreign Languages (by School Level), 1987, 1997, 2008

Source: Rhodes & Pufahl, 2009. Reproduced by permission of Center for Applied Linguistics

With an exclusive focus on English, NCLB requires schools to move language minority students into mainstream English-only classrooms as quickly as possible. Teachers and schools are under immense pressures to raise the test scores of these students and are increasingly focusing their instruction to the content covered by the tests, instead of providing the kind of instruction that addresses the full range of linguistic and educational needs of ELs (Meier & Wood, 2004; Menken, 2008). Curriculum and instruction, particularly in low-performing schools with high percentages of minority student populations, are increasingly driven by materials that are covered by the tests while non-tested subjects such as social studies, foreign languages, and music are neglected.

Foreign language teaching in public schools is not intensive enough to produce advanced bilingualism. Only a small percentage of foreign language programs in public elementary schools, where they exist, go beyond the introductory level. Rhodes & Pufahl (2009) found that of the 15% of all public elementary schools that offered any foreign language programs at all in 2008, 47% offered the exploratory model, which provides introductory exposure to the language. Language focus programs, which emphasize listening, speaking, reading, writing, and culture, were offered at 39% of public elementary schools with language programs. These programs may or may not expect students to gain proficiency in the language, depending on the goals of the particular program. Only 14% of public elementary language programs followed an immersion model, which provides students the opportunity to attain high levels of proficiency in the target language. Thus, foreign language teaching in K–12 schools lacks both *breadth* (in terms of the number of languages offered) and *depth* (in terms of opportunities to develop advanced proficiencies).

Heritage Language Education in Community-Based Programs

Other than formal school systems, community-based organizations provide heritage language education. Some heritage communities in the U.S. have well-developed weekend schools that offer language classes. For instance, about 150,000 students took Chinese language classes in community-based Chinese schools across the U.S. in 2007 (McGinnis, 2008: 231). There are approximately 1,200 Korean community language schools in the U.S. with a total student enrollment of about 60,000 (Lee & Shin, 2008). More than a third of these schools are located in the areas near Los Angeles and New York, with high concentrations of Korean immigrants. For many ethnic groups that are geographically more dispersed and are fewer in number, however, heritage language schools have not been part of their community structure. And where such schools exist, they generally face substantial obstacles in supporting language learning (Brecht & Ingold, 2002).

OUT OF THE MOUTHS OF BILINGUALS 4.2

Learning Chinese In A Community School

"Chinese was actually the first language I learned . . . since I lived in Taiwan for about five years. It was the only language. . . . And then when I got here, [my mom] still tried . . . actually made me and my brother go to I guess what they call Sunday school which is like a Chinese version of language school. So all throughout elementary school, middle school, and high school, I went to Chinese school Sundays. . . . When I was in 8th grade, my mom actually had an opportunity to send me and my brother to Taiwan. . . . And it was funny because after about two weeks there, I pretty much started speaking like a native. . . . After three months when we came back, my mom said, 'Wow, you guys sound completely different.'"

Kenny, a biracial Taiwanese American interviewed in Shin (2010: 209)

Community language programs in general have had little prestige and visibility in the broader community (Tse, 2001). They suffer from lack of recognition by public education systems, which generally view work done in heritage schools as extraneous and unrelated to mainstream education. Furthermore, many community-based schools are riddled with internal problems. Research has shown a weak correlation between community language school attendance and proficiency in the language in question (Sohn & Merrill, 2008). Teaching techniques that poorly address the learning styles of heritage learners, lack of motivation by students who resent having to go to school on weekends, and lack of professional development of teachers all contribute to low success rates (Lee, 2002). In addition, students are often turned off by instructional materials that have little direct relevance to their lives. For instance, in some Korean heritage programs, Korean history texts have been used to teach grammar, but with little or no background knowledge of Korean history, many students rapidly lose interest (Lee & Shin, 2008). Probably the biggest problem with community-based schools is that heritage learners see these programs as being completely removed from their regular American schooling experiences and providing little tangible benefit.

Although most community language programs operate independently from formal school systems, some heritage language sectors have been successful in increasing recognition of their languages by public educational entities. For instance, the inclusion of some heritage languages as part of standardized tests such as the SAT II and the Advanced Placement (AP) exams has led heritage students to see their languages as legitimate and valued entities. Since Korean and Japanese were included as SAT II elective subjects, interest in learning these languages among the heritage students and their parents increased markedly (Lee, 2002). Enrollment in Chinese language schools in southern California increased once students could receive foreign language credit from their local public schools for studying Chinese at community schools (Chen, 1996). The vast majority of the 5,129 SAT II Chinese Test takers in 2001 were heritage Chinese learners, and the same has been true of the AP exam in Chinese (McGinnis, 2008).

Given these figures, McGinnis (2008: 233) finds it ironic that heritage students who take the SAT II and the AP Chinese tests are not the "target audience" as defined by the Educational Testing Service (ETS) and the College Board, which administer these exams. McGinnis (2008: 233) portrays the ETS- and College Board-described "target audience" as a "student with from two to four years of classroom-based experience learning the language in question as a foreign language in a formal instructional setting." He argues that:

The challenge that lies ahead is to convince College Board officials that, rather than limiting their sales and distribution to the K–12 sector, they need to recognize that Chinese community schools can and should be part of the potential market for both the AP Chinese curriculum and test. However much Board officials believe that they are "not in the business of testing heritage learners," . . . they are in fact very much "in the business" of Chinese heritage language learner assessment.

(2008: 236)

Along the same lines, Fishman (2006: 417) makes an impassioned plea for the public to recognize the potential contributions of heritage languages to the greater society:

It is just as scandalous and injurious to waste "native" language resources as to waste our air, water, mineral, animal and various non-linguistic human resources. How long must languages and cultures be trivialized if they are learned at home, in infancy and childhood, and only respected if they are acquired later, during adulthood, when they are usually learned less well and at much greater cost in competence, time and money?

For language minority students in the U.S. with no opportunity to learn their languages in any type of program during their K–12 years, college may be the first time they may be able to take formal coursework in their native languages. This is the topic of the next section.

FOREIGN/HERITAGE LANGUAGE LEARNING
AT POST-SECONDARY INSTITUTIONS

In general, there is considerable interest in foreign language classes on U.S. college campuses. According to a Modern Language Association (MLA) survey, enrollments in languages other than English at American colleges and universities reached a new high of over 1.6 million course enrollments in 2009 (Furman, Goldberg, & Lusin, 2010). Figure 4.5 gives a historical view of modern language course enrollments in U.S. colleges and universities since 1960. Notice the continuous rise in enrollment numbers since 1995. But as a proportion of overall university student enrollments, enrollments in modern language courses were the same in 2006 and 2009 at 8.6 per 100 total enrollments (see Figure 4.6). Note that the 2006 and 2009 figures are significantly lower than the high of 16.5 enrollments per 100 overall enrollments in 1965 but are above the low of 7.3 enrollments per 100 overall in 1980. The MLA survey attributes the decline in foreign language enrollment ratio since 1965 to fewer and shorter language requirements found on U.S. college campuses in recent years than in the past (Furman et al., 2010).

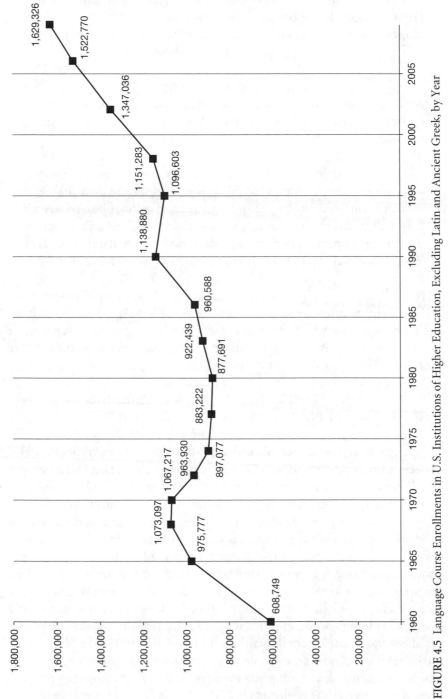

FIGURE 4.5 Language Course Enrollments in U.S. Institutions of Higher Education, Excluding Latin and Ancient Greek, by Year

Source: Furman et al., 2010. Reproduced by permission of the Modern Language Association

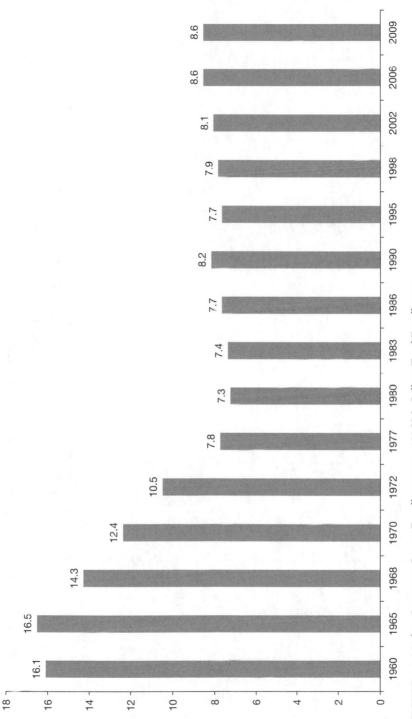

FIGURE 4.6 Modern Language Course Enrollments per 100 U.S. College Total Enrollments

Source: Furman et al., 2010. Reproduced by permission of the Modern Language Association

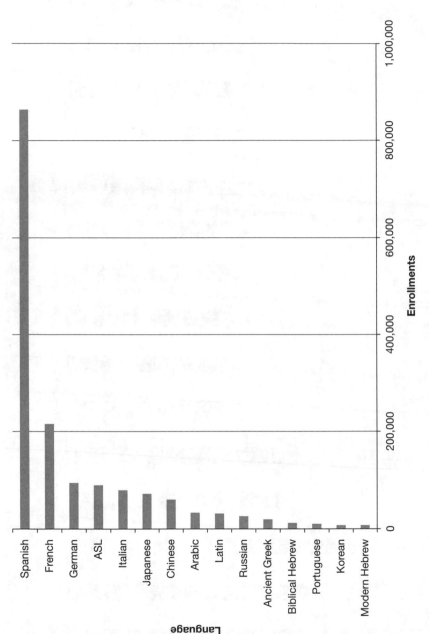

FIGURE 4.7 Most Studied Languages on U.S. College Campuses, 2009

Source: Adapted from Furman et al., 2010

Figure 4.7 shows the 15 most studied languages on U.S. college campuses in 2009. Spanish is by far the most popular foreign language of choice in U.S. post-secondary institutions and has four times the enrollments of French, which is ranked second. German, American Sign Language (ASL), and Italian have the third, fourth, and fifth highest enrollments respectively. The MLA survey reports that enrollments in languages outside the 15 most commonly taught languages, classified as "Less Commonly Taught Languages" (LCTLs), grew by 21% between 2006 and 2009, following a gain of 31% between 2002 and 2006. In total, 217 LCTLs were offered for study in 2009, 35 more than in 2006. Thus, compared to the K–12 level, far more languages are offered at the college level (i.e., there is *greater breadth*).

But once again, the problem of *lack of depth* I discussed earlier with regard to K–12 foreign language instruction applies to college-level programs as well. The majority of college students in the U.S. do not go on to advanced language studies. Figure 4.8 shows advanced course enrollments as percentage of all enrollments in the top 15 languages in 2009. Enrollments in introductory classes may reflect degree requirements, whereas enrollments in advanced classes may indicate possible language minors and majors, as well as courses taken as a part of professional preparation. As can be seen in Figure 4.8, advanced classes made up more than 20% of all undergraduate student enrollments in only five languages: Chinese, Russian, Portuguese, Biblical Hebrew, and Korean. In contrast, advanced courses made up less than 10% of all undergraduate student enrollments in ASL and Italian. For the LCTLs, the picture is not much better—advanced courses made up only 16.6% of all undergraduate student enrollments in LCTLs.

In terms of heritage language instruction, a considerable number of colleges and universities with significant heritage populations offer separate tracks for heritage and non-heritage learners in a variety of languages (Kondo-Brown, 2003). However, instructional materials and strategies, and assessment procedures and instruments for heritage populations are not adequately developed for many languages. Wang (2007) observes that post-secondary Chinese language programs that have experienced rapid growth in enrollment in recent years have been scrambling to figure out how to address the issues of accommodating students from very diverse backgrounds, including those who are completely new to the language (the truly foreign language learners), and heritage and non-heritage students who have received differing amounts of Chinese instruction in K–12 schools and/or community-based schools.

Heritage learners vary widely in background characteristics, language proficiencies, and attitudes toward their home languages and cultures (Peyton et al., 2001). Kondo-Brown (2005) compared the Japanese language proficiencies of three groups of Japanese as a Heritage Language (JHL) learners with

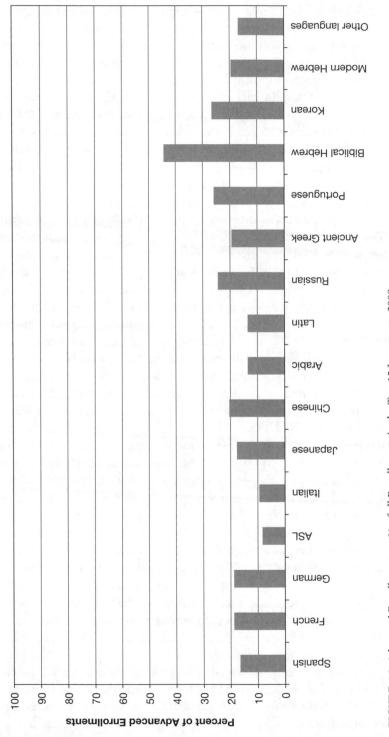

FIGURE 4.8 Advanced Enrollments as % of all Enrollments in the Top 15 Languages, 2009

Source: Adapted from Furman et al., 2010

those of Japanese as a Foreign Language (JFL) students. She found that there were striking similarities between the JFL group and two JHL groups (JHL students with at least one Japanese-speaking grandparent but no Japanese-speaking parent as one group, and JHL students of Japanese descent with no Japanese-speaking parent or grandparent as the other). In contrast, the third group of JHL students (those with at least one Japanese-speaking parent) proved to be substantially different from the other groups in (a) grammatical knowledge, (b) listening and reading skills, (c) self-assessed use of Japanese, and (d) self-ratings of a number of can-do tasks that represented a wide range of abilities. In other words, Japanese heritage students who grew up in homes where Japanese was not spoken on a day-to-day basis acted more like JFL students. This sort of information is critical in determining the type of placement and instruction that may be most beneficial to individual students, but is lacking for most languages.

Overall, heritage language education, as a field, is still very much in infancy. Much more research will be needed to understand the learning processes of heritage speakers in a variety of familial, community, and institutional settings.

PROMOTING HERITAGE LANGUAGES: WHAT NEEDS TO BE DONE

Given the state of the field, what can be done to promote languages other than English? In order for heritage languages to thrive, they should not only be valued by the ethnic communities involved, but also by English speakers in the wider society. There is a critical need to raise awareness of public school teachers and administrators of the need for heritage language education and maintenance (Compton, 2001). One way to do this is for heritage language communities to collaborate with public school systems to offer introductory language and culture classes for public school teachers as part of their professional development (Shin, 2006). In addition, teachers and administrators need to be informed about the critical importance of heritage languages in the lives of immigrant students, particularly the devastating effect on family relationships when parents and children cannot communicate with one another due to a language barrier (Fishman, 1991; Wong Fillmore, 2000). Whenever appropriate, teachers should encourage language minority parents to use their native language with their children at home.

Community-based programs can also collaborate with universities and professional organizations that value bilingualism. To illustrate, in 2005, the American Council on the Teaching of Foreign Languages (ACTFL) organized a national public awareness campaign called "The Year of the Languages." This campaign advanced the concept that every person in the U.S. should develop proficiency in at least one language in addition to English. Each month in the yearlong event, there was a focus on a different area—such as language policy, higher education, language advocacy, heritage languages, and early language learning—with specific events reflecting the monthly focus (Cutshall, 2004/2005). This is a terrific example of a mutually beneficial relationship that can be had when ethnic communities work in partnership with professional organizations.

In addition, heritage organizations, businesses, and places of worship need to actively reach out to the broader community by participating in local politics, events, and area development. Heritage language schools may provide classes for non-heritage speakers in the community who may be interested in learning the language and culture. Heritage language community organizations may also make their facilities (buildings, gymnasiums, playgrounds, meeting facilities, etc.) available for use by members of the larger community for purposes other than language instruction.

In the formal school setting, apart from offering a heritage language as a foreign language subject, a more effective method may be to integrate it more fully into the regular school-day curriculum. Two-way immersion education is one form of developmental bilingual education in which English-dominant and heritage-language-dominant students are placed in the same classroom for all or most of the instructional day and are given content and literacy instruction in both languages (Christian, 2008; see also Chapter 8). Two-way programs benefit English-dominant students by giving them extensive opportunities to develop functional literacy in the target language and interact socially with native speakers of that language. Two-way programs also contribute to the maintenance and development of heritage languages for heritage-language-dominant students.

In a study of 16 elementary two-way immersion schools, Lindholm-Leary (2001) found that Spanish speakers were highly proficient in their native language through sixth grade, and had consistently higher proficiencies in Spanish than Spanish speakers in transitional bilingual programs. In another study comparing Korean speakers in three types of programs—(1) two-way immersion programs, (2) modified bilingual programs with minimal Korean language support, and (3) English-only programs—Sohn & Merrill (2008) found that two-way immersion programs provide the greatest benefit to participating students. Korean speakers in two-way programs not only develop English language skills on a par with peers in English-only programs, but also maintain and develop their Korean language skills. Although more research is needed to fully understand the long-term effects of two-way programs, they seem to hold much promise in developing bilingual competence in both majority and minority language speakers.

Advances in electronic communication may provide new opportunities for language learning as well. In her study of Korean heritage learners' electronic literacy practices on a popular website called Cyworld.com, Jin Sook Lee (2006) shows that the online medium provided the students with authentic opportunities to use the target language within a social network of Korean speakers. She argues that the deviant language forms found in e-texts (e.g., contractions, omissions, and phonological adaptations) enable heritage language learners to engage in online interactions without the pressure of having to spell the words correctly, which is a requirement in traditional language classroom settings and a source of stress for heritage learners.

Web-based intercultural exchange programs may increase student engagement in a variety of languages. *Cultura* (http://cultura.mit.edu), a popular online program developed by the French program at MIT to enable cultural exchanges between American and French students, has been adapted to a number of other languages. The National Foreign Language Resource Center (NFLRC) at the University of Hawaii has offered training for language educators to create online cafés linking heritage learners of Filipino, Japanese, Samoan, and Chinese with native speakers of those languages. These programs help students to arrive at a deeper understanding of their own as well as their partner group's cultures and learn the target language more purposefully.

Creating "a language competent society" requires a concerted effort of educators, policymakers, families, and communities. As a society, we need to realize that the languages spoken by ethnic and linguistic minorities are a national asset, a resource that must not be wasted. Students who come from homes where languages other than English are spoken should be supported to maintain those languages while learning English. And students who speak English natively should be supported to learn another language not in a superficial way, but deeply enough to develop functional competence. We need to think of bilingual proficiency not as a luxury, dispensable when there are more pressing needs, but rather as a requirement in an increasingly global world. Most other countries are already doing that. It is time that the U.S. took more proactive steps toward increasing the bilingual competence of its citizenry.

FURTHER READING

- *Heritage Language Journal*—This is a peer-reviewed online journal (http://www.heritagelanguages.org/) devoted to the issues underlying the teaching and learning of heritage languages.
- Peyton, J., Ranard, D. & McGinnis, S. eds. (2001). *Heritage languages in America: Preserving a national resource.* McHenry, IL: Center for Applied Linguistics and Delta Systems.—This edited volume provides an excellent introduction and overview of heritage languages in the United States.
- Brinton, D.M., Kagan, O., & Bauckus, S. eds. (2008). *Heritage language education: A new field emerging.* New York and London: Routledge.—This

volume provides up-to-date research on policy and practice in heritage language education.

STUDY QUESTIONS AND ACTIVITIES

1. How are heritage language learners different from first and second language learners? What strengths do they bring to the language classroom? What advantages do heritage learners have in learning the language over traditional foreign language students?
2. What arguments can you make in support of promoting heritage language education? Other than to address the federal government's need for people with highly developed foreign language skills, what other reasons can you provide for strengthening heritage language education?
3. Interview a teacher or an administrator at a community-based heritage language school. Find out the linguistic backgrounds of the students and the kinds of language skills that are taught in the classes. What is the school's mission? What challenges does the school face in meeting the needs of its students? What types of collaborations, if any, does the school have with the K–12 public school system?
4. Interview several students who are currently attending a community-based heritage language school. How many hours of classroom instruction do they receive per week at the community language school? How many hours do they spend on homework outside of class per week? What do they like most about the school and what do they like least about it? What advantages and disadvantages do they see in learning the language?
5. Interview a university foreign language instructor who teaches both heritage and non-heritage learners. Are the instructional needs of heritage learners different from those of non-heritage learners? If so, in what ways? How are heritage and non-heritage learners differentiated in instruction and what kind of materials, strategies, and assessment procedures are available?
6. What actions can parents, teachers, school administrators, policymakers, and community and business leaders take to promote the teaching and learning of heritage languages?

Bilingualism and Identity

There is a reason why the language we inherit at birth is called our mother tongue. It is our mother, forgiving, embracing, naming the world and all its emotions. Though I have lived for the last forty years in cities where English or French is the language of the majority, it's Bangla that exercises motherly restraint over my provisional, immigrant identity.

—Bharati Mukherjee (2004: 11)

INTRODUCTION

The above excerpt comes from Wendy Lesser's (2004) book, *The genius of language*, in which 15 bilingual writers reflect on their mother tongues. The writers, all of whom are outstanding authors of various works in English, began their lives speaking languages other than English. Although the mother tongues of the 15 essayists are diverse—covering a wide range of languages from Czech to Gikuyu, from Polish to Bangla—one gets the sense that all of the writers have an intimate relationship with the first languages they learned as babies, whether or not they still speak them as adults. Indeed, as Li (2007) aptly points out in her analysis of identities of bilingual writers, "looking for home" is a perpetual theme in the works of bilingual writers, who are "souls in exile," endeavoring to reconcile languages and identities through writing. The intensely personal accounts in *The genius of language* illustrate the power of mother tongues over individual identities, which are shaped and re-shaped as the writers are exposed to other languages and cultures.

Amy Tan, author of *The Joy Luck Club* and one of the essayists in Lesser's book, reflects on her mother tongue, Chinese, and questions the common view that Chinese people are circumspect and do not know how to be direct in their speech. She opens her essay with a scene at a San Francisco restaurant where her mother offers the last scallop from a Happy Family seafood dish to her brother's wife [Sau-sau]:

> Sau-sau scowled. "*B'yao, zhen b'yao!*" (I don't want it, really I don't!) she cried, patting her plump stomach.
> "Take it! Take it!" scolded my mother in Chinese.
> "Full, I'm already full," Sau-sau protested weakly, eyeing the beloved scallop.
> "Ai!" exclaimed my mother, completely exasperated. "Nobody else wants it. If you don't take it, it will only rot!"
> At this point, Sau-sau sighed, acting as if she were doing my mother a big favor by taking the wretched scrap off her hands.
> My mother turned to her brother, a high-ranking communist official who was visiting her in California for the first time: "In America a Chinese person could starve to death. If you say you don't want it, they won't ask you again forever."
>
> (2004: 25)

Tan states that much is lost in translation of this interaction into English. True, Tan admits that Chinese people are culturally socialized to refuse things offered to them to show modesty, but she is troubled by one-dimensional, blanket statements such as, "Chinese people are so discreet and modest . . . In Chinese, there aren't even words for 'yes' and 'no' . . . If one is Chinese, one compromises, one doesn't hazard a loss of face by an overemphatic response." She finds it problematic that people think of the Chinese as fundamentally unable to assert themselves, saying no when they mean yes and yes when they mean no. She writes:

> Yet if I consider my upbringing more carefully, I find there was nothing discreet about the Chinese language I grew up with. My parents made everything abundantly clear. Nothing wishy-washy in their demands, no compromises accepted: "Of course you will become a famous neurosurgeon," they told me. "And yes, a concert pianist on the side."
>
> (2004: 30)

To Tan, human behavior is complex and influenced by social contexts and hidden intentions of individuals. **Cultural stereotypes**, like the statements about Chinese people that Tan finds problematic, fail to capture the varied lived experiences of individuals and their unique positions in the world. People's identities are not defined by any given category such as race, ethnicity, nationality, or gender, but are contested and negotiated through social interaction. For example, a natural response of someone who is discriminated on account of his/her ethnicity is to disassociate him/herself from the language associated with that ethnicity by temporarily suppressing it or denying knowledge of it. Since there are usually heavy costs associated with being identified as minorities, some people may even try to put some distance between themselves and others of similar backgrounds. Terms like "FOB" (fresh-off-the-boat) and "mojados" (wetbacks) are used by immigrants to describe recently arrived members of their own groups (Jeon, 2010). By distancing themselves from the more recent arrivals, the earlier immigrants negotiate a new identity, one that is not so stigmatized in the society.

In this chapter, I will examine the relationship between bilingualism and identity. According to Norton (1997: 410), **identity** refers to the ways in which "people understand their relationship to the world, how that relationship is constructed across time and space, and how people understand their possibilities for the future." Identity is dynamic, multifaceted, and negotiated through language (Cummins, 2000; Lam, 2004a; Leung, Harris, & Rampton, 1997; Nicholas, 2009; Nieto & Bode, 2011; Pavlenko & Blackledge, 2004; Rajadurai, 2010; Schecter & Bayley, 1997). I will show how identities are reflected in the way bilinguals use their languages and how people construct new identities through language. We will see that language and identity have been theorized differently in various disciplines such as sociology, cultural anthropology, psychology, and education. By drawing from different research traditions and making comparisons between methodologies where appropriate, I hope to introduce the reader to diverse ways of thinking about language and identity.

Also in this chapter, I will discuss language and identity in the classroom. Language teaching and learning are sociocultural phenomena, and constitute important sites for negotiating various identities (Kramsch, 1993). Because of the power differential in the languages involved in any bilingual situation (see Chapter 3), the language classroom is a place where questions of power, inequality, resistance, and struggle are very salient. When children who speak a minority language enter school, they are often labeled as being deficient in the language of school (e.g., "limited English proficient"). They are identified for what they cannot do rather than what they can, which leads to feelings of disempowerment and academic failure (Cummins, 2000). For teachers then, understanding the social context of education is as important as mastering the content material and pedagogical techniques. I will discuss how language and identity are constructed in the classroom and show ways in which educators can empower students through a better understanding of classroom power dynamics.

I first turn to a discussion of language and ethnic identity in multilingual societies.

LANGUAGE ATTITUDE AND ETHNIC IDENTITY

Ethnic identity is the behaviors, beliefs, values, and norms that define a person as a member of a particular ethnic group. In Chapter 3, I discussed the multilingual situation of Singapore, whose government's pro-Mandarin policy has resulted in a massive shift to Mandarin among speakers of different Chinese dialects such as Cantonese, Hakka, and Hokkien. Started in 1979, the Singaporean government's "Speak Mandarin" campaign has been so successful that whereas only 0.1% of the country's population spoke Mandarin as a mother tongue in 1965, the year Singapore became an independent republic, close to half of the population now use Mandarin at home (McKay & Bokhorst-Heng, 2008). This remarkable shift in language use is attributed to a widespread view among the different Chinese dialect groups that Mandarin is a unifying symbol of their ethnic identity.

In neighboring Malaysia, a negative attitude toward English-speaking Malays has resulted in particularly low levels of English proficiency among the ethnic Malays. Like Singapore, Malaysia is a multilingual, multiethnic country. Its population consists of 65% Malay, 26% Chinese, and 7.7% Indians (Rajadurai, 2010). Malay is the native language of most ethnic Malays and the national language, while English is widely regarded as a second language in the country. In addition to Malay and English, a number of Chinese dialects, Indian languages, and other minority languages are spoken in Malaysia. As a colonial language, English enjoyed a level of prestige that the other languages did not until Malay independence in 1957, when the Malay language became the official language and the medium of instruction at all levels of education.

Rajadurai (2010) observes that this shift in policy led to a gradual decline in English proficiency among Malaysians, particularly among the ethnic Malays. While the non-Malays have more or less retained their bi-/multilingual status, the Malays have become largely monolingual. Rajadurai (2010) attributes this uneven outcome in English proficiency to a general negative attitude among Malays toward English-speaking Malays. She notes that among the Malays, there is a widely held perception that English is "foreign, pagan, and, even, evil" and its speakers are "rude, snobbish, arrogant, un-Malay, and un-Islamic" (2010: 103). She contends that this prevailing negative attitude toward English prevents Malays in Malaysia from improving their English. Unlike the other ethnic groups in the country, she contends that the category "Malay" is associated with nonnegotiable linguistic, religious, and cultural loyalties—Malays are expected to speak Malay for participation, acceptance, and legitimacy in the Malay community.

The negative societal attitude toward English-speaking Malays drives some Malays to hide their knowledge of English. In another study of Malaysian identity, Kim (2003: 147) presents the following excerpt from her interview with

Soraya, a 25-year-old Malay woman, who lived in the U.S. from kindergarten through sixth grade:

> But it's quite embarrassing when you come back and you are a Malay and you don't know how to speak Malay . . . it's embarrassing. I didn't want to admit but somehow I knew I had to do it. Every time I spoke English, I had the American accent and people would think that I showed off, so I . . . I tried to hide it, and so when I went to secondary school in Kedah, I hid it all the more and I . . . I speak it less and less.

Azlina, another Malay participant in Kim's (2003) study, reported that she uses English most of the time on her college campus but avoids using it among friends back home:

> Because I don't want to look like I'm trying to boast. You are not in the "In" group anymore. I try not to speak English. If you want to be part of a group, you have to follow the rules, right? Yea[h], unwritten rules.
>
> (2003: 148)

But Azlina confessed that she sometimes deliberately used English to annoy her Malay friends who disapproved of her using English:

> When people irritate me, I'll change to English. And I don't just speak English, I'll speak with a little bit of slang. I know that when people irritate me, I use this as a form of shield. Even among my friends I'll try my best to speak in very good English. Partly as a shield. To make a point, okay, pay attention to me.
>
> (2003: 148)

Azlina commented that she finds Malaysians who speak English with a Western accent annoying. Therefore, when she is irritated and wants to annoy people who she knows resent Malays using English, she deliberately speaks English with a "put-on" British or American accent. Kim (2003) argues that this temporary shift in language draws negative attention to the speaker, resulting in her increased power over the audience. Azlina's strategic use of English here cannot be explained by a simple correlation between the use of Malay with a Malay identity and the use of English with a Western identity. Rather, Azlina's choice to temporarily mask (or unmask) English is determined by the specific social interaction.

OUT OF THE MOUTHS OF BILINGUALS 5.1

Quatro Formaggio Pizza, **Anyone?**

". . . I would like to pull the curtain a little to allow a glimpse at the intimate dance between my languages and my emotional responses to things . . . *Quatro formaggio pizza* makes my mouth water while four cheeses pizza leaves me unmoved. Only the English *jerk* captures all the things one associates with a real jerk. None of my other languages offers a word that comes even close."

(Todeva, 2009: 70)

For the ESL teacher in Malaysia, understanding the social realities of Malay learners of English is critically important. Given the prevailing negative attitude toward Malays who speak English, Rajadurai (2010) notes that for many students, the classroom may be the only place where any English use takes place. Given this insight, she argues that:

> learning institutions need to redefine themselves as sites where students can experiment, make mistakes, and practice using the L2 without fear of being judged, scorned, or derided. At the same time, these third spaces must provide scaffolding to support students and help prepare them for life in the real world. Students need to be equipped with some degree of perseverance, tenacity, and the will to succeed and navigate their way successfully in the various communities to which they belong or aspire to belong.
>
> (2010: 104)

Just as Malays who are trying to be accepted into Malay social groups might hide their knowledge of English, members of linguistic minority groups who want to be accepted as legitimate members of the mainstream group might hide their knowledge of their mother tongues. Shifting allegiance to the socially dominant language is a common pattern found among ethnic minority children as they try to come to terms with their minority status. This is the topic of the next section.

ETHNIC IDENTITY DEVELOPMENT: A MODEL

A number of researchers have proposed models of ethnic identity development, suggesting that ethnic minorities progress through a predictable path when coming to terms with their minority status. Drawing on the works of social psychologists (e.g., Phinney, 1989), Tse (1998) proposes a four-stage model of ethnic identity development that forecasts racial minorities' shifting attitudes toward the heritage and majority languages. "Stage 1—Unawareness" is a relatively brief period when ethnic minorities are not conscious of their minority status and/or of the subordinate status often associated with it. This stage typically occurs before major contact with other ethnic or racial groups, for example, before attending school or leaving an ethnic enclave. Preschool children in immigrant families can normally be found in this stage.

"Stage 2—Ethnic Ambivalence/Evasion" is characterized by ambivalent or negative feelings toward the ethnic culture and preferred identification with the dominant societal group. Starting formal schooling typically marks the beginning of Stage 2. This stage may span a relatively long period, for example, childhood through adolescence, and even through adulthood. In her analysis of the personal narratives of Americans of Asian descent, Tse (2000) states that the desire to be accepted by the dominant group, together with perceived failure to meet the criteria for group membership, led to feelings of alienation for several of the narrators, particularly when their distinctiveness was made salient. One of the narrators, Ben Fong-Torres, who as a child experienced shame and embarrassment at encountering a stereotypical Asian comic book figure, felt alienated when he was identified with that character:

> I remember the shock I felt in physical education class when Coach Kile, a handsome young man, looked at me early in the semester, clapped his hands, and yelled, "Let's go, Chop Chop!" . . . For a kid who was longing to belong, it was a devastating blow. Trying only to fit in, I had been singled out; I was that round little yellow-skinned guy in the comic book. I was the Ching-Chong Chinaman.
>
> (Tse, 2000: 194–195)

Many of the narrators in Tse's (2000) study saw language as a sign of ethnic group membership and tried to dissociate themselves from their heritage languages while identifying with English. David Mura recounted feelings of pride in his fluency in English and in his inability to speak Japanese because "I didn't want to be thought of as Japanese-American . . . I didn't want to be classified as one of the typical Asian science geeks, even though math was my best subject in high school" (Tse, 2000: 195). For many ethnic minorities, Stage 2 is a difficult period characterized by conflicting emotions and attitudes toward the mainstream society and their ethnic communities.

"Stage 3—Ethnic Emergence" is a time when ethnic minorities explore their heritage after confronting the fact that they are members of a minority group. In contrast to Stage 2 where ethnic minorities prefer associating with the majority group, the exploration during Stage 3 leads some to embrace their ethnicity in favor of the mainstream group. Finally, in "Stage 4—Ethnic Identity Incorporation," ethnic minorities discover and join their ethnic group (e.g., Mexican Americans, Chinese Canadians, etc.) and resolve many of the identity conflicts that were present in the previous stage. Because much of the confusion and uncertainty experienced during Stages 2 and 3 are resolved in Stage 4, this last stage is characterized by acceptance of oneself as an ethnic minority and improved self-image.

Tse (1998) qualifies her model by stating that not all racial and ethnic minorities go through the four stages. She observes that some ethnic minorities, including many adult immigrants, may never aspire to become a member of the dominant group, and therefore, never go through these four stages. Individuals are more likely to disassociate from a social group in favor of another if they believe that the boundaries between the old group and the new group are easily crossed. She argues that if ethnic minorities have strong ties to the ethnic culture and/or possess cultural markers that are not easily shed (e.g., an accent in English), joining the dominant group may never be seen as plausible or desirable.

Despite these qualifications, Tse's model is useful in predicting that heritage language acquisition is more likely to occur when someone is not in Stage 2. For optimal result, heritage language education needs to begin when children are in Stage 1 (i.e., preschool and early elementary years). Introducing the language in middle or high school is not very effective since this is when many ethnic minority youth are in Stage 2 and avoid being identified as members of their ethnic groups. Some language minority students take up heritage language classes for the first time in college, but this is often not as effective as starting earlier. Regardless of the stage one is in, Tse emphasizes the importance of heritage language group membership (e.g., positive peer relationships) in developing proficiency in the heritage language. Creating opportunities for positive social interaction in the language is essential.

Tse's model is supported by longitudinal investigations of bilingual children. Caldas & Caron-Caldas (2002) examined the evolving language preferences of their three French/English bilingual children, twin girls aged 13 and a boy aged 15. The children were raised in a predominantly French-speaking home in south Louisiana by the bilingual French/English-speaking authors, but spent summers in French-speaking Quebec. As the children moved into adolescence, they spoke significantly more English in their Louisiana home, but maintained their use of French in Quebec. The children's preference for English in Louisiana and French in Quebec was attributed to their desire to identify with monolingual peers in those settings. In a follow-up study, Caldas (2006) examined the changing bilingual self-perceptions of the three children from early adolescence through early adulthood. He found that the children valued their bilingualism much more as older adolescents than as younger adolescents. As older adolescents, they were less affected by peer pressure and had a greater sense of bicultural identity.

THE ROLE OF HERITAGE LANGUAGE
PROFICIENCY IN IDENTITY DEVELOPMENT

The research on the relationship between heritage language and identity development suggests that developing a strong sense of ethnic identity is crucial during adolescence when periods of identity crisis shape one's self-concept and self-esteem (Lee & Suarez, 2009; Phinney, Romero, Nava, & Huang, 2001; Tse, 2000). Lee & Suarez (2009) argue that for children who live at the intersection of two languages and cultures, depriving them of either language or culture does injustice to their sense of identity. They argue that children must be supported to develop in both languages and learn to be part of both cultures. Correspondingly, ethnic minorities with heritage language proficiency have been found to develop a stronger sense of bicultural identity than those without (e.g., Cho & Krashen, 1998; Jo, 2001; Lee, 2002; Lee & Suarez, 2009; Phinney et al., 2001; Rumbaut, 1994).

For example, in her study of the role of cultural identity and heritage language maintenance among second-generation Korean American university students, Lee (2002) found that heritage language proficiency tended to correlate with the degree of the participants' **bicultural identity**—that is, those who had greater Korean proficiency were more likely to identify themselves as *both* American *and* Korean. Lee & Suarez (2009) point out that immigrant children's sense of their "Americanness" is not diminished, but enhanced by a better understanding of their own ethnic identity and competence in their heritage language. Likewise, Portes & Rumbaut (2006) argue that immigrant groups that maintain their own ethnic language and culture *while* learning English and the U.S. culture have more positive acculturation experiences than those who switch over to English altogether.

The research by Pao, Wong, & Teuben-Rowe (1997) suggests that heritage language proficiency is strongly related to the identity of mixed-heritage individuals. The authors divided the participants into two groups based on language ability—a bilingual group and a monolingual English-speaking group. They found that the bilingual group had more support for the development of positive self-identities than did the monolingual group, who at times experienced feelings of isolation from both cultures. The bilingual participants believed that the ability to speak the languages of both of their parents was fundamental to their identity. In my own research on mixed-heritage individuals, I also found that the heritage language figures importantly in the participants' understanding of who they are (Shin, 2010). While some of the young adults in my study used their knowledge of the heritage language to gain greater access to and legitimacy in the ethnic community, some who never developed in that language lamented not being able to connect with their heritage-language-speaking parents and extended family members at a deeper level.

However, there are some studies which suggest that the relationship between heritage language proficiency and identity may not be so strong. For example, in her study of Hopi Indian youth, Nicholas (2009) showed that even without a strong proficiency in the Hopi language, youth learn to act, think, and feel Hopi through their active participation in their Hopi world. The Hopi youth who have no functional proficiency in the language nonetheless identified themselves strongly as Hopi and distinguished themselves from the Whites. Although the Hopi youth admitted that language is an important way of identifying with Hopi culture, they did not think language was necessarily a requirement for identification as Hopi. Similarly, in a study of Navajo and Pueblo Indian youth, Tiffany S. Lee (2009) found that while indigenous languages play an important role in contemporary youth identity, the youths' lack of proficiency in the heritage languages did not diminish their indigenous consciousness.

How do we make sense of these seemingly conflicting results? Which claim is right? Does heritage language proficiency matter or not in ethnic identity formation? Part of the answer to this question lies in the different populations studied. Lee (2002) and Tse (2000) base their research on children of Asian immigrants to the U.S. for whom language shift is ongoing in the family. As second-generation immigrants, these participants have grown up in homes where the immigrant language is spoken by the parents to varying degrees. Few of these children speak the heritage language well, while the majority of them, due to external pressures and/or personal choice, have neglected and developed little or no proficiency in that language. Language maintenance or shift is largely a matter of personal choice for these relatively recent immigrants, who are sometimes referred to as **voluntary minorities** (Ogbu, 1992). These are people who have voluntarily immigrated to the host country in search of a better life.

In contrast, the Native American youth in Nicholas's (2009) and Lee's (2009) studies are considered **involuntary minorities**, those who were originally brought into American society against their will through slavery, conquest, colonization, or forced labor, and were often denied the opportunity for full participation in the mainstream society. Feelings of language shame are endemic among indigenous communities after generations of oppression and cultural domination by the mainstream society. In a study of Native youth in the U.S. Southwest, McCarty, Romero, & Zepeda (2006) found that Navajo youth and their teachers had different perceptions of the number of Navajo speakers in their school. The teachers reported that between 30% and 50% of youth in their school could speak Navajo, whereas Navajo youth perceived this number to be between 75% and 80%. To explain this difference, the authors noted that many youth viewed speaking Navajo as an "emblem of shame" and hence give the impression they do not have Navajo language skills when in school (McCarty et al., 2006: 38).

Forced cultural assimilation of indigenous populations has been a common practice in the U.S. and in other parts of the world. For several decades, the U.S. government operated a program of boarding schools specifically designed to eradicate Native Americans' language and culture (Cultural Survival, 2011). Native American children were taken from their families, sent to boarding schools in faraway places and severely punished when caught speaking their native languages. This resulted in widespread language shame and language loss among indigenous peoples. Language shift is very advanced in many Native American communities—70 of the 139 Native American languages spoken today are expected to disappear in the next five years (Cultural Survival, 2011). In this context, Native youth must negotiate what it means to be a Native person in today's society *with* or *without* their language. Their identity cannot ride solely on their proficiency in their heritage language.

Aside from the differences in the populations studied, the conflicting results can be explained in part by different methodologies used in the studies. Lee (2002) used a 76-item written questionnaire which elicited participants' responses regarding their personal history, language skills, and cultural identity. Each of her 40 participants self-rated his/her proficiency and cultural identity on a five-point Likert scale in terms of how strongly he/she agreed with the statements. For example, participants could choose a number between 1 (strongly disagree) and 5 (strongly agree) on Korean orientation statements such as, "Knowing Korean will help me become successful" or, "I enjoy Korean music." They were presented with American orientation statements that mirrored the Korean statements, such as, "Knowing English will help me become successful" or, "I enjoy American music." The responses were put through a series of regression analyses to determine whether language proficiency had any effect on the participants' cultural identity. What Lee found was that Korean language proficiency had a significant effect on *both* the participants' Korean orientation *and* American orientation, leading her to conclude that a higher heritage language proficiency is related with a stronger sense of bicultural identity.

In comparison, Nicholas (2009) employed a case study approach involving in-depth interviews and participant observation. She provides rich, detailed descriptions of each of her three participants' backgrounds, including information on their personalities, physical characteristics, family makeup, hobbies, and career aspirations. As an "insider" researcher (Nicholas is a Hopi), she was able to observe informally the daily routines, conversations, and behaviors of her participants in the homes and the village. Building her analysis around these detailed observations and interviews, Nicholas presents a more intimate, personal account of identity. Her argument that even without a command of the Hopi language youth can develop a strong orientation to the Hopi way of life is supported by interview excerpts like the following:

> Yeah it's important to speak, but that's not all that counts. Because a Pahaana (Anglo) can learn how to speak it, speak the language, but they don't know the meaning behind it, or the actual culture, the in-depth stuff; [so] then they're not Hopi. They don't practice our religious ceremony[ies] and they don't *live* Hopi; [so] then they're not Hopi.
>
> (Dorian, age 19, a nonspeaker of Hopi;
> emphasis added by Nicholas) (2009: 321)

By staying away from pre-established identity statements such as those used by Lee (e.g., "I fit in well with Koreans," "I believe in American values"), Nicholas explores the issues of identity in a more open-ended manner. Had Nicholas adopted a survey method, she may not have been able to fully explain the intricacies of various Hopi religious ceremonies, farming rituals, and naming practices, all of which her participants considered to be crucial in their construction of a Hopi identity.

I am not implying that a qualitative method is better than a quantitative one. In fact, both methods are useful in their own ways. Questionnaires, popular in social science research, are better suited for studying large numbers of people because they are relatively easy to administer and analyze. Likert-scale and multiple-choice type questions used in questionnaires lend themselves well to statistical tests to show general trends, relationships, and correlations. On the other hand, qualitative studies usually require a significant amount of observations and interaction with participants and are therefore difficult to carry out with a large group. The important point to remember is that, as researchers, we need to avail ourselves of different methodologies, and know when to use which. We also need to be careful about making generalizations based on published research. Does heritage language proficiency matter in ethnic identity formation? Based on the above discussion, the answer is both yes and no, depending on the population involved and status of the language.

Research shows that the relationship between identity and language is in fact not linear and is complicated by interactions with a range of other factors such as social class, gender, geographic location, and generational differences (Lam, 2004a; Nguyen & Stritikus, 2009; Nieto, 2002; Phinney et al., 2001; Schecter & Bayley, 1997). For instance, in a study of the language socialization practices of four Mexican-descent families in northern California and in south Texas, Schecter & Bayley (1997) found that while all four focal children defined themselves as Mexican or Mexican American, only two of the families had aggressive Spanish maintenance strategies. Of the other two families, one combined some Spanish use in the home with instruction from Spanish-speaking relatives, whereas the family that had moved most completely into the middle class was the least successful in the intergenerational transmission of Spanish, despite a commitment to cultural maintenance.

Lee & Suarez (2009) contend that many immigrants experience what Bedolla (2003) calls "selective dissociation" with their heritage language and culture as a response to interactions in which their mother tongues become a source of shame rather than pride. They argue that when there are negative associations with one's culture and language, individuals tend to dissociate from the ethnic group, but in contexts where the heritage culture is viewed in a positive light, they desire close identification with the group. Thus, rather than being a fixed entity, identity is constructed and shaped through social interaction. This in fact represents the constructivist views on identity, to which I turn next.

ESSENTIALIST VS. CONSTRUCTIVIST VIEWS ON LANGUAGE AND IDENTITY: AN EXAMPLE

In the introduction, I stated that the link between language and identity has been theorized in various disciplines following different research traditions. Among them, constructivist frameworks have become particularly popular in the last 15 years (e.g., Kanno, 2003; McKay & Wong, 1996; Norton, 1997; Peirce, 1995) partly due to a growing dissatisfaction among researchers with essentialist models in which variations in language use are explained through correlations with pre-established social categories (see Auer, 2005). Quite simply, essentialist models view identity in terms of pre-supposed, measurable categories (e.g., age, gender, social class, ethnicity) whereas constructivist frameworks recognize the fluidity of identities as they are constructed in social interaction.

To take an example, Social Network Analysis, which has been used widely by sociolinguists to investigate language shift and maintenance among people living in bilingual communities, assumes that the mother tongue is an integral part of collective ethnic identity, and that maintenance of that language across generations is a key factor in the maintenance of such identities. Because close-knit social networks tend to exert pressure on people's language choice (Li & Milroy, 1995; Milroy, 1987), speakers with stronger ethnic ties are expected to make more use of the ethnic group's language and less use of the majority language than those with weaker ethnic ties.

The predictions of Social Network Analysis are borne out in some studies but not in others. In Li's (1994) study of Chinese immigrants in Tyneside, England, for example, participants who had a strong Chinese-based social network and interacted mainly with other Chinese people had Chinese-dominant language choice patterns. Likewise, those who had more non-Chinese ties adopted bilingual or English-dominant language choice patterns. But in Lanza & Svendsen's (2007) study of a multilingual Filipino community in Oslo, Norway, the participants who had a dense Filipino-based social network did not always use more Filipino with their children. Some chose to speak in Norwegian, while others spoke in Tagalog and English. In addition to these languages, some participants used other Filipino languages such as Cebuano, Bicolano, and Ilocano, as well as Spanish.

In discussing these results, Lanza & Svendsen (2007) recognize the limitations of an essentialist model such as Social Network Analysis in explaining the complex and multi-layered relationship between language choice and identity in a multilingual community. They contend that multilinguals have multiple identities and that while Social Network Analysis is a good predictive tool for assessing language choice in migrant communities, it should be supplemented with constructivist approaches to arrive at a fuller understanding of the communities in question. In the following, I discuss the constructivist views in more detail and consider their contributions to promoting a better understanding of the social contexts of language learning.

UNDERSTANDING THE SOCIAL CONTEXTS
OF LANGUAGE LEARNING

In the field of second language acquisition (SLA), examining the identity of second language learners has been a relatively recent phenomenon. Much emphasis has been placed on understanding second language learner errors, comparing them with native speaker norms. As such, the existing SLA research is skewed toward the acquisition of L2 grammar and morphology, and gives little recognition to the social contexts in which a second language is learned. The student is simply viewed as a language learner whose primary goal is to reach (near-)native proficiency in the target language.

One of the most widely recognized facts about second language learning is that some individuals are simply more successful in learning a second language than others despite equal instruction and materials (Gass & Selinker, 2008). Research has examined some of the factors that may be responsible for individual differences including age, aptitude, motivation, anxiety, and attitude. Krashen (1981), for example, has hypothesized that comprehensible input in the presence of a low affective filter facilitates SLA. In Krashen's view, this affective filter comprises the learner's motivation, self-confidence, and level of anxiety.

To lower student anxiety and increase self-confidence, language teachers have based their lessons on content that is likely to be familiar to the learner.

Teachers use a variety of student-centered teaching techniques to make the language classroom interesting and relevant to the students. One such technique is integrating students' own experiences into the language lesson. In many adult ESL classrooms, students are asked to write about their experiences in their home countries and present them to the class as a way of practicing their speaking, writing, and listening skills in English. Teachers do this activity in order to recognize students' different backgrounds and to promote a sense of community among the learners. But while some students appreciate the opportunity to share their stories with their teachers and peers, others find this to be of little benefit.

For example, Norton (1997: 412–413) presents the case of Mai, a young Vietnamese woman from her longitudinal study of five immigrant women in Canada. After completing a six-month ESL course offered to adult immigrants in Canada, Mai continued taking ESL courses at night in order to improve her English. Norton notes that Mai had to make great sacrifices to attend the evening classes after a long day at work and negotiating public transportation in an unsafe neighborhood. Given the sacrifices that Mai made to attend these evening courses, she expressed great frustration with one particular course she was taking. In an interview with Norton, Mai explained that the class was centered around students' presentations on life in their home countries. She described how frustrating it was to sit through a whole lesson and listen to one student speak:

> I was hoping that the course would help me the same as we learnt [in the six-month ESL course], but some night we only spend time on one man. He came from Europe. He talked about his country: what's happening and what was happening. And all the time we didn't learn at all. And tomorrow the other Indian man speak something for there. Maybe all week I didn't write any more on my book.

Norton reports that after struggling through this course for a number of weeks and coming to feel that she "didn't learn at all," Mai never returned to the class.

Norton (1997) argues that Mai's teacher's approach, though well-intentioned, did not do justice to the complexity of learner identities. She contends that whereas immigrant learners' experiences in their native country may be a significant part of their identity, these experiences are constantly being mediated by their experiences in the new country. Since the teacher did not provide learners with the opportunity to critically examine their experiences in Canada but focused solely on students' past experiences in their home countries, Mai had little investment in the presentations of her fellow classmates. Mai's story shows that language learners are not passive recipients of linguistic knowledge doled out by teachers. On the contrary, students actively engage in their own learning by reacting fiercely to teaching methods that they perceive to be a waste of their time and energy. These strong reactions are influenced by the learners' sense of who they are and what they imagine themselves to be in the future (Kanno & Norton, 2003).

Much of the research on identity and language learning advances the view that learning a second language is not simply an accumulation of skills through practice. Instead, scholars have highlighted the complex social interactions and power differentials that engage the identities of language learners. According to Kramsch (1993), sociocultural identities are not static, deterministic constructs that teachers and students bring to the classroom and then take away unchanged at the end of a lesson. Norton (1997) contends that every time language learners speak, they are not only exchanging information with their interlocutors; they are also constantly organizing and reorganizing a sense of who they are and how they relate to the social world. They are, in other words, engaged in identity construction and negotiation.

In a study of four Chinese-immigrant students in California, McKay & Wong (1996) found that second language learners are set up by relations of power and may set up their own counter-discourse that puts them in a more powerful position. For instance, one student in their study, Michael Lee, counteracted his powerless positioning as "ESL student" by not writing about suggested topics of family and school on the language assessment but by writing about his hobbies instead. Michael's mother had previously asked Ms. Romero, his ESL teacher, to take him out of ESL at the end of eighth grade but her request was denied based on his poor performance in ESL. Michael was getting Cs and Ds in ESL, especially in writing, though he received As in other courses. Then Michael tried to convince the Regular Core teacher to advance him to that level. Failing in his attempt, he wrote an essay entitled, "The Unlucky Day," concluding with the following paragraph:

> My ESL teacher, Ms. Romero, say I can not go to Mrs. O'Connor's class because of a lot of mistakes in my writing not even if I have pass . . . test. I don't care if I have to work twice as hard as every one in regular class but Ms. Romero just too stubborn. What the unlucky day!
>
> (McKay & Wong, 1996: 593)

McKay & Wong (1996) argue that Michael played the "good student" by adhering to the letter of the assignment while expressing a spirit of defiance. He seized agency in academic discourse to air his grievance about Ms. Romero and to counteract his powerless positioning as an "ESL student."

Lam (2004b) presents a case study of two young Chinese immigrants who had turned to a bilingual Chinese/English chat room to improve their English. She examines the language practices of this virtual community and how it provides an additional context of language socialization for the two teenage girls. Whereas at school the two girls had difficulty interacting with their English-speaking peers, on the Internet they were able to use English to create social and ethnic identifications with other young people of Chinese origin in different parts of the world. In analyzing the exchanges in the bilingual chat room, Lam (2004b) argues that a mixed-code variety of English that includes writing in romanized Cantonese was developed among the girls and their chat room peers to construct their relationships as bilingual speakers of English and Cantonese. For example, in the following chat extract from Lam (2004b: 55), notice the underlined sentence-final particles "ar" and "la" in lines 1, 2, 3, 12, 13, and 15. "Sure" is the nickname of Yu Qing, one of the participants in Lam's study, and "CHoCoLaTe" is a girl in the Netherlands:

1	sure	choco . . . >_< can't send mail to u <u>ar</u> (PT: neutral softener or downtoner) . . . . Next time give my (sic: me) your add <u>la</u> (PT: indicates request) . . . can't send at your web site
2	CHoCoLaTe	sure> how come <u>ar</u> (PT: indicates question)?
3	sure	i don't know <u>ar</u> (PT: softener) . . . when i click on it . . . a juno web jump out
4	CHoCoLaTe	huuh?
5	CHoCoLaTe	very strange
6	sure	choco do u know y?
7	sure	and i can't go your web site everytime . . . sometimes can't find the site
8	CHoCoLaTe	very strange (emoticon of a sad face)
9	sure	too bad
10	CHoCoLaTe	<u>haiya</u> ("yes" or a sigh in Cantonese)
11	sure	uh?
12	CHoCoLaTe	u can mail me on the other emew accont <u>ar</u> (PT: softener) ^^
13	sure	but i don't have <u>ar</u> (PT: softener)
14	sure	what about I give u my add. then u send a hello to me.. then I got your add or
15	CHoCoLaTe	sure> my other account <u>ar</u> (PT: seeks confirmation)?
16	CHoCoLaTe	oke ^^

Lam (2004b) notes that the Cantonese particle "ar" is used as a softener or a down-toner, to signal a question, or to seek confirmation, while "la" indicates a suggestion or plea for a course of action. She argues that this mixed language variety served to create a collective ethnic identity for these young people and specifically allowed the two girls to assume a new identity through language, which follows neither the social categories of English-speaking Americans nor those of Cantonese-speaking Chinese. In Chapter 6, I will explore the social functions of bilingual code-switching in greater detail.

EDUCATION FOR EMPOWERMENT

Finally, I turn to a discussion of what it means to educate students for empowerment. The research on school experiences of language minority students shows that societal and school structures have a significant impact on students' identity (e.g., Cummins, 2000; García & Bartlett, 2007; Gibson, Gándara, & Koyama, 2004; Lee, 2009; Nieto & Bode, 2011; Shin, 2007; Suárez-Orozco & Suárez-Orozco, 2001). These investigations have often been framed in terms of **cultural assimilation** or **cultural pluralism** (Bartlett & García, 2011; Valenzuela, 1999). Cultural assimilation is the process whereby a minority group gradually adapts to the customs and attitudes of the dominant group. Cultural pluralism describes a situation where smaller groups within a larger society maintain their cultural identities, and their values and practices are accepted by the wider culture.

In her study of students attending an all-Mexican, inner-city high school in Houston, Texas, Valenzuela (1999) argues that the school's assimilationist policies diminish students' native language and culture. This kind of "subtractive schooling," she asserts, results in reduction of students' social capital required for academic success. In contrast, Bartlett & García (2011) document the successful efforts of one New York City high school to educate Dominican immigrant youth. The authors examine the language and cultural challenges that the immigrant teens face, and how the school works with the community to respond to those challenges. Bartlett & García (2011) attribute the students' success to an "additive" approach taken by the school staff—the students are viewed as emergent bilinguals with potential to succeed academically and socially, and not as failed attempts at assimilation into mainstream culture. The students' ethnic community is encouraged to participate as partners in their education and to contribute the "funds of knowledge" that exist in their communities to this educational partnership (González, Moll, & Amanti, 2005; Schecter & Bayley, 1997).

Cummins (2000) argues that to educate the whole child in a culturally and linguistically diverse context, it is necessary to nurture intellect and identity equally in ways that challenge "coercive relations of power." According to Cummins (2000: 44), "coercive relations of power" refer to "the exercise of power by a dominant individual, group, or country to the detriment of a subordinated individual, group, or country." He gives as an example that, in the past, dominant group institutions (e.g., schools) have required that minority groups reject their cultural identity and abandon their languages as a necessary condition for success in the mainstream society.

"Collaborative relations of power," on the other hand, refers to the empowerment of minority individuals or groups (Cummins, 2000). Cummins points out that interactions between teachers and students are never neutral with respect to societal power relations and that empowerment derives from the process of negotiating identities in the classroom. In varying degrees, these negotiations either reinforce or challenge coercive relations of power in the wider society. For example, Cummins states that acknowledging culturally diverse students' religion, culture, and language as valid forms of self-expression is to challenge coercive relations of power. He contends that students whose identities are affirmed by educators are more likely to succeed academically than those whose voices are silenced.

Other researchers support Cummins's assertion. Nieto (1992) reports that the academically successful students from various cultural backgrounds in her study had a positive sense of cultural identity. She presents the case of Manuel, a 19-year-old Cape Verdean who had a negative attitude toward immigrants taking on Americanized names and identity:

> That's something that a lot of kids do when they come to America. They change their names. Say you're Carlos, they say, "I'm Carl." They wanna be American; they're not Cape Verdean . . . . That's wrong. They're fooling themselves . . . . I identify myself as Cape Verdean. I'm Cape Verdean. I cannot be an American because I'm not an American. That's it.
>
> (1992: 176)

Another student in Nieto's study, James, a Lebanese Christian, stated:

> First thing I'd say is I'm Lebanese . . . . I'm just proud to be Lebanese. If somebody asked me, "What are you?" . . . everybody else would answer, "I'm American," but I'd say, "I'm Lebanese" and I feel proud of it.
>
> (1992: 136)

Although both Manuel and James clearly took pride in their cultural roots, Nieto notes that the pride these youth felt was not without conflict, hesitation, and contradiction. One of the most consistent outcomes in her study was "the striking combination of *pride* and *shame* that the young people felt about their culture" (Nieto, 2002: 107). This is because "a positive sense of cultural identity flies in the face of the assimilation model held out as the prize for sacrificing ethnicity, language, and even family loyalties" (Nieto, 2002: 106–107). Language minority students are presented with a choice of *either* holding onto their native language and culture *or* accepting assimilation, with no options in the middle. This, Nieto contends, creates a great deal of internal conflict, which leads to academic failure, or even depression. Vinh, a student from Vietnam in Nieto's (1992) study, is a case in point:

I've been here for three years, but the first two years I didn't learn anything. I got sick, mental. I got mental. Because when I came to the United
States, I missed my [parents], my family and my friends, and my Vietnam
.... I am a very sad person. Sometimes, I just want to be alone to think
about myself.... Before I got mental, okay, I feel very good about myself,
like I am smart.... But after I got mental, I don't get any enjoyment
.... I'm not smart anymore.

(1992: 146)

Nieto (2002) argues that students and teachers need to construct curricula that
affirm all students while also challenging the idea of fixed or idealized identities. Understanding the multiplicity and fluidity of student identities is a first
step in this transformative education.

SUMMARY

In this chapter, I examined the relationship between bilingualism and identity.
I began with the premise that language is intimately connected to
one's identity, and that to understand the educational and social aspects of
bilingualism one must carefully consider issues of identity. From the examples
involving Mandarin in Singapore and English in Malaysia, we saw that language attitude and ethnic identity have a significant influence on people's
language behaviors in multilingual societies. Bilingual language choice and
preference change according to people's conceptions of who they are and how
they wish to be perceived by other people. For English-speaking Malays in
Malaysia, this often means hiding their knowledge of English in the presence
of other Malays. For language minority children and adolescents, this often
involves identifying with the socially dominant language.

I discussed Tse's four-stage model of ethnic identity development which
predicts ethnic minorities' shifting attitudes toward the heritage and majority
languages as they come to terms with their minority status. Although this
model by no means accounts for the identity development of all ethnic
minorities (and is rather essentialist in its orderly sequential conception of
identity development), it is useful in predicting that heritage language education is most likely to succeed when ethnic minorities are not in Stage 2
(Ethnic ambivalence/evasion). I discussed the research which suggests a strong
link between greater heritage language proficiency and better self-esteem
among ethnic minority youth. I also explained that we must be careful about
generalizing results to different populations given that the relationship between
identity and language is complicated by interactions with a range of other
factors such as language status, social class, geographic location, and generational differences.

I discussed the role of essentialist frameworks such as Social Network Analysis (Milroy, 1987) in predicting the language use patterns of bilingual speakers. These theories try to link bilinguals' language behavior with pre-determined categories such as the degree of ethnic social ties. I showed that essentialist models, though insightful in their own right, do not adequately explain the negotiated, constructed, and conflicted nature of identity. What is increasingly preferred are the more interpretive, constructivist accounts which conceptualize identity as fluid and dynamic. People's constructions of gender, age, race, ethnicity, nationality, religion, and socioeconomic status provide them with multiple identities, which complement and conflict with one another. People do not establish these identities by themselves but negotiate them through social interaction with others. The process of constantly positioning and re-positioning oneself relative to others evades easy categorizations.

We saw that this view of identity is increasingly adopted by educators who are committed to improving the education of linguistically and culturally diverse students. Because societal and school structures tend to privilege the views of the dominant groups at the expense of the minority groups, educating cultural minority students requires nurturing students' intellect and identity in ways that challenge societal power structures (Cummins, 2000; Nieto, 2002). As Cummins (2000) argues, empowerment derives from the process of negotiating identities in the classroom, and educators who affirm culturally diverse students' religion, culture, and language as valid forms of self-expression and identities are more likely to be effective than those who do not. Affirming diversity requires not merely tolerating the presence of different languages or cultures, but actively acknowledging, promoting, and celebrating individual identities as they are continuously created, re-created, and negotiated.

FURTHER READING

- Cummins, J. (2000). *Language, power and pedagogy: Bilingual children in the crossfire.* Clevedon, UK: Multilingual Matters.—Jim Cummins, a leading authority in bilingual education, shows the ways in which power relations in the wider society affect teacher–student interaction in the classroom.
- Lesser, W. ed. (2004). *The genius of language: Fifteen writers reflect on their mother tongues.* New York: Pantheon Books.—This is a wonderful collection of essays by first-rate writers who examine their transition from their native languages to English.
- Nieto, S. (2002). *Language, culture, and teaching: Critical perspectives for a new century.* Mahwah, NJ: Lawrence Erlbaum.—In this highly readable book, Sonia Nieto encourages critical reflection on classroom practices related to linguistic and cultural diversity.

STUDY QUESTIONS AND ACTIVITIES

1. How do you identify yourself ethnically/racially/culturally? What is the relationship between the way you identify yourself and your proficiency in the language associated with that group? What cultural practices, customs, and beliefs factor into your identity? Are there circumstances when your preferred identity conflicts with the way others see you? What do you do when this happens?

2. In what ways are language learning and identity related? Why is it important for language teachers to understand societal attitudes to speakers of various languages?

3. What does it mean for linguistically and culturally diverse students to feel "disempowered" in school? What are some ways in which educators can empower students? What obstacles stand in the way of educators' efforts to affirm diversity?

6

Social and Conversational Aspects of Code-Switching

INTRODUCTION

In this chapter, I will examine the social and conversational attributes of code-switching, the alternating use of two or more languages within the same conversation. Bilinguals most often switch languages in ordinary conversations when they are in the company of other bilinguals. Code-switching is perhaps the most obvious indication of one's bilingual abilities, since very few bilinguals keep their two languages completely separate (Gardner-Chloros, 2009; see also Chapter 1). But monolinguals often have negative attitudes toward code-switching and think that it represents a deficient knowledge of language and a grammarless hodgepodge. Bilinguals themselves may feel embarrassed about their code-switching and attribute it to careless or lazy language habits. Pejorative names such as "Spanglish" or "Tex-Mex" (mixture of Spanish and English by bilingual speakers in the American Southwest) and "Franglais" (mixture of French and English in parts of French-speaking Canada) reflect these negative attitudes.

However, a great deal of research in the last several decades has shown that contrary to popular assumptions, code-switching is rather orderly, triggered by social and situational contexts, and used as a conversational resource by bilingual speakers (e.g., Auer, 1998; Callahan, 2004; Chanseawrassamee & Shin, 2009; Gardner-Chloros, 2009; Gumperz, 1982; Isurin, Winford, & de Bot, 2009; Milroy & Muysken, 1995; Myers-Scotton, 1993a, 1993b; Zentella, 1997). A large amount of evidence indicates that code-switching requires unusually high grammatical sensitivity and that individuals who code-switch do not lack syntactic knowledge (Gumperz & Cook-Gumperz, 2005). Readers interested in the grammatical theories of code-switching are referred to key literature on the topic (see Belazi, Rubin, & Toribio (1994) for the Functional Head Constraint; Di Sciullo, Muysken, & Singh (1986) for the Government Constraint; MacSwan

(2006) for the Minimalist Program; Myers-Scotton (1993b) for the Matrix Language Frame Model; Poplack (1980, 1981) for the Equivalence Constraint and the Free Morpheme Constraint).

But in this chapter, I shall focus on the social and conversational aspects of code-switching. Drawing on a diverse array of examples from both formal and informal conversations, popular music, and computer-mediated communication, I will show how bilinguals use code-switching as a communicative resource. We will see that "prescriptive 'rules' such as speaking only one language at a time are deliberately and playfully broken" in popular music (Gardner-Chloros, 2009: 29) and in online communication (Danet & Herring, 2007). We will also see how bilinguals utilize code-switching to convey a variety of social meanings including toning down a statement that might otherwise sound too strong, interjecting to grab the floor in the conversation, and expressing solidarity with members of the same ethnic group. In all these discussions, we will see that bilinguals' ability to mix two or more languages emerges as a valuable linguistic resource.

OUT OF THE MOUTHS OF BILINGUALS 6.1

The Many Functions of Code-Switching

". . . I code-switch from English to Serbian and vice versa, only when I know that my interlocutor is versed in both languages . . . I resort to it if I want to signal that a particular expression in Serbian or English really encapsulates what I want to say. For instance, I tend to use the word *humble* when speaking Serbian, probably because it does not have a good translation equivalent. Besides this, I have noticed that I sometimes switch into my mother tongue when I talk to my good friends who live in Britain or the USA, when we are in the company of native speakers and converse in English. That bit of Serbian is invested with a special role – solidarity building, bonding, or evoking something from our shared past."

(Popovic, 2009: 47)

We will also examine attitudes toward code-switching in the classroom. Code-switching is generally frowned upon by language teachers who believe that it detracts from students' learning of the target language (see also Levine, 2011; Raschka, Sercombe, & Huang, 2009; Turnbull & Dailey-O'Cain, 2009). In many classrooms, students are instructed to speak only in the target language without resorting to their native languages, which are viewed as an unnecessary crutch that gets in the way of proper second language development. The same holds true for immigrant children in majority language schools who are told to speak only in the language of the school. The argument goes, if immigrant students come to school lacking the language of school, they should be provided with as many opportunities to speak in that language as possible. Children's native languages are seen to have no place in the curriculum, and students are expected to leave their home languages behind as they come into the school.

Even in bilingual two-way immersion, there is an emphasis on keeping the two languages completely separate. In a study of a second-grade two-way Spanish-English immersion program in California, Palmer (2009) notes that code-switching during class time is generally viewed as an error and that children are reminded to stay with the "correct" language at any given time. The expectation is that students make a clean mental break from one language as they move to another with no mixing in between. But as we will see in this chapter, insisting on artificially separating two languages has little research basis. As Cummins (2008) points out, there already exists extensive empirical evidence for interdependence across languages. Cummins and many other scholars argue that second language acquisition can be greatly facilitated by allowing students to use their first languages to make sense of second language structures.

Similarly, a great deal of research shows that literacy skills transfer between languages—that is, students apply reading and writing skills they have acquired in one language to learning to read and write in another language (Bialystok et al., 2005; Lanauze & Snow, 1989). The two languages in a bilingual's linguistic repertoire are a lot more intertwined than what is commonly envisioned as two separate compartments in the brain (Cummins, 1996). Instructional assumptions that insist on a strict separation of two languages simply do not reflect the linguistic realities of bilingual students. We will examine the important roles of the first language and of code-switching in the classroom and discuss what it means to teach and learn in a "multilingual classroom community of practice" (Levine, 2011: 168).

But first, let us examine the nature of bilingual conversations.

REVISITING DIGLOSSIA

In Chapter 3, I discussed the concept of diglossia, a language situation where two distinct varieties, each with its own set of social functions, coexist as standards throughout a community. One of these varieties is used in ordinary conversations in the home and in the community (the Low variety) whereas the other variety is used for more formal purposes, mainly in prestigious domains such as government, media, and education (the High variety). In a diglossic community, specific language situations call for the use of one language or the other, and individual language choices are constrained by societal norms.

Fishman (1971) applies the diglossia concept to bilingual face-to-face interactions and suggests that certain conversational activities prompt the use of one language or the other. Consider Extract (1) below from Fishman (1971: 37), an excerpt from an office conversation between two Puerto Ricans:

Extract (1)
[Boss has been dictating a letter to Mr. Bolger to his secretary, Spanish in italics]

Boss: . . . Sincerely, Louis Gonzalez
Secretary: Do you have the enclosures for the letter, Mr. Gonzalez?
Boss: Oh yes, here they are.
Secretary: Okay.
Boss: Ah, this man William Bolger got his organization to contribute a lot of money to the Puerto Rican parade. He's very much for it. *¿Tu fuiste a la parada?*
Secretary: *Sí, yo fuí.*
Boss: *¿Sí?*
Secretary: *Uh huh.*
Boss: *¿Y cómo te estuvo?*
[etc., continues in Spanish]

Here, Fishman finds a systematic correlation between the use of Spanish and an informal chat about going to the Puerto Rican parade, and between English and a business-related activity.

While Fishman's analysis seems appropriate for the above extract, it does not always work in other cases. In fact, in many bilingual situations, speech activities are not tied to one particular language, and even among those which tend to occur more often in one language than in another, the correlation is never strong enough to predict language choice with certainty (Auer, 1995). Auer (1995) points out that in Fishman's Puerto Rican example above, it is conceivable that the Puerto Rican boss might deal with his secretary in Spanish around the office all the time and choose to use English even to talk about the Puerto Rican parade. He suggests that the mere fact of juxtaposing two languages can have a signaling value of its own. Auer argues that it is often impossible to fully explain the conversational meaning of code-switching by any kind of a fixed association between languages and speech activities.

CONVERSATIONAL CODE-SWITCHING

If language choice and speech activities are not linked in any fixed way, then what explains code-switching? John Gumperz (1982), whose pioneering work on discourse strategies has been highly influential in sociolinguistic research, argues that code-switching is a communicative option available to the bilingual speaker in much the same way that switching between styles or dialects is an option for the monolingual speaker. By building up a contrast in languages, code-switching conveys the speaker's momentary attitudes, communicative intents, and emotions to other participants in the conversation.

Under the heading of "conversational code-switching," Gumperz describes the strategies bilinguals use to choose their language. He argues that code-switching is "an element in a socially agreed matrix of **contextualization cues** and conventions used by speakers to alert addressees, in the course of ongoing interaction, to the social and situational context of the conversation" (Gumperz, 1982: 132). Basically, contextualization cues are communicative devices like intonation, gesture, speech tempo, and volume, which people use to communicate metaphoric information about how they intend their words to be understood by others in the conversation (Gumperz, 1982: 61). Thus, a statement uttered in anger might be said in a louder voice, in a faster tempo, and accompanied by violent gestures. All of these contextualization cues help communicate the speaker's angry feelings to other participants in the conversation. Gumperz's argument is that code-switching works very much like these contextualization cues.

Gumperz derives the conversational meaning of code-switching through a turn-by-turn sequential analysis, in which the language choice in one utterance is compared against the language choice in the preceding utterance. Following this approach, Gumperz (1982: 75–84) lists the following discourse functions of code-switching:

(a) quotations (reported speech)
(b) addressee specification
(c) interjections
(d) reiteration
(e) message qualification
(f) personalization *vs.* objectivization.

An illustration of how code-switching contextualizes quotations (reported speech) is found in Romaine's (1995: 162) example of a young Papua New Guinean girl narrating a story in a cartoon she has just seen on video. While the girl retold the story in Tok Pisin, she reported the speech of one of the characters in English: Lapun man ia kam na tok, "OH YU POOR PUSIKET," na em go insait [The old man came and said, "Oh, you poor pussycat," and then he went inside]. Romaine notes that the girl's switch to English here is socially appropriate because the cartoon characters are white and the setting is obviously not Papua New Guinea. It would, therefore, have been highly unlikely that the man in the cartoon would know Tok Pisin, which explains why the girl used English to quote him directly.

An example of code-switching used for reiteration can be found in my own study of Korean American bilingual first-graders. Extract (2) comes from a conversation between two girls working on a classroom activity (Shin, 2005: 19). Korean is in italics.

Extract (2)
1 Yooni: CAN I USE YOUR ERASER?/
2 Grace: (1.5)
3 Yooni: *Na*   ERASER   *sse-to-toy?/*
        I   eraser   use-even-okay
        (Is it okay if I use your eraser?)
4 Grace: *Ne*   *iss-cyanha*   *keki*   *ey/*
        You   have not   there   LOC
        (You have it over there.)

In line 1, Yooni asks to borrow Grace's eraser even though she has her own. As Grace does not respond (as shown by the 1.5-second silence), Yooni rephrases her request in Korean in line 3. Yooni may have interpreted Grace's lack of response as a sign of misunderstanding or rejection of her request. Had Yooni been a monolingual English speaker, she may have repeated her request in English in a louder voice, maybe even pointing her finger at the eraser for further clarification. But as a bilingual, Yooni has the option of switching languages, *in addition to* these other contextualization cues (e.g., speaking in a louder voice and using gesture) to communicate her meaning. In this way, code-switching serves as an *additional* conversational tool for bilingual speakers.

Myers-Scotton's "Markedness Model"

Gumperz's analysis of code-switching as an interactional strategy is further developed by Myers-Scotton (1993a) in her "Markedness Model." Myers-Scotton argues that bilingual speakers are aware of the social consequences of choosing a specific language (or, mixing languages) in a particular context. She contends that in any given circumstance, a particular language variety is the expected or **unmarked language**, while the other variety is the unexpected or **marked language**. Myers-Scotton contends that bilingual speakers are endowed with a knowledge of socially relevant markedness associated with expected practices in a given community, and that speakers who make the unexpected or marked choices do so for specific reasons. Thus, in most post-colonial multilingual societies, switching to the local ethnic language to talk about one's family would be "unmarked" (i.e., there is nothing remarkable about this language choice), whereas switching to the local ethnic language in a public speech would be "marked" (i.e., listeners would wonder why the speaker chose this unexpected variety and try to figure out the speaker's intentions).

Myers-Scotton observes that one of the most common uses of code-switching as a marked choice is to express authority, anger, or annoyance. In Extract (3), from Myers-Scotton (1993a: 133), a passenger on a bus in Nairobi is talking to the conductor in Swahili, the unmarked choice for bus transaction. English is in italics.

Extract (3)
Passenger: Nataka kwenda Posta.
             "I want to go to the post office."
Conductor: Kutoka hapa mpaka posta nauli ni senti hamsini.
             "From here to the post office, the fare is 50 cents."

(Passenger gives the conductor a shilling, from which he should get 50 cents in change.)

Conductor: Ngojea *change* yako.
             "Wait for your change."

(Passenger says nothing until some minutes have passed and the bus is nearing the post office where the passenger plans to get off.)

Passenger: Nataka *change* yangu.
             "I want my change."
Conductor: *Change* utapata, Bwana.
             "You'll get your change."
Passenger: *I am nearing my destination.*
Conductor: *Do you think I could run away with your change?*

Myers-Scotton argues that the passenger switches from Swahili (the "unmarked" choice) to English (the "marked" choice) to reinforce his annoyance at not having received his change. She points out that the passenger is using English to show off his education and assert his authority. But the conductor, by also switching to English, asserts his own position as the passenger's equal.

To illustrate code-switching as an "unmarked" choice, Myers-Scotton (1993a: 116) provides an extract from an office interaction in Kenya. In Extract (4), Edward is visiting his relative, John, an executive in a soft-drink bottling company in Nairobi. Myers-Scotton states that both English and Swahili are the unmarked choice for office interactions. Notice that John speaks English to his white-collar subordinate, but when he calls to the receptionist to get a soft drink for Edward, he switches to Swahili. Then he switches back to English to lecture a salesman. Myers-Scotton contends that while John might speak in either Swahili or English to his higher-level staff members, in this conversation he uses English because it is the more unmarked choice for expressing authority. Swahili is italicized.

Extract (4)

Subordinate: (entering John M.'s office and speaking to Edward M. just after John M. has stepped out for a minute) Where has this guy gone to?

Edward: He's just gone out. He will soon be back.

John: (to subordinate when he returns) Why did you change the plan of our stand at the showground? Who recommended the change? . . .

Subordinate: (looking guilty) Nobody told me.

John: Go and change it according to our previous plan. Also make sure that the painting is done properly.

John: (to Edward when subordinate has left) I've told this man how to build our stand, but he went and did a different thing. *Ni mtu mjeuri sana.* ("He's a stubborn person.") I'll make him pay for the paint he spoilt.

John: (calling to the receptionist) *Letea mgeni soda anywe.* "Bring the guest a soda so that he may drink."

Receptionist: (to Edward) *Nikuletee soda gani?* "What kind of soda should I bring you?"

Edward: *Nipe Pepsi.* "Give me a Pepsi."

Salesman: (entering) *Sikuweza kufika kwa sababu nilikuwa mgonjwa.* "I couldn't come because I was not well."

John: Well, I wanted you to explain something about one of your receipt books . . . There's a mistake somewhere. Take it back and make the totals again.

John: (to Edward when salesman leaves) This one will not earn any money at the end of this month. He has a big shortage.

Although it is claimed to be both comprehensive and predictive, capable of associating the social symbolism of particular languages with the conversational strategies of speakers, Myers-Scotton's Markedness Model presents difficulties in that it is not always possible to determine which languages become marked or unmarked in a given bilingual interaction (see also Alfonzetti, 1998; Auer, 1995; Li, 2005; Shin & Milroy, 2000). In some cases, mixing itself may be the unmarked variety. Gafaranga (2005) showed that Kinyarwanda-French code-switching by his bilingual Rwandese participants already constituted their language "code" and that they used the mixed variety in exactly the same way as monolinguals use one language. He disagrees with the "language-reflects-society" view put forth by Myers-Scotton and other scholars, and contends that code-switching must be analyzed on a case-by-case basis by taking into account the conversational structure of the interaction. This is exactly what Auer (1995) accomplishes with his conversation analytic framework, to which I turn next.

Auer's Conversation Analytic Framework

Auer (1995) presents a very different development of Gumperz's interactional paradigm. Critical of Gumperz's characterization of speakers' language choices as realizations of a pre-established set of functions (e.g., quotation, interjection, reiteration), Auer argued that not only was such a list theoretically problematic, but it could also never be complete in principle. He suggested that the problems posed by a functional analysis of code-switching could be solved by adopting the framework of **Conversation Analysis (CA)** (see Atkinson and Heritage, 1984; Levinson, 1983). In Auer's view, the CA approach has at least two advantages. First, it recognizes "the fact that whatever language a participant chooses for the organization of his or her turn . . . exerts an influence on subsequent language choices by the same or other speakers" (Auer, 1984: 5). Second, it "limits the external analysts' interpretational leeway because it relates his or her interpretations back to the members' mutual understanding of their utterances as manifest in their behavior" (Auer, 1984: 6).

Auer (1995) draws a useful distinction between "participant-related code-switching" and "discourse-related code-switching." Participant-related code-switching is used to negotiate the proper language for the interaction— ideally, one that is both socially appropriate and accommodates the language competences and preferences of everyone in the conversation. Discourse-related code-switching, on the other hand, sets up a contrast that structures some part of the conversation (e.g., to mark out an off-topic sequence).

Below, I present a conversational sequence from my study of bilingual Korean-English-speaking children, where examples of both participant-related and discourse-related code-switching are illustrated (Shin, 2005). Note that this conversation takes place in a mainstream American first-grade classroom. Mrs. Kim, the teacher, immigrated to the U.S. at the age of seven with her family from Korea. Though she is bilingual in English and Korean, Mrs. Kim had specifically instructed her Korean students at the beginning of the school year not to speak to her in Korean out of consideration for the non-Korean students in her class. But she did not interfere with her students speaking Korean among themselves.

In Extract (5), from Shin (2005: 86–88), Mrs. Kim gave Jae and Abel the task of studying a snail. She asked them to measure the length of the snail, identify the different body parts, and determine how far it travels in a given amount of time. After Mrs. Kim walks away from them in line 21, Jae and Abel begin talking about cooking and eating snails. In line 33, Abel switches to Korean and says that one can eat the snail shell because it is hard, which Jae corrects by saying that one cannot eat it. Abel then says that one can die from swallowing a hard shell. In line 38, Jae explicitly tells Abel to speak English. This ends the use of Korean for the rest of the activity and the conversation continues solely in English. In Auer's framework, the switch to English in lines 38 and 39 would constitute a participant-related code-switch since Jae's preference for English was the motivation for the switch.

In contrast, Jae's initial switch from English to Korean in line 24 is a discourse-related code-switch, which marks out the beginning of a side sequence where the boys talk about whether they could eat snail shells. Note that when Abel says that he eats snail shells, Jae's disagreement is accompanied by a code-switch into Korean despite Jae's usual preference for English. In line 27, Abel then switches into Korean and agrees with Jae. Li & Milroy (1995) report a similar pattern in their study, where Chinese-English bilinguals used code-switching to contextualize disagreement. In both Li & Milroy (1995) and Shin (2005), preferred responses (e.g., agreement) are accompanied by language alignment while dispreferred responses (e.g., disagreement) are accompanied by code-switching. In this example, Jae disagrees with Abel with a different language choice from the previous turn while Abel agrees with Jae in the same language Jae used in the previous turn.

Extract (5)

Abel and Jae follow the movements of a snail assigned to them. They measure the length of the body, how long it travels, etc. Abel and Jae have been speaking exclusively in English for ten minutes. Mrs. Kim approaches their desk and checks on their progress. Korean is in italics.

1   Mrs. Kim: OKAY/
2   HOW LONG IS IT/
3   MEASURE IT/

4 Jae: UH/
5   THREE INCH/
6 Abel: MINE ˌIS/
7 Mrs. Kim: ˈTHREE WHAT?/
8 Jae: (2.0) ˌTHREE
9 Mrs. Kim: ˈTHREE INCHES? ˌOH OKAY/
10 Jae: ˈTHREE INCHES/
11 Mrs. Kim: DID YOU MEASURE IT?/
12 Abel: YEAH/
13 Mrs. Kim: OKAY SO IF THAT'S SNAIL'S LENGTH/
14   PUT A SPACE BETWEEN THIS/
15   OKAY SNAIL'S LENGTH HOW LONG IS IT/
16   WRITE IT IN/
17 Jae: (3.2) THREE/
18 Mrs. Kim: OKAY NOW LOOK AT THE EYES/
19   LOOK AT THE EYES/
20   AND THEN LOOK AT THE MOUTH/
21 Jae: EAT IT/
(Mrs. Kim walks away from Jae and Abel.)
22 Abel: WELL THE SHELL/
23   I EAT IT/
24 Jae: SHELL   *nun   mos   mek-ci*/
               shell   TOP   cannot eat-right
               (You can't eat the shell, can you?)
25   *ike-n   pelyeya-toy*/
               this-TOP   discard-must
               (You should throw this out)
26   *ike   man   mek-ko*/
               this   only   eat-and
               (and eat only this)
27 Abel: *e*/
               yeah
               (Yeah.)
28 Jae: WE NEED TO COOK IT/
29   PUT THIS RIGHT KID=/
30 Abel: =AND PUT IN *elum* AND WE COULD EAT IT RIGHT=/
               and put in   ice   and we could eat it right
               (and if you put ice in it you could eat it, right?)
31 Jae: =YEAH/
32   ˌ(unintelligible)
33 Abel: ˈ*ike   nemwu   ttakttakhay-se   meke*/
               this   too   hard-because   eat

	(You eat this because it's too hard)
34 Jae:	*mos* *meke/*
	Cannot eat
	(You can't eat it.)
35 Abel:	*e* *ttakttakhay/*
	Um hard
	(Yeah, it's hard.)
36 Jae:	[(unintelligible)
37 Abel:	[(unintelligible) *ha-myen* *cwuke/*
	do-if die
	(You die if (unintelligible).)
38 Jae:	(emphatically) SPEAK ENGLISH/
39 Abel:	OKAY/
40	(touches the head of the snail) OOOOH/
41 Jae:	NO LEAVE IT/
42	EY IT'S GONNA GO IN/
43 Abel:	IF YOU SCARE HIM/
44	HE'S GONNA GO INTO THE SHELL RIGHT?/
45 Jae:	ABEL JUST SEE/
46	(3.5) NOW WE DID MOUTH EYE FEET FEET FEET/
47	FEET FEET LEAVE HIM ALONE LIKE THAT ABEL/
48	IT'S GONNA GO IN/
49	SEE ITS FEET/
50 Abel:	(3.5) (softly) IT'S GOING/
	(Note: [[shows point at which overlap occurs.)

By comparing the language choice in one utterance against the language choice in the previous turn, Auer's (1995) sequential analysis shows ways in which bilinguals use code-switching to structure their conversation and to negotiate the language for the interaction. As the conversation proceeds, individuals carefully monitor other participants' speech production and adapt their own language choice to their assessment of the bilingual abilities and preferences of the other participants. In sum, bilinguals use code-switching as an *additional* means to communicate their intentions and preferences to other participants in the conversation. This conclusion directly contradicts the view that code-switching is evidence of some sort of communicative deficit in bilinguals.

Next, we will see how bilinguals use code-switching to wield power over others.

USING CODE-SWITCHING TO WIELD POWER

In a study of the code-switching behaviors of two six- and seven-year-old Hungarian-English bilingual girls in a pretend-school activity, Bolonyai (2005) shows that the girls used English to gain access to the conversational floor and exert influence over each other. Both children come from first-generation Hungarian American immigrant families where the parents are bilingual, middle-class professionals who value maintaining Hungarian in their children. In Extract (6), from Bolonyai (2005: 17–18), Emma's mother asks the girls about cats in Hungarian. English is italicized. Emma raises her hand to answer, but when Linda answers without being called upon (line 289), Emma uses English to confront Linda for taking her turn (line 290). But Linda maintains control over the floor by using strategies such as laughing, interrupting, and ignoring Emma (lines 291, 293, 295, 297, 300, 302, 306).

Notice that Emma challenges Linda's aggressive control of the floor by switching languages. First, Emma tries to insert her contribution in Hungarian (line 294), but when she is interrupted, she tells Linda to stop in Hungarian (line 296). As Linda keeps interrupting (line 297), Emma switches to English to complain (lines 298, 303). After Mother selects Emma as next speaker, Emma starts her response in English (line 305). But just as Emma was about to switch back to Hungarian, Linda cuts in again (line 306). Then in line 307, Emma switches to English to complain to Linda yet again that it is not her turn.

Bolonyai (2005) argues that in this pretend-school activity, switching to English enables the girls to exert power and symbolic dominance over each other because they associate English with knowledge and authority. Had the girls been monolingual, they would have competed for control of the floor by using other contextualization cues such as laughing, interrupting, and louder utterances (which Linda uses extensively, in fact). The difference between bilinguals and monolinguals is that bilinguals have the *additional* option of switching languages, over and above these conversational resources.

Extract (6)

287   Mother: Mit esznek a cicák?
                "What do kittens eat?"
288   Emma: (waving her hand to be called on) Uh!   [Uh!
289   Linda: (blurting out)   [*Hot dogs!* (laughing)
290   Emma: *It's not your turn,* Linda.
291   Linda: (laughing) *Hot dogs and chicken bones.* (laughing)
292   Emma: (bidding for the floor) Linda?
293   Linda: *Chicken* (laughing).
294   Emma: Uhm, szeretnek enni, uh, nema **cat**   [
                "Uhm, they like to eat, eh, not a cat."   [

295 Linda: [(bursting into laughter)
296 Emma: Ne csi [náljad!
              "Don't [do this!"
297 Linda: [*Fish!*
298 Emma: Linda?! *I'm getting tired of it.*
299 Mother: (To Linda) Mehet?
              "Could she continue?"
300 Linda: (laughing resumes)
301 Emma: Linda?!
302 Linda: *I said*
303 Emma: [*She won't leave me alone! She won't let me talk!*
304 Mother: Jó, mondjad most már Emma.
              "All right, go ahead and say it now, Emma."
305 Emma: *That cats' teeth can grow. And whenever they grow, they wanna*
              bite. So they wanna bite stuff. Oh, a cica   [
                                                "Oh, the kitty" [
306 Linda: (interrupting Emma)   [*Their teeth fall*
              out sometimes.
307 Emma: *Uhh!* Linda?! *It's not your turn!*
                            (Note: [[shows point at which overlap occurs.)

   I now turn to a discussion of code-switching in computer-mediated communication.

CODE-SWITCHING ON THE INTERNET

By and large, code-switching in online contexts has been observed to resemble
face-to-face, conversational code-switching (Androutsopoulos, 2006, 2007;
Danet & Herring, 2007). In a study of German-based diasporic websites fre-
quented by members of various ethnic groups (e.g., Indian, Persian, Greek),
Androutsopoulos (2006) shows that code-switching is used by the bilingual
participants to contextualize a shift in topic or perspective. In the Greek forum,
for instance, Androutsopoulos observes that switches to Greek in largely
German discussion threads contextualized contributions as non-threatening
to recipients (e.g., teasing). Conversely, when a discussion thread was in
Greek, German did the contextualizing. In the joke-telling area of the Persian
forum, users selected Persian to narrate the jokes but used German to
comment on them. In line with Auer's conversation analytic framework,
Androutsopoulos (2006) argues that switches away from the generally expected
base language (i.e., German) typically signal playfulness. When the other
language is used as the base code, he notes that German is selected for
comment and critique.

印象中上回麗麗學姐的 suggestion 好像沒什麼回應ㄚ ³~~~~

"From what I can recall no one seemed to respond to Lily's last suggestion…"

FIGURE 6.1 An Example of an English Word Embedded in a Chinese Sentence

Source: Su, 2003. Reproduced by permission of Wiley-Blackwell

While online code-switching is in many ways similar to language mixing in face-to-face interactions, one of the biggest differences between the two is that online communication requires writing. Code-switching on the Internet may involve switching between different orthographies, which users manipulate to produce various effects. To take an example, Su (2003) examined Taiwanese college students' use of Chinese and English orthographies on electronic bulletin board systems (BBSs). She notes that while the main language on Taiwanese BBSs is Mandarin (which is written in standardized, traditional Chinese characters), English words or expressions sometimes appear in this Chinese-dominant environment (see Figure 6.1). But when English phrases are written in Chinese characters rather than in the Roman alphabet (see Figures 6.2 and 6.3), Su (2003) shows that it indicates playfulness on the part of the writer.

In Figures 6.2 and 6.3, the actual Chinese characters found in the BBSs are indicated by an arrow. Pinyin, a Mandarin Romanization system, indicates how the Chinese characters are read. In Figure 6.2, for example, the three Chinese characters read as "ou-mai-ga," which approximates the English pronunciation of the phrase, "Oh, my god." However, as the gloss shows, the phrase written in Chinese means something totally different from the original English expression. Su (2003) notes that the high-low-high-falling tone contour of the three characters mimics the English intonation of the expression, "Oh, my god." The deletion of "d" in the final position of "god" indicates that the syllable has been phonologically adapted into Chinese, making the phrase sound as if it were produced by a Taiwanese person, rather than a native English speaker.

Similarly, in Figure 6.3, the low-high-falling tone contour of "gu-nai" resembles the intonation associated with the phrase "good night." But again, the phrase written in Chinese characters means something entirely different from the English expression. Su (2003) contends that writing English phrases using Chinese characters

plays down the stiffness and arrogance often linked in Taiwan with the use of English, a language with international status and overt prestige, lending this alternative linguistic practice a sense of locality and congeniality while simultaneously maintaining a level of sophistication associated with English.

→ | Character | 噢 | 買 | 尬 |
|---|---|---|---|
| Pinyin | ou | mai | ga |
| Gloss | interjection | to-buy | to-embarrass |
| Tone Contour | high-level | low-dipping | high-falling |
| Intended Meaning | "Oh, my god." | | |

FIGURE 6.2 An Example of Stylized English Used in Taiwan-Based Electronic Bulletin Board Systems

Source: Su, 2003. Reproduced by permission of Wiley-Blackwell

→ | Character | 古 | 耐 |
|---|---|---|
| Pinyin | gu | nai |
| Gloss | ancient | endure |
| Tone Contour | low-dipping | high-falling |
| Intended Meaning | "Good night." | |

FIGURE 6.3 Another Example of Stylized English Used in Taiwan-Based Electronic Bulletin Board Systems

Source: Su, 2003. Reproduced by permission of Wiley-Blackwell

In fact, among the Taiwanese college students Su studied, Chinese rendering of English expressions was much more widely used than English itself.

Similarly, in a study of Internet Relay Chat exchanges of Cantonese-speaking university students in England, Fung & Carter (2007) show that transliterated Cantonese words or phrases inserted in an otherwise English discourse qualify the writers' feelings. Extracts (7) and (8), taken from Fung & Carter (2007: 46), illustrate this. Cantonese is in italics.

Extract (7)
Kit: no,   *'ho   ho   may'*
                (very   very   delicious)
                (it's very delicious)
REL: . . . . hhaha !! ok   *la* !! need to do some work   *la* !
                                            (DM)   (DM)
Kit: ok, cu tommorrow

Extract (8)

Ying: Bill . . . . *ho   charm ho   charm ar* . . . i just failed my java exam . . .
       (very bad   very bad   DM)
       (it's very bad)

Notice that *la* and *ar* in Extracts (7) and (8) are discourse markers (DMs) in Cantonese, which are typically found at the end of utterances and are grammatically optional (i.e., their absence does not make the utterance ungrammatical). But, as Fung & Carter (2007) point out, discourse markers perform an important function of displaying the emotional status of the bilingual participants. *La*, for instance, is an assertive particle which expresses mutual agreement—it establishes common understanding of situations and feelings among the participants. Since it is difficult for non-Cantonese speakers to decode the meanings of these and other Cantonese expressions embedded in an otherwise English text, Fung & Carter (2007) argue that code-switching helps to reinforce solidarity among the Cantonese-English bilingual users in this online environment. To understand the bilingual chat interactions, one must be familiar with the beliefs, assumptions, and attitudes of the members of this close-knit speech community, which are manifested in their language mixing behaviors and are off-limits to non-Cantonese speakers.

CODE-SWITCHING IN POPULAR MUSIC

Bilingual musicians and song writers exploit the creative capacities afforded by code-switching to push artistic boundaries and to bolster their messages. In Japanese and Korean popular music (J-Pop and K-Pop), English is mixed to assert "a new identity" and to represent "a discourse of resistance" (Lee, 2004; Moody, 2006; see also Chapter 2). Lee (2004: 429) argues that English mixing in K-Pop enables Korean youth "to challenge dominant representations of authority, to resist mainstream norms and values, and to reject older generations' conservatism." Kachru (2006: 227) states that in popular songs in India, mixing Hindi with English offers

additional opportunities to express social and political commentary, employ fresh metaphors, imagery, and rhymes, and represent what is increasingly a familiar theme—that of the expatriate NRI (Non-Resident Indian) from the West visiting or returning to India with an affluent life style, and often skewed values.

Omoniyi (2006) shows that code-switching is also common in Nigerian hip-hop music, where Yoruba, Standard English, and Pidgin English are frequently mixed to express a new hybrid identity and to reconcile the conflicting demands of globalization and localization.

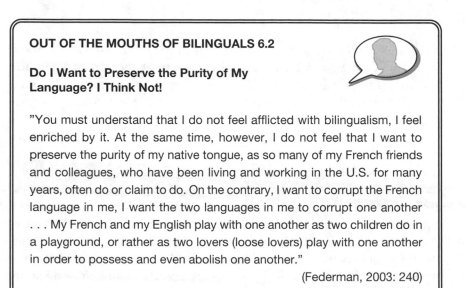

OUT OF THE MOUTHS OF BILINGUALS 6.2

Do I Want to Preserve the Purity of My Language? I Think Not!

"You must understand that I do not feel afflicted with bilingualism, I feel enriched by it. At the same time, however, I do not feel that I want to preserve the purity of my native tongue, as so many of my French friends and colleagues, who have been living and working in the U.S. for many years, often do or claim to do. On the contrary, I want to corrupt the French language in me, I want the two languages in me to corrupt one another . . . My French and my English play with one another as two children do in a playground, or rather as two lovers (loose lovers) play with one another in order to possess and even abolish one another."

(Federman, 2003: 240)

While code-switching is typically carried out by bilingual artists, not all code-switching is done by those who are proficient in the languages involved. Sarkar & Allen (2007) state that Quebec rap lyrics often include inserts from languages in which the rappers do not have functional competence. One of the local rappers they interviewed, SP, makes extensive use of words and phrases from Haitian Creole in his raps despite his partial grasp of the language. Originally from upstate New York, SP was raised in Quebec by Congolese parents:

> I speak Creole if I have to. It's like, sometimes, people just think I'm Haitian and . . . I'll just answer, like, Yes, No, or . . . But I understand, 'cause I grew up with a lot of Haitians . . . . Their parents used to talk to me in Creole.
>
> (Sarkar & Allen, 2007: 125)

Sarkar & Allen (2007) explain that since Haitians form the largest single group within Quebec's Black community, non-Haitians who wish to belong to this community use Haitian Creole to participate on an equal footing with Haitians. As Sarkar & Winer (2006: 189) point out, these "crossings" into other people's languages (see also Leung et al., 1997) "are fundamentally linked by a positioning of multilingualism as a natural and desirable condition, whether or not everything is then comprehensible to everyone."

CODE-SWITCHING IN THE CLASSROOM

Finally, I turn to a discussion of code-switching in the classroom. As I pointed out in the introduction to this chapter, many language teachers discourage code-switching because they believe that it hinders students' learning of the target language. In a study of the code-switching practices of Taiwanese EFL teachers, Raschka et al. (2009) state that policy-makers, at both the national and school level, tend to view code-switching as undesirable within the language classroom, and promote an "English-only" rule. However, as the authors point out, total immersion in English is virtually impossible in foreign language classrooms, especially when everyone in the classroom (including the students and the teacher) speaks the same first language. They argue that "English-only" is a lazy rule in that it means that teachers do not have to think about when and where code-switching occurs and in what contexts it may be pedagogically useful.

Similarly, Levine (2011) discusses his experience as a director of a university German language program, who required his graduate student instructors to adopt a "German-only" approach in the classroom, only to find out that the instructors and the students frequently and openly broke the rule. He explains how he came to abandon his "German-only" policy (Levine, 2011: xiv):

> This became especially apparent in the occasional, candid remarks made by some students on course evaluations and elsewhere about the L2 use "policies" in their classes. Some people expressed that they felt not only frustration about it, but even anxiety. These comments . . . led me to rethink my position on exclusive L2 use, fueled also by my observations during classroom visits that even in the most stringent exclusive-L2-use classes, many learners *still* made frequent use of that forbidden code: English!

Levine notes that not only was his "German-only" rule unrealistic, it also prevented him from providing students with effective language instruction that built on the students' knowledge of their first language.

If the above-mentioned "English-only" and "German-only" rules are ineffective, unrealistic, and even lazy, then why do educators insist on them? Turnbull & Dailey-O'Cain (2009) note that much of the "target-language-only" assumptions are based on several influential theories on language learning. Krashen's (1985) **comprehensible input hypothesis**, for instance, argues for exposing learners to a great deal of comprehensible target-language input (i.e., give learners lots of opportunities to hear and read the target language). Swain's (1985) **comprehensible output hypothesis** contends that not only do learners require comprehensible input, but they also need meaningful opportunities to produce output in the target language (i.e., speaking and writing). As Turnbull & Dailey-O'Cain (2009) point out, extreme proponents of "target-language-only" have interpreted these theories to mean that all the listening, reading, speaking, and writing must always and only be in the target language, with no recourse to the students' first languages. Like-wise, translation between students' first and second languages is discouraged as this is viewed as a reversion to the outmoded **grammar translation method** of language teaching (Cummins, 2008).

However, as Cummins (2008) points out, there already exists extensive empirical evidence for interdependence between students' first and second languages (for a review, see Cummins, 1996). Cummins (2008) states that within bilingual and second language immersion programs, strong relation-ships between the first and second language are observed for literacy-related aspects of language—that is, students use their first language to make sense of second language input, and the second language in turn exerts an influence on the first language. He notes that students in bilingual programs spontaneously focus on similarities and differences in their languages despite the lack of explicit support for this strategy in the classroom.

Furthermore, we have seen in this chapter that code-switching is a useful communicative resource for bilinguals. Whereas monolinguals rely on style switching and voicing, bilinguals employ these strategies in addition to their bilingual resources (Gumperz & Cook-Gumperz, 2005). In a study of bilingual third graders in Arizona, Sayer (2008) points out that insisting on artificially separating bilingual students' two languages in the classroom is counterproductive as this does not reflect their normal language use patterns. He analyzed a structured reading activity involving bilingual students, and showed that the children used Spanish-English code-switching as a resource for meaning-making and negotiating literacy. Similarly, Gumperz & Cook-Gumperz (2005) argue that students' use of their first language allows them to apply their knowledge of one language to learn the grammar and semantics of another language.

Given what we know about code-switching and the role of students' first languages, what can teachers do? McKay & Bokhorst-Heng (2008: 173) recommend that educators minimize negative attitudes toward code-switching and encourage a view of bilingualism as a resource. They argue that educators need to consider how students' other language(s) can productively be used within the educational context, and examine their own assumptions about code-switching. To promote literacy engagement in both students' first and second languages, Cummins (2008) recommends creating dual language multimedia books or projects. (To see sample student works, visit the Thornwood Public School Dual Language Showcase at: http://www.thornwood ps.ca/dual/index.htm.) Cummins also recommends engaging students in computer-mediated sister class exchanges to create literature and art in both **L1** and **L2** and to explore socially relevant issues.

SUMMARY

In this chapter, I have discussed the social and conversational aspects of code-switching. Language purists would say that code-switching is a lazy, corrupted form of speech. However, we saw evidence that far from being a communicative deficit, code-switching is a valuable linguistic resource for bilinguals. We saw that having access to two languages, bilinguals have more ways to convey their meanings and intentions than do monolinguals. I discussed Gumperz's influential theory on conversational code-switching, which maintains that code-switching is a communicative option available to the bilingual speaker in much the same way that switching between styles or dialects is an option for the monolingual speaker. By building up a contrast in languages, code-switching conveys the speaker's attitudes, preferences, and emotions to other participants in the conversation. Viewed in this way, there is nothing really special about code-switching. In fact, code-switching is quite unremarkable in that it is used by bilinguals as but one of a host of contextualization strategies to communicate their meanings.

I discussed two separate developments of Gumperz's analysis of code-switching as an interactional resource. Myers-Scotton's Markedness Model argues that bilingual speakers are aware of the social consequences of choosing a specific language in a particular context. According to this model, speakers who choose the marked variety in a given social circumstance do so for specific reasons such as to show authority or displeasure. The conversation analytic framework developed by Auer (1995) shows ways in which bilinguals use code-switching to structure their conversation and to negotiate the language for the interaction. His turn-by-turn analysis is useful in revealing that as the conversation proceeds, individuals carefully monitor other participants' speech production and change their own language choice to fit their assessment of the bilingual abilities and preferences of the other participants.

We saw that bilinguals use code-switching for a variety of social purposes such as to exert power over others and to show solidarity with members of the same ethnic group. We also saw that code-switching can signal playfulness in some contexts whereas it can represent a "discourse of resistance" in others (Lee, 2004). In all of these examples, the ability to switch between languages emerges as an important communicative asset.

I also discussed negative attitudes toward code-switching in the school setting. Language mixing is generally discouraged by teachers who believe that it is distracting and robs students of the opportunity to practice the target language. However, we saw that forcing students to speak only the target language in the classroom is counterproductive because it prevents students from making connections to what they already know. Perhaps more importantly, insisting on rigidly separating two languages disregards what it means for bilingual students to live with two languages. The two languages in a bilingual's linguistic repertoire are a lot more meshed together than what is commonly envisioned as two separate compartments in the brain. Students' bilingual abilities, as manifested in code-switching, should be supported, promoted, and celebrated as tools for learning rather than be dismissed as a hindrance to acquiring new languages and skills.

FURTHER READING

- Gardner-Chloros, P. (2009). *Code-switching.* Cambridge: Cambridge University Press.—In this book, Penelope Gardner-Chloros introduces the reader to the sociolinguistic, psycholinguistic, grammatical, and developmental aspects of code-switching.
- Levine, G.S. (2011). *Code choice in the language classroom.* Bristol, UK: Multilingual Matters.—In this book, Glenn Levine argues that the foreign language classroom should be viewed as a "multilingual classroom community of practice" and provides sample classroom activities that engage students in the co-construction of language choice conventions.
- Zentella, A.C. (1997). *Growing up bilingual: Puerto Rican children in New York.* Oxford/Malden, MA: Blackwell.—In this book, Ana Celia Zentella describes the individual code-switching styles of five Puerto Rican children growing up in New York City's Spanish Harlem and the development of their Spanish and English over time.

STUDY QUESTIONS AND ACTIVITIES

1. Why is bilingual speech looked upon as deficient and undesirable? How is code-switching a communicative resource for bilinguals? How do bilinguals use code-switching as an *additional* means to communicate their intentions and preferences to other participants in the conversation?
2. Gather samples of code-switching in conversation. Keeping in mind the functions of code-switching you read about in this chapter, try to determine what communicative purposes might be served by the code-switches found in your samples. What particular functions of code-switching did you find most often? How frequently did code-switching occur? Would you say that

the code-switches were more deliberate or more spontaneous? Ask the participants in the conversation for their opinions.

3. Observe a foreign language classroom. How much time does the instructor spend in the target language? How much time is spent in the native language of the students? When does the instructor switch to the students' native language? What functions do the switches serve? When do the students code-switch? In your opinion, how would the learning of the target language be affected if the instructor and the students were not allowed to code-switch at all?

Educating English Learners

INTRODUCTION

In this chapter, I discuss some of the major policies and pedagogical issues related to educating ELs, the fastest growing segment of the American school population. One in five school-age children (ages five to 17) in the U.S. (11.2 million) speaks a language other than English at home (U.S. Department of Education, National Center for Education Statistics, 2011). About half of this group, or 5.3 million school-age children, are ELs, students who are not fully proficient in English (U.S. Department of Education, National Clearinghouse for English Language Acquisition and Language Instruction Educational Programs, 2011).

ELs (also referred to as "**English Language Learners**," or "**ELLs**") are among the students placed most at risk for academic failure—on practically every educational measure, ELs perform at lower levels than almost any other category of students (Gándara & Hopkins, 2010b). In California, for example, with a third of the nation's ELs, the overwhelming majority of schools in Program Improvement status for failing to meet NCLB benchmarks are schools with high proportions of English learners (Gándara & Hopkins, 2010b: 17; more on this legislation later in this chapter). Since an increasingly larger portion of the nation's report card depends on the academic performance of ELs, educators and policy-makers are paying more attention to improving the education of this group.

One of the most intensely debated issues surrounding the education of language minority students has been the question of what language should be used for instruction. School districts with large numbers of Spanish-speaking ELs have provided various forms of bilingual education in Spanish and English to a subset of this population. A small percentage of these programs are geared toward helping students maintain the use of Spanish while they learn English (i.e., "developmental bilingual education programs"), whereas most other models offer instruction in Spanish for a limited amount of time, and drop it as soon as students are deemed sufficiently proficient in English to be mainstreamed into English-only instruction (i.e., "transitional bilingual education programs").

Regardless of the amount of Spanish used in these programs however, bilingual education has often been wrongly blamed for the poor academic performance of Hispanic students (see also, Chapter 1, Myth #5). Some groups opposing bilingual education for immigrant children have argued that teaching in Spanish prevents students from learning the English they need to succeed in school. They argue that if children come to school lacking proficiency in English, they need maximum exposure to English in school in order to learn it (i.e., the "maximum exposure hypothesis"). This hypothesis has led to the claim that immersion in English is the most effective means to ensuring the learning of English and improving academic performance.

But simply teaching in two languages does not automatically lead to academic failure. Many non-language factors including the student's socioeconomic status and prior education as well as overall school climate influence the academic performance of ELs. In fact, ELs are over-represented in schools in urban areas with high concentrations of minority and poor students (Fry, 2008). In these schools, many students struggle academically regardless of whether they are ELs or English speakers. In addition, many ELs are educated in schools in which they make up either a majority or substantial minority of the student population and therefore have limited opportunities to interact with native speakers of English, who can serve as good language models (Valdés, 2001).

Many ELs struggle with reading, writing, and oral language in English, which interferes with their academic work in all subjects. One of the biggest challenges facing ELs is going beyond the intermediate level of English to develop advanced language skills. While many immigrant students make fairly rapid progress from beginning to intermediate levels of proficiency in English, few progress beyond the intermediate level to achieve the high levels of English literacy that are required to meet grade-level standards in content areas (August & Shanahan, 2006; Bielenberg & Wong Fillmore, 2004/2005).

Many ELs are fluent in the **conversational English** needed for everyday interaction, but have considerable difficulty in navigating the dense, decontextualized language of **academic English** (Scarcella, 2002; Short & Fitzsimmons, 2007). A consensus is emerging in the field of EL education, that ELs should be explicitly taught the features of academic English (Saunders & Goldenberg, 2010; Spada & Lightbown, 2008). In this chapter, I will show how academic English is structurally different from everyday spoken English and what teachers can do to draw students' attention to linguistic form within a meaning-driven study of content area texts.

This chapter is organized as follows. I will first show some statistics on the growing numbers of ELs in the U.S. I will discuss geographic distribution of ELs across the U.S. and their language backgrounds. I will then provide a brief history of the policies that have guided the instruction of language minority children in the U.S. I will discuss how English, itself an immigrant language, has come to dominate the American linguistic landscape, and major policies and legal precedents that have guided immigrant education. I will describe how federal support for language minority students has evolved over the years and what impact the NCLB has had on EL education.

I will also discuss some state-level educational policies that have restricted the use of languages other than English in the classroom. We now have data on the educational outcomes for ELs since the passage of Proposition 227 in California (1998), Proposition 203 in Arizona (2000), and Question 2 in Massachusetts (2002), anti-bilingual education legislation which has significantly curtailed the use of languages other than English in EL education in these states. Despite what has been widely claimed to be the panacea for the poor academic performance of ELs, English-only instruction has not closed the achievement gap between ELs and non-ELs in these states (Rumberger & Tran, 2010). After at least five years since the passage of these laws, ELs in all three states maintain the same relative (and very low) position academically compared to their English-speaking peers and in some cases are doing worse (Mahoney, MacSwan, Haladyna, & García, 2010; Uriarte, Tung, Lavan, & Diez, 2010; Wentworth, Pellegrin, Thompson, & Hakuta, 2010).

I will then provide a synthesis of the available research on academic language, and show how ELs could benefit from an instruction on language structure. There is currently a renewed interest in **focus on form**, an approach to second language teaching that explicitly draws learners' attention to the structure of language within a meaning-driven content-based lesson (Doughty & Williams, 1998; Ellis, 2002). This approach is contrasted with **communicative language teaching**, whose primary goal is to promote meaningful social interaction in the second language. In communicative language teaching, the acquisition of language forms and rules are seen to be an implicit process, not requiring overt instruction. Focus on form, on the other hand, involves occasionally shifting students' attention to linguistic features triggered by perceived problems with comprehension or production during an otherwise meaning-based lesson (Long & Robinson, 1998). It is important to understand that focus on form is not a proposal to revert back to a structural syllabus (e.g., the grammar translation or **audiolingual methods**). I will show what focus on form looks like in a content classroom and why it is important to train content teachers to address language issues in their classrooms. Finally, I will discuss policy implications for improving the education of ELs.

THE GROWING ENGLISH LEARNER POPULATION

The EL population is the fastest growing segment of the American school population. As can be seen in Figure 7.1, while there was only a 7% increase in total PreK–12 enrollment between 1998/99 and 2008/09 (from 46.2 million to 49.5 million), the EL enrollment during the same period rose by 51% (from 3.5 million in 1998/99 to 5.3 million in 2008/09). The EL student population is expected to continue growing in the next decade. It is projected that by 2020, there will be 17.9 million school-age children of immigrants in the U.S. (Fry, 2008).

Figure 7.2 shows a state-by-state breakdown in the number of ELs. In terms of total EL enrollment, the top five EL states are California (1,512,122), Texas (713,218), Florida (257,776), New York (229,260), and Illinois (208,839). EL enrollment as a proportion of total student enrollment in a given state varies substantially across the U.S. Figure 7.3 shows that the "EL-heavy" states, where ELs account for more than 10% of the total PreK–12 student population, are concentrated in the western and southwestern part of the U.S., near the U.S.–Mexico border. California, in particular, has the highest percentage of ELs—one in four students in California schools are ELs.

Although historically, the western and southwestern states have had the highest concentrations of ELs, much of the recent growth in EL population has been observed in the eastern part of the U.S. (see Figure 7.4). This increase is attributed to a robust growth in jobs in construction, agribusiness, and service sectors through the 1990s and the early part of the twenty-first century (Maxwell, 2009). While the global economic recession and rising anti-immigrant sentiments in recent years have had a dampening effect on immigration, immigrant students and families can now be found practically everywhere in the U.S.

While ELs as a group speak more than 150 languages, Spanish is by far the most common first language spoken by ELs. According to an analysis of the 2009 American Community Survey by the Migration Policy Institute, 73.1% of all EL students in the U.S. spoke Spanish as their first language (Batalova & McHugh, 2010). This was followed by Chinese (3.8%), Vietnamese (2.7%), French/Haitian Creole (2.1%), Hindi (1.8%), Korean (1.5%), and German (1.5%). More than two-thirds of ELs spoke Spanish as their first language in 28 states. Among these, 13 states, including those with traditionally large numbers of Spanish speakers (e.g., California and Texas) as well as the more recent destinations for immigrants (e.g., Wyoming, Arkansas, and Colorado), had more than 80% of their ELs coming from Spanish-speaking homes.

Contrary to a popular assumption that all ELs are recent arrivals, 57% of adolescent ELs were actually born in the U.S. (Batalova, Fix, & Murray, 2005).

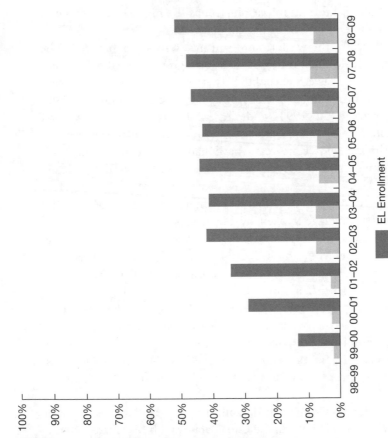

Year	Total PreK-12 Enrollment	PreK-12 Growth Since 1997–98	Total EL Enrollment	EL Growth Since 1997–98
98–99	46,153,266	0.00%	3,540,673	0.00%
99–00	47,356,089	2.61%	4,416,580	24.74%
00–01	47,665,483	3.28%	4,584,947	29.49%
01–02	48,296,777	4.64%	4,750,920	34.18%
02–03	49,478,583	7.20%	5,044,361	42.47%
03–04	49,618,529	7.51%	5,013,539	41.60%
04–05	48,982,898	6.13%	5,119,561	44.59%
05–06	49,324,849	6.87%	5,074,572	43.32%
06–07	49,863,427	7.89%	5,218,800	47.40%
07–08	49,914,453	7.98%	5,297,935	49.63%
08–09	49,487,174	7.22%	5,346,673	51.01%

■ EL Enrollment

▨ PreK–12 Enrollment

FIGURE 7.1 The Growing Numbers of English Learners in the U.S., 1998/99–2008/09

Source: U.S. Department of Education, National Clearinghouse for English Language Acquisition and Language Instruction Educational Programs (NCELA), 2011

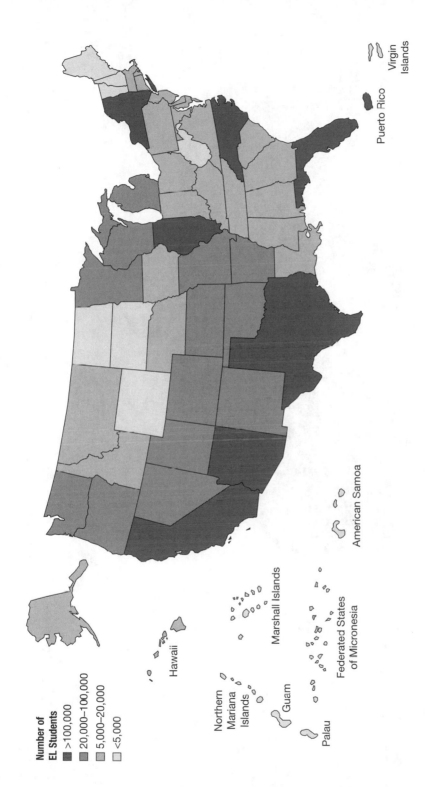

Number of EL Students
- ■ >100,000
- ▨ 20,000–100,000
- ▨ 5,000–20,000
- □ <5,000

Hawaii

Northern Mariana Islands

Palau

Guam

Marshall Islands

Federated States of Micronesia

American Samoa

Puerto Rico

Virgin Islands

FIGURE 7.2 Number of English Learners in the U.S., 2008/09

Source: U.S. Department of Education, National Clearinghouse for English Language Acquisition and Language Instruction Educational Programs (NCELA), 2011

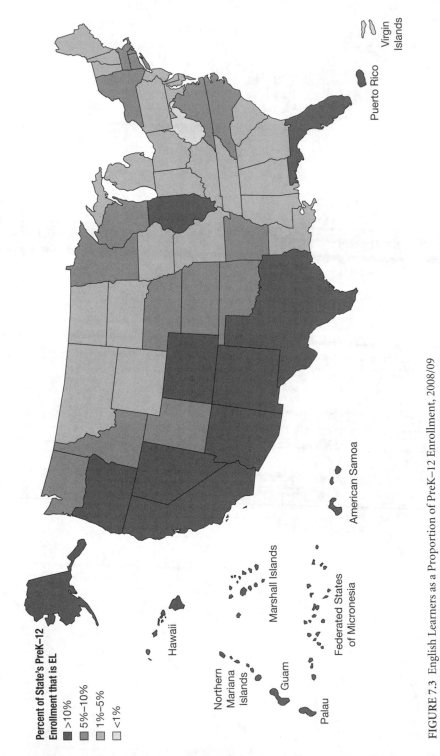

Percent of State's PreK–12 Enrollment that is EL

■ >10%
■ 5%–10%
□ 1%–5%
□ <1%

FIGURE 7.3 English Learners as a Proportion of PreK–12 Enrollment, 2008/09

Source: U.S. Department of Education, National Clearinghouse for English Language Acquisition and Language Instruction Educational Programs (NCELA), 2011

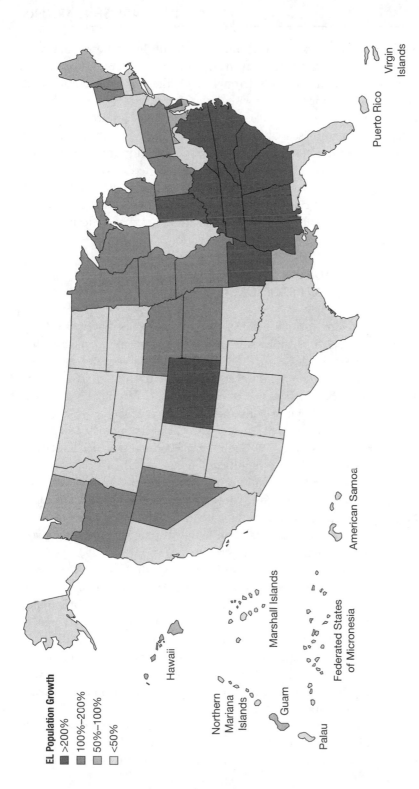

EL Population Growth

- ■ >200%
- ■ 100%–200%
- ■ 50%–100%
- □ <50%

Hawaii

Northern
Mariana
Islands

Guam

Palau

Marshall Islands

Federated States
of Micronesia

American Samoa

Puerto Rico

Virgin
Islands

FIGURE 7.4 English Learner Population Growth, 1998/99–2008/09

Source: U.S. Department of Education, National Clearinghouse for English Language Acquisition and Language Instruction Educational Programs (NCELA), 2011

ELs come from diverse backgrounds. Some EL students live in homes in which no English is spoken, while others come from families that have shifted mostly to English. Some ELs may identify strongly with their heritage culture and language, while others identify only with American culture. Some ELs live in economically depressed areas, while others live in affluent suburbs. Some ELs may be high achievers in school while others struggle academically. Some students come to American schools with strong education from their home countries whereas others have had limited or interrupted schooling. In sum, there is no single profile for an EL. With such diversity, it is difficult to craft a single set of policies that can adequately address the needs of every learner. Any proposed educational plan will have to be tailored specifically to the characteristics and needs of the local EL population.

LANGUAGE POLICY IN THE UNITED STATES: A HISTORICAL OVERVIEW

Contrary to what some people believe, the U.S. does not have an official language. Even though English acts as the *de facto* official language in the government, media, and education, the U.S. Constitution does not specify an official language of the country. However, there are currently 31 states which have adopted official English laws that require official government business to be conducted solely in English. This includes public documents, records, legislation, and regulations, as well as hearings, official ceremonies, and public meetings. Organizations such as U.S. English and ProEnglish, which have been campaigning to adopt English as the official language of the U.S., argue that making English official will unite Americans by providing a common means of communication among its citizens. These groups portray using languages other than English in public domains to be un-American and unpatriotic. But the fact that some groups should insist on "English-only" is intriguing given America's highly multilingual past (and present).

At the time of initial European colonization, North America was vastly multilingual. An estimated 500 to 1,000 Native American languages were spoken in fifteenth-century North America at the time of Christopher Columbus (Grosjean, 1982: 82), and other immigrant languages were widely used before the time of the founding of the U.S. English was first introduced in America as a colonial language, as were two other major colonial languages, Spanish and French (Wiley & Lee, 2009). Spanish and French in particular were commonly spoken in a significant portion of America that would eventually become the U.S. (Gándara et al., 2010).

English is also an immigrant language in America. Since the seventeenth century, England, Scotland, Wales, Ireland, Canada, and other former British colonies have been major sources of U.S. immigration because these countries were favored under a restrictive quota system (Wiley & Lee, 2009). Thus, one of the reasons that English has come to dominate the linguistic landscape of the U.S. is that so many immigrants have come from English-speaking countries.

To understand the current context of EL education, it is important to review some of the major language and educational policies of the past. Since the early eighteenth century, the use of languages other than English in education has been controversial. Depending on the relationship of the U.S. with the countries from which immigrants came, there were alternating cycles of acceptance and rejection of non-English immigrant languages (Gándara et al., 2010: 22). These cycles are aptly captured by Ovando (2003), who divides the history of language-in-education policies in the U.S. into four main periods: *permissive* (1700s–1880s), *restrictive* (1880s–1960s), *opportunist* (1960s–1980s), and *dismissive* (1980s–present). Following Ovando (2003), I highlight the major policies and practices during these periods.

The Permissive Period: 1700s–1880s

Ovando (2003: 3–4) describes the period between 1700 and 1880 in the U.S. as "inconsistent and contradictory regarding the ideology, policies, and politics of language diversity." He states that,

> though some states published official documents in minority languages, the U.S. Congress consistently refused to do so. Some states authorized bilingual education while others mandated English-only instruction . . . . Responses to language diversity were shaped by the changing local-ized political, social, and economic forces rather than by systematic ideas about language itself.

On the whole, however, Ovando portrays eighteenth- and nineteenth-century America as tolerant toward non-English immigrant languages in part because "if individuals did not like their neighbors, they could keep clearing the land and move" (2003: 4).

By the latter half of the nineteenth century, bilingual or non-English instruction was provided in many public and private schools:

> German in Pennsylvania, Maryland, Ohio, Indiana, Illinois, Missouri, Nebraska, Colorado, and Oregon; Swedish, Norwegian, and Danish in Wisconsin, Illinois, Minnesota, Iowa, North and South Dakota, Nebraska, and Washington; Dutch in Michigan; Polish and Italian in Wisconsin; Czech in Texas; French in Louisiana; and Spanish in the Southwest.
>
> (Kloss, 1998, cited in Ovando, 2003: 4)

Although this period can be characterized as permissive toward non-English languages, Ovando (2003) notes that nineteenth-century education in America did not actively encourage bilingualism. Rather, it promoted linguistic assimilation of immigrants, only without the kind of active coercion seen in later decades.

The Restrictive Period: 1880s–1960s

Ovando states that the period spanning the 1880s to the 1960s was a turning point in which a number of repressive language policies appeared. Among these was the federal government's policy to "civilize" Native Americans by subduing their cultures and forcing them to use English. Beginning in 1879, federal officials began separating Native American children from their families and forcing them to attend off-reservation boarding schools. Students were severely punished when caught speaking their native languages, even if they could speak no English (Crawford, 2004: 92). Such repressive policy has had a deleterious effect on language maintenance among Native Americans. It has been estimated that of the 175 American Indian languages still spoken today, only 20 will survive to 2050 (Crawford, 2004).

One factor that was strongly linked to restrictive language policies around the turn of the twentieth century was a dramatic increase in the number of new immigrants to the U.S. A call for Americanization of new immigrants was made, with competence in English becoming associated with loyalty to the U.S. (Baker, 2006). Furthermore, European nationalism at the turn of the twentieth century began to exert its influence on America and "increasing fear about the importation of foreign ideologies into the U.S. resulted in a call for all immigrants to be assimilated into one cultural and linguistic mold" (Ovando, 2003: 5). English-only school laws were adopted in Illinois and Wisconsin in 1889, and the Naturalization Act of 1906 required immigrants to speak English before they could become naturalized U.S. citizens.

With the entry of the U.S. into World War I, extreme anti-German sentiments spread. The German language was portrayed as a threat to the unity of the U.S., and laws forbidding the use of German in schools, in the media, and even in public were passed. By 1923, the legislatures of 34 states had dictated English-only instructional policies in all private and public elementary schools (Baker, 2006). Just as Hispanics are the largest minority group in the U.S. today, Germans were the most substantial and active minority group at the turn of the twentieth century—about 9 million Americans spoke German natively in 1910 (Grosjean, 1982). But Germans in the U.S. have since become almost completely assimilated into English-speaking American society. World War I brought about extreme pressure on German Americans to assimilate, and "children were humiliated in school, and many reacted by rejecting their background and refusing to speak German in public or even with their parents" (Grosjean, 1982: 90).

The prevailing approach to educating language minority students during this period was sink-or-swim (or submersion). The schools did not provide any linguistic or academic accommodations to students who came from non-English-speaking homes. Ovando (2003) notes that most educators and policy-makers felt that it was up to the language minority students, not the schools, to make the linguistic, cultural, and cognitive adjustments necessary to achieve academically in English. When these students did not do well academically, their home cultures and languages were often blamed. In fact, many immigrant students failed in school. In 1911, the U.S. Immigrant Service found that 77% of Italian, 60% of Russian, and 51% of German immigrant children were one or more grade levels behind compared to 28% of American-born White children (Kloss, 1998).

The Opportunist Period: 1960s–1980s

Ovando (2003) points out that World War II served as the first wake-up call for the U.S. to recognize its inadequacies in foreign language instruction. Language, math, and science became a high priority in the national defense agenda during the Cold War period. The National Defense Education Act of 1958, spurred in large part by the launch of *Sputnik* by the Soviet Union the year before, raised the level of foreign language education in the U.S. However, Ovando observes that the U.S. government's investment in foreign language education was not without contradiction—although the National Defense Education Act provided federal funding to support the study of foreign languages by English monolinguals, it did little to tap the linguistic resources already present in the country (i.e., the language skills of linguistic minorities; see also Chapter 4). Significant effort was invested in teaching foreign languages to English-speaking Americans while the same languages possessed by immigrants were purged through English-only education.

The 1960s saw a number of landmark legislations and legal challenges with regard to language minority education. More opportunities for bilingual education, albeit patchy and half-hearted, became available in the context of the Civil Rights Movement. The Civil Rights Act of 1964 prohibited discrimination on the basis of a person's color, race, or national origin, and led to the establishment of the Office for Civil Rights. There were also changes in immigration laws which helped to revive bilingual education. The Immigration Act of 1965 terminated an earlier national origin quota system which restricted the number of immigrants admitted from Southern and Eastern Europe, as well as from the Middle East and Asia. As a result of this legislation, larger numbers of Asians and Latin Americans started to enter the U.S., leading to a major demographic shift in the U.S. Much of the linguistic and ethnic diversity seen in America today is a direct outcome of this legislation.

Title VII of the Elementary and Secondary Education Act (ESEA), also known as the Bilingual Education Act (BEA), was passed in 1968. This policy was designed to address the needs of students with limited English proficiency. But the primary instructional model endorsed by the federal government was transitional bilingual education, which provides native language instruction for a limited period as a temporary bridge to English-only instruction (see also Table 1.2). In addition to bilingual education, the BEA allocated some funds for ESL programs. But the amount of federal support for these programs was always far less than was necessary to meet the needs of all the children who were eligible, and many school districts continued to ignore the needs of language minority students and failed to provide any accommodation (Wiley & Lee, 2009).

A major court decision that set a legal precedent for language minority education during this period was *Lau v. Nichols*. This case involved a class-action suit on behalf of Kinney Lau and 1,789 other Chinese-background students in San Francisco public schools (Crawford, 2004). The lawsuit alleged that these children were being denied equal educational opportunities because of their limited English skills. San Francisco school officials denied that there was any discrimination against the Chinese students because they were neither segregated nor treated differently from their English-speaking peers in the district. The school officials stated that the same instruction was offered to all students, regardless of national origin.

Federal district and appeals courts sided with the San Francisco school officials, but in 1974, this case reached the U.S. Supreme Court, which unanimously rejected the decision of the lower courts (Crawford, 2004). The Supreme Court ruled that merely providing non-English speaking students with the same facilities, textbooks, teachers, and curriculum does not constitute equality of treatment since these students are effectively foreclosed from any meaningful education due to their limited language abilities. In other words, schools were obligated to help non-English speakers learn English so that they can have equal access to instruction given in English.

However, the Supreme Court did not mandate any specific program. Rather, it left it to the schools to determine what type of accommodation would facilitate the acquisition of English while making instruction in English comprehensible. Naturally, some confusion ensued, and many programs with a wide range of differing quality were labeled *bilingual* regardless of whether any model of bilingual education was actually used (Wiley & Lee, 2009).

In 1975, the Office for Civil Rights investigators made preliminary visits to 334 school districts with large numbers of language minority children and found that most districts had "utterly failed to meet their responsibilities" (Crawford, 2004). Thus, a set of guidelines, called Lau Remedies, were drawn up by the Office for Civil Rights. The guidelines instructed districts on how to identify and evaluate children with limited English skills, what instructional treatments would be appropriate, when children were ready for mainstream classrooms, and what professional standards teachers should meet (Crawford, 2004). The Office for Civil Rights embarked on a campaign of aggressive enforcement of the Lau Remedies, and many school districts undergoing compliance reviews adopted bilingual education for fear of losing federal funding.

The Dismissive Period: 1980s–Present

Ovando (2003) states that the battle against bilingual education began to gain momentum in the 1980s. Political activist groups such as U.S. English, English Only, and English First appeared on the scene and campaigned vigorously against bilingual education. The debate over bilingual education reached a climax when California voters decided in 1998, through passage of Proposition 227, that English should be the primary medium of instruction for language minority students. Proposition 227 mandates that ELs be taught "overwhelmingly in English" in **Structured English Immersion (SEI)** classes and then transferred to a mainstream English-only classroom.

Voters in Arizona and Massachusetts approved similar measures in 2000 and in 2002 respectively. Anti-bilingual education activists claimed that children were staying too long in bilingual programs, which prevented them from learning the English they needed to succeed in school. However, student performance data from these states since the implementation of the anti-bilingual education laws show that ELs are not learning English any faster than before the policies went into effect. Likewise, the academic achievement gaps between ELs and English speakers in these states remain largely unchanged.

The passage of Proposition 227 in 1998 had an almost immediate effect of reducing the number of students receiving bilingual instruction in California from 29% to 8% (Gándara et al., 2010). Wentworth et al. (2010) used five years of California Standards Test data (from 2003 to 2007) to examine Proposition 227's impact on EL achievement. They report that there has been no discernible closing of the achievement gaps between ELs and English speakers, and found some evidence that the first cohort of students studied may have been hurt (as shown in their lower test scores) from having bilingual education abruptly pulled from their instruction following the passage of the legislation.

In Arizona, the passage of Proposition 203 in 2000 resulted in a sharp drop in enrollment in bilingual education programs. For example, in 1997, 32% of

Arizona's ELs were enrolled in bilingual education programs, but in 2004, only 5% were (Mahoney et al., 2010). Using student scores on SAT-9, a standardized test that reflects national curriculum content standards, Mahoney et al. (2010) compared the academic achievement among **reclassified ELs**—ELs that have tested at proficient levels on an English language exam and no longer receive ESL instruction—before the passage of Proposition 203 (1997–2000) to the academic achievement among similar students after the passage of the proposition (2001–2004). They found that student gains before and after Proposition 203 were nearly identical for ELs and English speakers. In other words, Proposition 203 did little to close the achievement gaps between the two groups.

When Mahoney et al. (2010) examined post-Proposition 203 student scores for Arizona's Instrument to Measure Standards (AIMS), an annual test designed to measure Arizona's content standards, they found that while there were large gains for third-grade reclassified ELs, there was a dramatic decline in achievement for fifth- and eighth-grade reclassified ELs. The authors point out that responding to the demands of the regular school curriculum becomes increasingly difficult as children advance through the grades, as early deficits resulting from incomprehensible instruction make it harder for students to keep up. This result is confirmed by other large-scale investigations which found that EL children enrolled in English-only programs often do well initially, but do less well in later years (e.g., Ramirez, Yuen, Ramey, & Pasta, 1991).

In Massachusetts, the passage of Referendum Question 2 replaced a wide-ranging set of bilingual programs with SEI. Examining four years of data immediately following the passage of Question 2, Uriarte et al. (2010) found that there were substantial decreases in the identification of students who, because of limited English proficiency, required programs for ELs. Instead, enrollments of ELs in special education increased during the same period. The authors point out that while proponents of Question 2 promised more rapid acquisition of English for ELs in Massachusetts and a rise in academic achievement and a narrowing of the achievement gap, pass rates on Massachusetts Comprehensive Assessment System (MCAS) actually declined for ELs in English language arts and math, and the improvements in pass rates, when found, were smaller than those for other groups. The achievement gaps in both math and English language acquisition, but especially in math, widened between ELs and students in general education. The authors also show that while dropout rates generally increased in Boston public schools between 2003 and 2006, the magnitude of the increase among ELs was significantly larger than that among other student groups.

Overall, ELs in California, Arizona, and Massachusetts are doing worse academically than their peers in states without restrictive language policies.

Using data from the 2005 National Assessment of Educational Progress (NAEP), the only ongoing national assessment that measures what students in grades 4, 8, and 12 know and can do in several content areas, Rumberger & Tran (2010) examined the achievement gap between ELs and English speakers among states across four areas—reading and math in grades 4 and 8. They found that states with restrictive language policies (California, Arizona, and Massachusetts) tended to have larger achievement gaps than those without such policies (Nevada, New Mexico, and Texas), especially in grade 4.

All of these findings confirm what we know from the past 40 years' research on immigrant education—primary language instruction, or instruction in the primary and second languages simultaneously, results in superior outcomes compared to English-only instruction in improving the English language development of language minority children (August, Goldenberg, & Rueda, 2010). Most research on positive models of immigrant education points to the importance of children maintaining the ability to function in their heritage culture as they adapt to a new one (Portes & Rumbaut, 2001). Similarly, development of English language proficiency depends on the overall quality of the programs for ELs and their integration into a healthy school environment, as well as children's prior schooling and language resources in the family (Suárez-Orozco & Suárez-Orozco, 2001; Suárez-Orozco, Suárez-Orozco, & Todorova, 2008).

OUT OF THE MOUTHS OF BILINGUALS 7.1

A Young Bilingual Interpreter

"Being bilingual gives me satisfaction and pride. When you are bilingual you can help other people, especially the needy ones. The other day I went to the pharmacy with my mom. There was an elderly couple. They did not know any English. They did not know how to explain what they needed. I helped them to fill out the prescription. At that moment I felt very proud of speaking two languages. I also feel very proud of being bilingual, because I can read, write and communicate in two languages. I feel secure to go everywhere with my parents and without them."

—Angel, an elementary bilingual student writing on the topic of "Being Proud To Be Bilingual," posted on the Project Based Technology Integrated Learning (PBTIL) website (n.d.)

With the passage of NCLB in 2002, federal policy for language minority students changed significantly. Heralded as an unprecedented, bi-partisan effort to improve every child's academic performance and increase school accountability, NCLB requires annual testing of all students in reading and math in grades 3 through 8. NCLB requires each state to set academic achievement benchmarks for adequate yearly progress (AYP) so that by school year 2013/14, *all* students are reading and doing mathematics at grade level. Under NCLB, schools are required to report the scores of different subgroups of students separately. This disaggregation of test scores ensures that the traditionally underperforming students—those who tend to be poor and of minority backgrounds—are no longer concealed in school aggregates.

While NCLB has the potential to close the achievement gap between minority and poor students and their mainstream peers by holding schools accountable for the academic progress of *all* categories of students including English learners, it does not encourage the development of languages other than English. With an exclusive focus on English, NCLB requires schools to teach language minority students English and move them into mainstream English-only classrooms as quickly as possible. Unlike previous legislations, NCLB assigns little value to the bilingual abilities of language minority children (see also Crawford, 2004; Shin, 2006).

Another problem with NCLB is its heavy emphasis on high-stakes testing and rapid sink or swim English immersion (Menken, 2008; Wright, 2007). Many schools have adopted scripted one-size-fits-all curricular programs which consume large amounts of instructional time, leaving less time for ESL and content area instruction that is tailored to the English proficiency and literacy levels of individual students (Wright, 2005). Many argue that far from increasing the ability of public schools to serve poor and minority children, NCLB punishes these students by driving their schools to focus on testing and test preparation (Meier & Wood, 2004).

Much remains to be seen as to how EL education will be shaped at the national level in the years to come. But one thing is for certain—educating ELs will be an increasingly critical issue for local, state, and federal governments as the nation undergoes a significant demographic shift. Improving the educational outcomes for ELs will "contribute to the nation's longer-term health by building the human capital necessary for continued economic growth and democratic participation" (Working Group on ELL Policy, 2010). All students, including ELs, must have access to high-quality curriculum and instruction, effective teachers, and supportive school environment to be successful. They must also receive specific help in mastering the language of schooling. This is the topic of the next section.

ACADEMIC LANGUAGE DEVELOPMENT OF ENGLISH LEARNERS

Many ELs have difficulty with reading, writing, and oral language in English, which interferes with their academic work in all subject areas. In order to help ELs succeed in school, teachers need to know the specific linguistic challenges faced by ELs in different subject-matter classes, including textbook difficulty, demands made by classroom interactions, and characteristics of the language challenges present in standardized tests (Valdés, 2001). This kind of academic language is different from the English used in everyday conversations and requires at least several years to develop (Cummins, 2000).

Scarcella (2003: 10–11) defines academic language as "a variety or register of English used in professional books and characterized by the specific linguistic features that are used in particular situational contexts." Chamot & O'Malley (1994: 40) define it as "the language that is used by teachers and students for the purposes of acquiring new knowledge and skills . . . imparting new information, describing abstract ideas, and developing students' conceptual understanding." Saunders & Goldenberg (2010: 49–50) define academic language as "the specialized vocabulary, grammar, discourse/textual, and functional skills associated with academic instruction and mastery of academic material and tasks." Students need academic language to perform sophisticated tasks such as synthesizing and evaluating information, arguing persuasively for or against a point of view, and analyzing a set of data.

Academic language is different from one content area to another. Thus, the language of mathematics is different from the language of social studies, from that of science, and so on. Different disciplines require knowledge of specific technical vocabulary and make use of different grammatical forms and discourse patterns. For example, in order to write an analysis of data presented in a graph in a math class, students would need to know the vocabulary of graphs as well as the sentence structures and discourse features required for writing an analysis (e.g., "The population of X decreased from 1965 to 1990. Then the population increased from 1990 to 2005. The population of Y increased slowly from 1965 to 1985, then increased more rapidly from 1990 to 1995. Between 1965 and 2005, Z showed the greatest increase in population."). In an English language arts class, students may need to know the differences between an informal summary of a short story written in their reading journals and a formal summary of a journal article written for a term paper, including use of expressions such as "According to the author" and "The author maintains" (Dutro & Kinsella, 2010).

Advanced language development for ELs requires teachers to understand the specific textual demands of a discipline. Schleppegrell, Achugar, & Oteíza (2004) believe that history provides a particularly good example of discipline-specific literacy demands because it is constructed through texts that cannot easily be experienced hands-on. They show that many ELs have difficulty in identifying the events that are relevant to the historical content. To help students to identify historical events, the authors recommend analyzing the verbs. They classify the verbs used in history texts into (1) action verbs (e.g., *fight, defend, build, vote*); (2) saying and thinking-feeling verbs (e.g., *said, expressed, suppose, like, resent*); and (3) relating verbs (e.g., *is, have, is called*). This categorization helps students understand when authors are writing about events (action verbs), when they are giving opinions or telling what others have said (saying and thinking-feeling verbs), and when they are giving background information (relating verbs).

What makes history texts particularly difficult is that even when students do this type of analysis, they find that verbs are sometimes used in unconventional ways or metaphorically, as in Examples 1 and 2 from a text about the Missouri Compromise (Appleby et al., 2000: 437–438, cited in Schleppegrell et al., 2004: 77):

1. By 1819 the Missouri Territory *included* about 50,000 whites and 10,000 slaves.
2. The admission of a new state would *upset* that balance.

The authors point out that while the verb *included* is usually used as an action verb (e.g., to be *included* in a game), in this text, it functions as a relating verb that establishes the situation in the Missouri Territory at the time of the Compromise debate. In 2, the verb *upset* is used metaphorically. The authors observe that these academic uses of verbs can make it difficult for ELs to make sense of what is happening in the text.

OUT OF THE MOUTHS OF BILINGUALS 7.2

A Bilingual Teacher Helps Spanish Speakers with English Spelling

"I have observed that some Spanish-speaking children who are used to spelling easily in Spanish are disappointed to find it difficult to spell in English. But when they phoneticize the English word in the same way they learned to do in Spanish, then it no longer is a problem. For example, the children take the word *beautiful* and sound it out in Spanish: (bĕ)(ah)(oo)(tĭ)(fōōl). Then they write the word as they hear it in Spanish. This way they can remember all the vowels in the English word."

(Igoa, 1995: 159)

In my own research on the development of academic English by high school ELs, I found that the students' lack of knowledge of the grammar of academic English can also get in the way of their adequately understanding the texts (Shin, 2009). Consider the following three sentences from an article that the students read about disputes over trademarking Ethiopian coffee beans (from *The Economist*, 2006, cited in Shin, 2009):

(1) No wonder Starbucks, [a global coffee chain that prides itself on being socially responsible], has reacted like a scalded *barista* to criticism from Oxfam, [a development charity] . . . (2) [Although it denies being behind coffee-industry lobbying against the Ethiopian government], Starbucks argues that trademarking coffee beans might introduce legal complexities that will deter firms from buying trademarked beans, [thereby hurting farmers instead of helping them] . . . (3) Indeed, Mr. Holt's suggestion [that the Ethiopian government is being frustrated in its attempts to help coffee growers become more entrepreneurial] is laughable.

Each of the bracketed clauses in (1) is a type of nonrestrictive relative clause also known as an appositive, a group of words following an expression that further defines that expression (Celce-Murcia & Larsen-Freeman, 1999: 596). The first bracket in (1) contains a relative clause, "that prides itself on being socially responsible." The bracketed clauses in (2) are adverbial phrases. The main sentence in (2) contains a relative clause, "that will deter firms from buying trademarked beans." In (3), the long embedded clause, "that the Ethiopian government is being frustrated in its attempts to help coffee growers become more entrepreneurial" is a complement to the complex noun phrase, "Mr. Holt's suggestion." Notice that this complement clause has a passive construction in which the implied agent (i.e., Starbucks, coffee-industry lobbyists) is not explicitly mentioned because it was stated in the preceding passage. Formal writing in English is replete with such complex syntactic constructions, and failure to grasp the structural complexities at the sentence level prevents ELs from adequately comprehending the texts.

HOW SHOULD ACADEMIC LANGUAGE BE TAUGHT?

Teachers should teach the structural aspects of academic language explicitly to students, and ELs need to concentrate on form, in addition to engaging in communicative language use. Spada & Lightbown (2008) argue that explicit instruction in the structural features of academic English facilitates students' second language learning in a way that relying solely on meaning and communication-oriented instruction does not. Similarly, Ellis (1996) contends that advanced proficiency and accuracy in spoken and written production are essential for effective functioning in an academic setting, and that attaining high levels of proficiency requires specific instruction. Research showing the value of explicit instruction on form confirms these assertions (see also Doughty & Williams, 1998; Hinkel & Fotos, 2002).

Norris & Ortega (2000) conducted a meta-analysis of 79 studies that examined the effectiveness of various types of language programs. Despite its limited applicability to K–12 EL education (only 20% of the studies they analyzed involved elementary and secondary students; the rest involved college-age or adult learners), Norris & Ortega's meta-analysis showed that explicit instruction on language form consistently produced better student results than implicit instruction. Norris & Ortega classified an instructional treatment as explicit when the instructors presented a language form to the students and provided opportunities for them to practice it with many examples. Explicit instruction also involved instructors engaging students in tasks containing many examples of a particular form and then directing students' attention to it so that students can arrive at the rule by themselves or with the teacher's guidance. In contrast, instructional treatments were classified as implicit if the teachers did not explain the language form and did not direct students' attention to it. The authors point out that, in terms of student learning, explicit instructional approaches were on average more than twice as effective as implicit approaches.

Research on what has come to be known as focus on form has been motivated by the findings that suggest that when classroom second language learning is entirely experiential and meaning-focused, some linguistic features do not ultimately develop to target-like levels (Harley, 1992; Harley & Swain, 1984). For example, even after many years in French immersion programs in Canada, many students have difficulty using the *tu* and *vous* forms appropriately and marking gender on articles. Swain (1998) notes that although many of these students are able to get their meanings across in French, they often do so with non-target-like morphology and syntax. She concludes that an input-rich, communicatively oriented classroom does not provide all that is necessary for the development of target-like proficiency. Swain has long emphasized the role for output (speaking and writing) in second language learning (Swain, 1985).

We should note that focus on form is different from what Long & Robinson (1998) refer to as focus on forms—that is, isolated instruction in linguistic forms that often takes place in primarily grammar-based classrooms. In these classrooms, students might learn how to transform a sentence into the passive voice (e.g., The kids put on the show → The show was put on by the kids) or pluralize nouns (e.g., book → books, match → matches, sheep → sheepØ, goose → geese). The goal of these lessons is to have students rehearse and memorize individual rules of the target language. While it is certainly important for ELs to master discrete rules such as these in order to use English accurately and fluently, a mere collection of language rules is not sufficient for ELs to access grade-level content in the various subject areas.

What ELs need is meaning-driven academic discussions of content with specific attention to form. Doughty & Varela (1998: 115) provide the following criteria for a content-based lesson with a focus on form:

1. The target of the focus on form should arise incidentally in the otherwise content-based lesson.
2. The primary focus should remain on meaning or communication.
3. The teacher should draw students' attention to form rather than leaving it to chance that students will notice linguistic features without any pedagogical assistance.

In a lesson with a focus on form, teacher discussions of structural aspects of language are carried out with specific reference to performing the academic task at hand. Students' learning of the structural rules of language is not an end goal but a means to accessing the content.

What does focus on form look like in the content classroom? Doughty & Varela (1998) provide an example from their study of intermediate ELs in middle school science classes. The teacher in the treatment group analyzed students' writing in their weekly lab reports and noticed that many of the students had particular difficulty with past time reference. Although students were having difficulty with other forms as well (comparatives and superlatives, third person singular -*s*), the teacher selected simple past and conditional as the form in focus because errors of time reference were quite common among the ELs and resulted in oral and written reports that unsuccessfully communicated the predictions and outcomes of the science experiments.

Throughout the treatment period, whenever past or conditional errors occurred in speaking or writing, the instructor of the treatment group drew students' attention to the problem and then immediately provided corrective feedback in the form of a **recast**, a reformulation of an incorrect utterance that maintains the original meaning. Each procedure focused on only one learner error of past time reference and involved repetition of the student's incorrect utterance with a rising intonation and a corrective recast with a falling intonation. Thus, each procedure looked something like the following (Doughty & Varela, 1998: 124):

José: I think that the worm will go under the soil.
Teacher: I *think* that the worm *will* go under the soil?
José: (no response)
Teacher: I *thought* that the worm *would* go under the soil.
José: I *thought* that the worm *would* go under the soil.

Doughty & Varela (1998) report that the effects of the intonational focus and corrective recasting during science lab experiments were substantial. Learners in the treatment group improved in both accuracy and total number of attempts at past time reference, particularly in the oral reporting of the science labs. The progress made by the control group (which received no focus on form instruction) was much less significant than the improvement seen in the treatment group.

Overall, to successfully focus on form, content area teachers need to become more aware of the linguistic challenges of their specific disciplines at the grammatical, phonological, and discourse levels (Wong Fillmore & Snow, 2000). In order to help students develop an "ear" for academic English, teachers may wish to increase the amount of students' exposure to academic texts by reading to them out loud, focusing their attention on specific features of English, and getting them to use these features in their own writing and speech (Scarcella, 2002). Teacher training courses need to ensure that teachers are equipped with the skills necessary for focusing students' attention on form and that they have an understanding of the potential advantages and disadvantages of the different procedures involved. Furthermore, teachers need to be trained to analyze and reflect on their own as well as others' techniques for addressing form. Accomplishing this will require a significant change in the way content area teachers are prepared, and a shift in teacher identity from mainly content experts to those who are also well versed in the language demands of their subject areas.

CONCLUSIONS

In this chapter, I discussed some of the major policies and pedagogical issues related to educating ELs, the fastest growing segment of the American school-age population. There are more than 5 million ELs in the U.S., comprising more than 10% of the national public school enrollment. Although it used to be the case that immigrants were found in only certain parts of the U.S., they now reside in practically every corner of the country. A number of states, particularly in the Southeast and Midwest, have seen dramatic increases in their EL populations in the last decade. Because ELs perform at lower levels than almost any other category of students and because entire schools can be sanctioned based on the poor performance of their EL student groups under NCLB, improving the educational outcomes of ELs has become an urgent problem for many school districts.

One of the most politicized issues surrounding EL education has been the question of what language(s) should be used for instruction. Should language minority children be instructed in English only or should they receive instruction in English and in their native languages? Although there is ample research evidence that suggests that there are clear benefits to bilingualism and educating students in two languages, English-only advocates have argued that bilingual education prevents children from learning the English they need to succeed in school. They have claimed that only systematic immersion in English will improve the school performance of ELs. However, one needs only to look at the latest EL outcomes in California, Arizona, and Massachusetts, states that have passed anti-bilingual education legislation, to see that English-only education has not closed the achievement gaps between ELs and English speakers. After at least five years since the passage of these laws, ELs in all three states are still doing poorly and in some cases are doing worse.

What we can learn from the numerous language policies throughout the history of the U.S. is that English-only education neither leads to faster learning of English nor produces better academic results for language minority children. If anything, sink or swim in English only makes school subjects more unattainable and leads to student failure. Rather than undermine the languages that students bring from home, what schools need to do is treat students' bilingual abilities as a resource (Working Group on ELL Policy, 2010). However, one would be foolish to believe that simply teaching in two languages will ensure good education. As David J. Francis, Director of the federally funded National Center for Research on the Educational Achievement and Teaching of English Language Learners, puts it,

> You can have bilingual instruction and do it poorly, and you can have English-only instruction and do it poorly . . . My argument has been to figure out what it is we can do best, do it well, and worry less about the language of instruction.
>
> (quoted in Viadero, 2009: 4)

If language of instruction is not the be-all and end-all in EL education, then what is? The fact that there is no one archetype of the typical EL means that it is difficult to create a blanket policy to help them succeed academically. For some, the answer may be moving them out of isolation in sheltered ESL classes and integrating them more with English speakers. For others, it may involve one-on-one tutoring in various content areas. Teachers should have high expectations for ELs and help them acquire the same content and high-level skills that are expected of all students (Working Group on ELL Policy, 2010). ELs should not be allowed to fall behind in content area classes just because they are learning English (Valdés, 2001). In fact, English learning and content learning have to occur in tandem. To help students gain access to the language of schooling, teachers need to teach the structure of academic English explicitly. Training content area teachers to become experts in the languages of their disciplines requires significant shifts in the way teachers are prepared but the payoff from a judicious focus on form could potentially be very large.

FURTHER READING

- Crawford, J. (2004). *Educating English learners: Language diversity in the classroom* (5th ed.). Los Angeles: Bilingual Education Services.—In this highly readable introduction to EL education, James Crawford provides an excellent review of U.S. language policies and educational program alternatives for language minority students.
- Gándara, P. & Hopkins, M. eds. (2010). *Forbidden language: English learners and restrictive language policies.* New York: Teachers College Press.—This book features chapters on educational outcomes for English learners in California, Arizona, and Massachusetts, three states which have adopted restrictive language policies, and offers suggestions for effective instruction of English learners.
- Wiley, T.G., Lee, J.S., & Rumberger, R.W. eds. (2009). *The education of language minority immigrants in the United States.* Bristol, UK: Multilingual Matters.—Based on cutting-edge research and policy analyses, this collection will be of value to those interested in promoting educational equity and achievement for immigrant language minority students.

ONLINE RESOURCES

- http://www.migrationinformation.org/integration/ellcenter.cfm—Migration Policy Institute has an online ELL Information Center with videos, fact sheets, and maps of the ELL student population across the United States.
- http://ellpolicy.org/—The Working Group on ELL Policy brings a research perspective to developing recommendations, sharing information, and fostering dialogue among educators, policy-makers, and other stakeholders about current policy issues affecting ELs.

STUDY QUESTIONS AND ACTIVITIES

1. Explain the "maximum exposure hypothesis" in your own words and explain how this view is not supported by existing linguistic and social evidence. Present an alternate, more linguistically sound conceptualization of the bilingual capacities of children learning two or more languages and research findings that support it.
2. Describe specific ways in which teachers and school administrators can promote the continual development and maintenance of ELs' native

languages and why doing this is necessary. In addition, explain ways in which your suggestions can benefit non-ELs in your schools.

3. How is academic English different from conversational English? Analyze a paragraph from a content area textbook and identify vocabulary, grammar, and discourse features that might be difficult for ELs. What can teachers do to help students learn these successfully?

4. Observe a content area class (e.g., math, science, history) in which ELs are present. With the permission of the teacher, talk to the ELs about what they find hard to understand. Do you suspect any of the students' difficulties might be due to their lack of understanding of academic English? Share your findings with the teacher and ask for his/her ideas.

8

Educational Models that Promote Additive Bilingualism

Bilingual education has the potential of being a *transformative* school practice, able to educate all children in ways that stimulate and expand their intellect and imagination, as they gain ways of expression and access different ways of being in the world.

—Ofelia García (2009: 12)

INTRODUCTION

In this chapter, I describe program options for educating children in more than one language. Aside from learning another language through informal interaction in the family and community, children can significantly expand their bilingual capacities by being schooled in two or more languages. This chapter is about the institutional practices that facilitate the acquisition of two or more languages. To most people, bilingual education simply means teaching students in two languages. In reality, there is a wide range of program options with various goals, target students, and amount of time spent in instruction in each language (Baker, 2006; Cummins, 1996; García & Baker, 2007; Hornberger, 1991). Programs may also differ in terms of teaching methodologies and how the two languages are perceived in the wider community. What often makes conversations about bilingual education confusing is that the same terms can be used to describe programs with very different goals and outcomes.

Take for example the term **immersion**, which can have different outcomes for different populations. People who have lived in other countries often attest to the usefulness of being immersed in another language. An American college student who had spent a year abroad in Mexico once told me that living with a Mexican family with whom she spoke in Spanish all the time was far more effective than taking four years of high school Spanish. She was certain that the best way to learn a second language was through total immersion. This sentiment is echoed in public opinions about Canadian French immersion programs, which for several decades have produced functional bilinguals in French and English. Canadian students in French immersion programs learn to speak, read, and write both French and English while making good academic progress (more on Canadian French immersion programs later in this chapter). Their success is often cited by English-only advocates in the U.S. for placing immigrant students in Structured English Immersion (SEI). "If Canadian students who are immersed in French learn French well," they argue, "then immigrant children should be immersed in English to learn English well."

However, there are crucial differences between students in French immersion programs and immigrant children in American schools. Students in French immersion programs are mostly English-speaking Canadians from middle-class backgrounds who are taught through the medium of French. Canadian parents who enroll their children in these programs do so because they believe that having proficiency in Canada's two official languages will be beneficial for their children. What makes these programs a positive experience for students is that children who enter the program in kindergarten are often allowed to use their home language for up to one and a half years for classroom communication, and there is no pressure to speak the school language in the playground or cafeteria (Baker, 2006). The child's home language is valued and not looked down upon.

In contrast, ELs in American schools are by definition native speakers of minority languages. When they enter American schools, many are placed in SEI, whose primary goal is to teach students English. With little or no support provided in the students' native languages, the effective outcome of such program is submersion, or, sink or swim in English (Baker 2006: 216–217; see also Chapter 7). Home languages are seen to have no place in the school curriculum and many students lose them in the process of learning English.

In classifying bilingual education programs, it is useful to refer to Cummins's (1996) distinction between the *means* and the *goals* of a particular program. When defined in terms of the *means*, bilingual education simply refers to the use of two (or more) languages to varying degrees in instructional contexts. Proficiency in two languages is not necessarily a desired outcome. For example, transitional (or early-exit) bilingual education programs provide native language instruction to immigrant students only as a temporary bridge to learning English (see Table 1.2, p. 18). Snow & Hakuta (1992: 390) comment that the effect of transitional bilingual education programs in the U.S. is monolingualism in English: "What it fosters is monolingualism; bilingual classrooms are efficient revolving doors between home-language monolingualism and English monolingualism." Transitional bilingual education is an example of a **weak form of bilingual education** and often results in subtractive bilingualism, where students' native languages are replaced with the majority language (Baker, 2006, 2007).

When defined in terms of *goals*, bilingual education may actually be delivered in only one language for a period of time. For instance, immigrant students may be taught almost exclusively in their native language, say from kindergarten to grade 1 or 2, so that they can learn to read and write in the language they already speak. This is done to help students establish a strong foundation in the minority language, which is weaker and lower in status than the majority language. After the initial grades, these programs maintain close to 50% of instruction in the minority language throughout elementary school. These programs promote additive bilingualism, where a second language is acquired with the expectation that the mother tongue will continue to be learned and used (Baker, 2007). Developmental (or late-exit) bilingual education in the U.S. (see Table 1.2, p. 18) is an example of such a **strong form of bilingual education** (Baker, 2006). Research overwhelmingly supports strong forms of bilingual education in developing bilingual skills.

There are mainly two types of strong forms of bilingual education: (1) enrichment bilingual education, and (2) **maintenance bilingual education** (Hornberger, 1991). The main difference between enrichment and maintenance programs is the first language of the students in the program. Enrichment models are most often associated with relatively privileged majority language speakers learning through a second, third, or even a fourth language. I will describe two such programs in this chapter: Canadian French immersion and the European Schools. Maintenance models, on the other hand, are most often associated with minority language speakers who have varying degrees of proficiency in their native language and wish to maintain it while learning a second language. I will discuss two such programs: Indigenous language immersion and Developmental bilingual education. I will then describe two-way (dual) immersion, which incorporates elements from both enrichment and maintenance programs. In two-way immersion, **language majority** and language minority children help each other in learning both languages in the same classroom. Both groups of students become proficient in the other group's language while making good progress in academic subjects.

One of the biggest challenges facing bilingual education is the public's lack of interest in such programs. Despite well-documented effectiveness, education in two or more languages is actually taken up by only a small portion of the population in the U.S. (Crawford, 2004). Even in officially bilingual Canada, only about 7% of the eligible students participated in French immersion programs in 2002 (Canadian Council on Learning, 2007). But as Ofelia

García (2009) argues in her book, *Bilingual education in the 21st century: A global perspective*, modern societies cannot afford to educate students in only one language. She contends that bilingual education is the right choice for *everyone*, and that it is the most appropriate form of education for preparing children to live and succeed in a globalized world. In line with García's arguments, this chapter attempts to stimulate conversations about the role of bilingual education in expanding the language capacities of individuals and societies.

I first turn to Canadian French immersion programs.

CANADIAN FRENCH IMMERSION

Canadian French immersion began in 1965 in St. Lambert, Quebec with the explicit goal of enabling children to become bilingual in French and English without sacrificing their academic achievement (Canadian Council on Learning, 2007). Since then, immersion education has spread rapidly throughout Canada as well as in other parts of the world. There are several types of immersion programs that differ in terms of (1) when students are introduced to French instruction and (2) the amount of instruction given in French. "Early immersion" begins in kindergarten or grade 1, while "delayed immersion" does not begin until the middle elementary years, and "late immersion" in middle school. In "total French immersion," all classes are taught in French, usually for the first three years of the program. English language arts classes are introduced around the third or fourth grade, followed by a gradual increase in English instruction for other subjects. In "partial French immersion," around 50% of classes are taught in French throughout the program. In French immersion programs, the same academic content is taught as in the regular English program.

A substantial body of research shows that French immersion programs are effective in meeting students' language and academic achievement goals. In terms of French language proficiency, immersion students outperform English-speaking students enrolled in basic French programs, where French is taught as a subject for about 20 to 40 minutes a day (Cummins & Swain, 1986; Genesee, 1987). The level of French proficiency attained by immersion students depends on the age of introduction to French and on the extent of French instruction. Total-immersion students tend to outperform partial-immersion students (Genesee, 1987; Swain & Lapkin, 1982), and early-immersion students generally do better than delayed-immersion and late-immersion students (Weschc et al., 1996).

However, immersion students often do not develop native-like proficiency in French despite many years of participation in the program (Genesee, 2006). This has led some researchers to question the effectiveness of a mainly communicative approach to language teaching used in these programs, and turn to focus-on-form, a teaching method that highlights specific linguistic structures and forms within the context of communicative language instruction (Swain, 1998; see also Chapter 7). It is important to remember, however, that while French immersion students do not often develop native-like proficiency in French, they are still far more proficient in French than students who take French as a foreign language subject.

In terms of English language proficiency, early total-immersion students (those who receive no instruction in English for the first few years of their programs) initially do worse than non-immersion students on English language tests. However, their English skills generally improve after the first year of English language arts instruction introduced in grade 3 or 4. Turnbull, Lapkin, & Hart (2001) found that early-immersion students in grades 3 and 6 performed as well as their non-immersion peers on English reading and writing tests. In addition, 15-year-old French immersion students do better on reading assessments than non-immersion students, even when tested in English (Statistics Canada, 2004).

In terms of academic achievement in the content areas, immersion students perform as well as (and in some cases better than) non-immersion students on tests of science and mathematics (Turnbull et al., 2001). Bournot-Trites & Reeder (2001) examined the effect of teaching math in French on math assessments given in English. They compared the math achievement scores of students enrolled in different types of French immersion programs in Vancouver. In one immersion program, math classes were taught in French up to grade 3, after which the students were taught math in English. In another immersion program, math classes continued to be taught in French in grades 4 through 7. The study found that students who continued learning math in French performed better on math tests (administered in English) than those who stopped receiving math instruction in French after grade 3. These results support the linguistic interdependence principle, which states that instruction in French not only develops French skills, but also improves a deeper conceptual and linguistic proficiency that is related to the development of English literacy (Cummins, 1996).

Statistics Canada (2004) reports that students in French immersion programs generally come from higher socioeconomic backgrounds than non-immersion students, and there are more girls than boys. Since socioeconomic status is widely known to be strongly related to academic achievement, one might suspect that the positive student outcomes are an effect of immersion students' higher socioeconomic status. However, even after controlling for socioeconomic background, the Statistics Canada report found a substantial lead in the achievement of immersion students over non-immersion students in many Canadian provinces. The report also found that the average reading performance of immersion students was significantly higher than for non-immersion students even when boys and girls were considered separately.

One of the challenges facing French immersion programs is student attrition—many students drop out of the program especially after grade 8 (Canadian Council on Learning, 2007). Among the reasons for the attrition are a shortage of qualified teachers with content area expertise to teach advanced courses in French and a lack of appropriate learning materials at the advanced levels. Despite these difficulties, French immersion has been an educational program of remarkable success and growth. Today, immersion education can be found all over the world, with the original model adapted in various ways to suit the needs of local populations (see also Johnson & Swain, 1997).

Next, I discuss the European Schools, another strong form of bilingual education.

EUROPEAN SCHOOLS

First established in Luxembourg in 1953, the European Schools system provides multilingual and multicultural education to the children of the relatively elite civil servants working for the European Community (EC). European Schools form a network of 14 schools in seven countries (Belgium, the Netherlands, Germany, Italy, United Kingdom, Spain, and Luxembourg) with a total enrollment of 22,500 (Schola Europaea, 2007–2009). As a system, the European Schools offer 15 different language sections (Czech, Danish, German, Greek, English, Spanish, Finnish, French, Hungarian, Italian, Lithuanian, Dutch, Polish, Portuguese, and Swedish), representing the native languages of the students. At any given European School, there may be anywhere between three and 12 language sections. More languages are likely to be added as other countries join the EC.

Young children entering the program are taught in their native language (L1) but also receive compulsory second language (L2) instruction (chosen from among English, French, and German, which are known as the "working languages") during primary school. English is by far the most popular L2, chosen by 59% of the students in the European Schools, followed by French (23%) and German (18%) (Schola Europaea, 2011). As children progress through the grades, they receive part of their education in their native language and part of it in the "working language." Starting in the second year of secondary school, all students must study a second foreign language (L3), which could be any language available in the school. Students may choose to study a third foreign language (L4) from the fourth year of secondary school. This could also be any language available in the school. Thus, by the time students graduate from secondary school, they are functionally bilingual, if not multilingual in several European languages.

One of the specific goals of the European Schools is to promote multi-lingual/multicultural interaction through weekly "European Hour," which brings together children from all language sections for cultural, artistic, and games activities (Schola Europaea, 2007–2009). Although every child has second language instruction in one of the "working languages," not everyone shares the same combination of languages. During the European Hour, students are purposefully assigned to linguistically heterogeneous groups so that they can learn to communicate and work collaboratively with speakers of other languages. The outcome of such deliberate mixing of different nationalities is the development of a supranational European identity and promotion of European multiculturalism (Swan, 1996). Teachers typically use their first language, one of the "working languages," or a combination of languages at their disposal during the European Hour (Muller & Baetens Beardsmore, 2004).

How do students and teachers communicate in such a linguistically diverse environment? In a study of students' and teachers' communication strategies during a European Hour class at the Brussels III European School, Muller & Baetens Beardsmore (2004) show that only two out of the 20 children they observed did not speak any of the three working languages well enough to communicate without difficulties. But at no time was there a complete breakdown of communication, as students frequently used their various language combinations to act as interpreters for one another. Naturally, code-switching played a significant role in the students' and teachers' communication strategies. This is exemplified in the following excerpt from Muller & Baetens Beardsmore (2004) (note that T = Teacher, M = Male, It = Italian, and Fr = French):

Excerpt 1
Two male Italian-speaking students (MIt1 and MIt2) are trying to get clarification from the teacher, Chantal.

MIt1:   *Chantal.*
MIt2:   *Chantal.*
MIt2:   Che vuol dire? (to MIt1) [It.]
MIt1:   Si puo encolare questa parte (points at a cut-out) i poi colare con un filo. [It.]
MIt2:   *Il dit qu'il peut coller puis il le retaille et il fait . . . .* (to T—turns his head to MIt1) [Fr.]
MIt1:   Lascia libera questa parte e poi mete un filo. (to MIt2) [It.]
MIt2:   *Ah, il a dit qu'il . . . eh . . . qu'il colle et puis il laisse une partie libre.* (to T) [Fr.]
T: *Mais un tout petit peu, oui.* [Fr.]

Translation of Excerpt 1

MIt1: Chantal.

MIt2: Chantal.

MIt2: What do you want to say?

MIt1: Whether I can glue this part and then stick a thread to it.

MIt2: He says that he can stick it and then he cuts it out again and he . . . .

MIt1: Leave this part free and then put a thread.

MIt2: Oh, he said that he . . . er . . . he glues and then he leaves one part free.

T: But only a little bit, yes.

Like Canadian French immersion, the European Schools can be considered a strong form of bilingual education because they produce graduates who are not only bilingual but also academically successful—student achievement is not compromised as a result of the program's heavy emphasis on multi-lingualism and multiculturalism (Baetens Beardsmore, 1993; Housen, 2002). Students in the European Schools perform well on educational assessments. In 2011, overall pass rate for the European Baccalaureate, taken at the end of the seventh year of secondary school, was 98% (Schola Europaea, 2011). Furthermore, in a school environment where children are explicitly taught to respect one another's languages, students learn a second, third, or even a fourth language to high levels while being firmly rooted in their first language. These benefits make the European Schools a distinctively enriching educational experience.

But what about children in less privileged linguistic circumstances? What can schools do when children's native languages are socially stigmatized? How can students be helped to maintain their mother tongues while they learn additional languages and academic content? These questions are addressed by successful programs in indigenous language immersion, to which I turn next.

INDIGENOUS LANGUAGE IMMERSION

McCarty & Watahomigie (1998) state that nearly 2 million American Indians, Alaska Natives and Native Hawaiians live in the U.S., representing over 500 tribes and 175 distinct languages. Yet only 20 of those languages are currently being transmitted to children (McCarty, 1998). Without inter-generational transmission, the rest are expected to disappear in the next several decades. During the first half of the twentieth century, education of indigenous peoples in the U.S. was marked by systematic attempts to purge the heritage languages and cultures from the Native American psyche. Native children were forcefully taken from their families and sent away to boarding schools in distant places where they were humiliated and beaten when caught speaking their native languages (Dick, 1998). Submersed in English-only classrooms, many children struggled in school and grew up ashamed of their languages.

OUT OF THE MOUTHS OF BILINGUALS 8.1

Navajo Children in Boarding Schools

"My formal education began at the age of seven in a boarding school 35 miles from home. My first teacher was a Navajo woman. I remember she spoke only English and constantly reminded us that we had to speak, read, and write in English. It was confusing and difficult; we had to struggle. The schools operated on a military system, and if we were caught speaking Navajo, the dormitory matrons, who were Navajo, gave us chores like scrubbing the floors. Some students had their mouths "washed" with yellow bar soap. This shows that even for Navajo educators and school employees, school was not a place for Navajos to be Navajos."

(Dick, 1998: 23–24)

Crawford (2004) points out that for indigenous peoples in particular, language serves as the central storehouse of tribal history, customs, and values. Because indigenous cultures are based on oral traditions passed down from one generation to the next, language death often means the death of the culture as well—little is left of the group's memory and ways of interacting with the world. For children, language loss often results in the erosion of cultural identity and self-esteem, factors that are linked to academic achievement. Thus language plays a central role in the education of indigenous children.

Among the best known indigenous language immersion programs in the U.S. are the bilingual education programs on the Navajo nation, the largest Indian reservation in the U.S. Rough Rock was the first school to teach in the Navajo language, and became a model for many indigenous communities (McCarty, 2002). With a locally elected, all-Indian governing board, Rough Rock reflected Navajo attitudes, values, and styles of interacting—school was no longer perceived as "an alien institution run by outsiders" (Crawford, 2004: 277). At Rough Rock, specific classrooms and teachers are designated solely for Navajo language instruction. In these classrooms, Navajo social-living lessons (e.g., weaving, silversmithing, and leather crafts), as well as formal language instruction, are carried out in Navajo (McCarty, 1998).

Evaluations of the Rough Rock program over a six-year period show consistent improvements on both local and national achievement measures, including qualitative assessments of students' Navajo and English writing (McCarty, 1998). For a full five years, students at Rough Rock performed better on local tests of Navajo and English than similar cohorts with little or no time in the program. At Rock Point, another school which offers a K–12 program with literacy and content classes in Navajo, student outcomes have been as significant in English as they have been in Navajo (McCarty & Watahomigie, 1998). In both programs, students develop Navajo literacy at no cost to their development of English literacy and academic achievement.

In New Zealand, concern over the extensive loss of the Maori language led to the creation of programs in which only Maori was spoken (May & Hill, 2005). Total-immersion preschool programs called *Te Kohanga Reo* ("language nests") were first established in 1982 and have become famous for their early language success with Maori speakers (Baker, 2006). By 1995, close to 50% of all Maori preschoolers attended *Te Kohanga Reo,* and the New Zealand government now funds all programs (García, 2009). Other indigenous language education programs, such as those in Hawaii, have used the total-immersion model to teach children Hawaiian, a language that had drastically declined in use. Known as *'Aha Pūnana Leo,* the Hawaiian immersion program first began in private preschools but later expanded to public elementary schools. Although the total-immersion model postpones English instruction until the fifth grade, students outscore their English-speaking counterparts on standardized tests over the long term (Crawford, 2004). The original program has been greatly expanded to include secondary schools, and it is now possible for students to receive university education in Hawaiian (Ng-Osorio & Ledward, 2011).

One of the challenges facing indigenous language immersion programs is dealing with rapid language shift in the student population. Crawford (2004) states that when bilingual education began at Rough Rock and Rock Point, at least 90% of the students started school as monolingual Navajo speakers. More than three decades later, that pattern has changed dramatically—virtually all children now speak some English upon entry and barely 50% are assessed as proficient in Navajo. May & Hill (2005) also point out that currently most students and teachers in Maori-medium education are L1 speakers of English and L2 speakers of Maori. Thus they argue that labeling Maori-medium education as "maintenance-oriented" is not entirely appropriate since many children are having to learn Maori for the first time in school. As language shift accelerates across communities and more and more students come to school not speaking their native languages well, there is a need for rethinking the role of these programs as not only "maintenance-oriented" but also "developmental" (García, 2009).

Another challenge facing indigenous programs is securing financial resources. Because government funding for bilingual education has been inconsistent, other sources of private and community-based funds are necessary for program continuity and success. However, local resources are often inadequate to fully sustain these programs, leading to cuts in program offerings (Crawford, 2004). Furthermore, resistance to bilingual education often comes from the parents themselves (Crawford, 2004). Many parents who have experienced discrimination on the basis of their native language want their children to learn only the socially dominant language. Parents may also forgo bilingual education out of fear that it might hurt their children's academic performance. Thus, ensuring a successful program requires convincing parents that bilingual education not only promotes language acquisition but also positive academic skills.

Next, I discuss developmental bilingual education for immigrant children, another linguistic minority group.

DEVELOPMENTAL (LATE-EXIT) BILINGUAL EDUCATION

As a strong form of bilingual education, developmental (late-exit) bilingual education enables language minority students to continue developing their home languages while learning a second language and academic content (Lindholm-Leary & Genesee, 2010). All students in developmental bilingual programs are mother tongue speakers of one language (e.g., Spanish) being schooled in a majority language (e.g., English) environment. However, students often enter these programs with varying proficiencies in Spanish and English—some students may have recently arrived as immigrants and therefore speak no English while others were born in the U.S. and are already bilingual. Typically, about 90% of the instruction in kindergarten and first grade is provided in the home language while 10% is given in English. The English portion of the instruction gradually increases through the grades to about 50% by the late elementary years.

Research shows that sustained use of the home language in instruction has academic benefits for language minority students. In their synthesis of the research on ELs, Genesee, Lindholm-Leary, Saunders, & Christian (2006) state that students in late-exit bilingual education programs outperform students in early-exit programs and that bilingual proficiency is positively related to academic achievement in both languages. A large-scale study by Ramirez et al. (1991) compared the academic performances of 2,352 Latino elementary schoolchildren in three types of classrooms: (1) English-only, (2) transitional (early-exit) bilingual, and (3) developmental (late-exit) bilingual. Although there were no differences among the program types in student achievement in third grade, students in late-exit programs were doing better in math, English language arts, and English reading than students in the other programs by sixth grade.

In another study involving 42,000 bilingual students in five school districts in various regions of the U.S, Thomas & Collier (2002) compared the achievement on standardized tests of English learners enrolled in different kinds of programs. They found that programs that used students' home languages in bilingual education produced better results in English reading than programs that used English only. They also found that developmental and two-way bilingual education programs produced better results in English reading than transitional (early-exit) bilingual education programs. Other evaluations of bilingual education programs have consistently favored models that allow children to develop their native language to high levels of proficiency while learning English (Snow, 1990). A review of studies by Francis, Lesaux, & August (2006) revealed that language minority students receiving instruction in both their native language and English did better on English reading assessments than language minority students instructed only in English at both the elementary and secondary levels.

Despite their documented effectiveness, developmental bilingual education programs are rare in American public schools today as bilingual education has come under attack in several states with large numbers of immigrant students (see also Chapter 7). Since the passage of anti-bilingual education legislation, Proposition 227 in California and Proposition 203 in Arizona, only around 8% of ELs in California and 5% of ELs in Arizona are receiving any type of bilingual education (Gándara & Hopkins, 2010a). Interestingly enough, even as the number of developmental bilingual education programs has been decreasing, two-way immersion has been growing in popularity. Next I discuss why that is the case.

TWO-WAY (DUAL) IMMERSION

Two-way (dual) immersion programs first started at the Coral Way Elementary School in Miami in 1963, when political refugees fleeing Fidel Castro's Cuba created a program to educate their children in both Spanish and English (Baker, 2006). The Cubans were motivated to teach their children Spanish because many of them believed that the Castro regime would not last and they would be able to return to Cuba. The bilingual program at Coral Way Elementary was special in that it was open to both Spanish-speaking Cuban children and local English-speaking children with the goal of bilingualism for both groups. Indeed, the program had very good results. Crawford (2004) explains that in English reading, both the Spanish-speaking and English-speaking groups did as well as or better than their counterparts in monolingual English schools, and the Cuban children achieved equivalent levels in Spanish. Although the English-speaking group did not quite reach national norms in Spanish reading achievement, the program was largely deemed successful and became a model for other school districts.

Since the establishment of the Coral Way program, the number of two-way immersion programs has grown considerably in the U.S. There are now 400 dual immersion programs in 30 states and Washington DC (Center for Applied Linguistics, 2011). Three hundred and seventy-five of them (94%) pair Spanish with English while the remaining programs have French, Chinese, Japanese, and Korean as the target languages. Two-way immersion typically involves about equal numbers of language majority and language minority children learning both languages and academic content in the same classroom. Each group serves as native language models for the other group, and students learn each other's languages through social interaction. According to Christian (1994), a typical two-way immersion program has the following goals:

- *Language development*: Students will develop high levels of proficiency in their first language and in a second language.
- *Academic development*: Students will perform at or above grade level in academic areas in both languages.
- *Social development*: Students will demonstrate positive cross-cultural attitudes and behaviors and high levels of self-esteem.

In terms of amount of instructional time spent in each language, most two-way immersion programs employ either a 50/50 model or a 90/10 model. In the 50/50 model, 50% of the instruction is in one language and the other 50% is in the other language. This ratio is maintained more or less throughout all grades. In the 90/10 model, the minority language is given much more weight toward the beginning of the program in kindergarten and first grade—about 90% of instruction is provided in the minority language and 10% in English. Instruction in English gradually increases through the grades until the program becomes about 50/50. Research shows that students in 90/10 programs tend to become more fully bilingual than those in 50/50 programs (Lindholm-Leary, 2001). In terms of which language is used when, some programs may use one language for instruction in the morning and the other language in the afternoon, while other programs may use the languages in alternating days or weeks. Some programs may teach certain subjects (e.g., math, science) in one language and other subjects (e.g., social studies, art, music) in the other language.

Two-way immersion offers a number of benefits. First, by having both language majority and language minority children learn side by side in the same classroom, it is more inclusive than traditional bilingual education programs serving only minority language speakers. Crawford (2004: 289) states that "a program model open to all children could hardly be branded a 'special interest' subsidy" and that English-speaking parents, who are "more accustomed to activism and more likely to influence politicians, [could] become effective ambassadors for bilingual education."

For English-speaking students who would not otherwise have significant exposure to another language, two-way immersion gives them an immersion experience. An important difference between two-way immersion and one-way immersion (e.g., Canadian French immersion) is that English speakers in two-way immersion have the additional benefit of interacting with classmates who arc native speakers of the target language. For language minority children, two-way immersion provides them with an educational environment where their native language is valued as a resource. This is in sharp contrast to English-only programs where it is often treated as a problem. In addition, by promoting the development of both basic and advanced literacy in the native language and in English, dual immersion allows language minority students to gain important content knowledge that in turn will make English more comprehensible (Christian, 1994).

Fred Genesee, as cited in Crawford (2004: 290), states that

> including students from both language groups creates a learning environment that can be truly bilingual and bicultural. Sustained contact with members of the target language group of the same age as the learners may be necessary if students are to develop fundamentally more tolerant and positive attitudes toward each other.

The society ultimately benefits from having bilingual citizens who are positively disposed toward people of other cultural backgrounds and who can meet national needs for language competence (Lindholm-Leary, 2001).

A growing body of research shows that two-way immersion is effective in meeting the language and academic needs of both language majority and language minority students (e.g., Genesee et al., 2006; Lindholm-Leary, 2001; Lindholm-Leary & Block, 2010; Oller & Eilers, 2002; Thomas & Collier, 2002). Lindholm-Leary (2001) conducted one of the most comprehensive evaluations of two-way programs. Analyzing data from 18 schools, she analyzed student outcomes in different program types including both 90/10 and 50/50 dual immersion models, transitional bilingual education, and mainstream English-only programs. She examined students' proficiencies in English and Spanish, academic achievement, and attitudes.

In terms of L1 development, Lindholm-Leary (2001) found that both English-dominant students and Spanish-dominant students in two-way immersion programs scored high in oral and academic skills in their respective native languages. In terms of L2 development, she found that English speakers in 90/10 programs did better in oral Spanish than English speakers in 50/50 programs. But English speakers failed to acquire the levels of Spanish proficiency that the native Spanish speakers did. This may be due to the fact that the main source of Spanish input for these children was in school whereas the

Spanish speakers had Spanish input at home as well. For Spanish-speaking students, no difference in English language proficiency was found between the 90/10 and 50/50 programs, leading to the conclusion that more English instruction does not necessarily lead to better English proficiency. Compared to Spanish speakers in transitional bilingual education and English-only programs, Spanish speakers in dual immersion did better in English despite having received less instruction in English. Dual immersion students also did better in math than English-speaking students in English-only programs. Furthermore, two-way immersion students had very positive attitudes toward the programs, teachers, the classroom environment, and other cultures.

A typical two-way immersion program is composed of two populations: (1) Latino, low-income, native Spanish speakers, and (2) White, middle-class, native English speakers (Howard & Sugarman, 2001). However, where dual language programs are implemented in schools that are predominantly Hispanic, English-speaking Hispanics, often also from lower income backgrounds, constitute the "English-speaking group" (Lindholm-Leary & Block, 2010). Lindholm-Leary & Block (2010) asked the question of whether the positive outcomes of dual language programs found with the middle-class White English-speaking populations can be generalized to dual language programs located in low-income, predominantly Hispanic schools. Their analysis of students' standardized test scores showed that the answer is yes—Hispanic students participating in dual language programs in predominantly Hispanic/low-income schools achieve at similar or higher levels compared to their mainstream peers in tests of English. In addition, the students achieve at or above grade level in Spanish.

OUT OF THE MOUTHS OF BILINGUALS 8.2

"A Multilingual American"—An Oxymoron?

"I've been told I shouldn't exist. I am a white, suburban, middle-class, third-generation United States citizen, the product of public schools . . . and I am multilingual. I can speak three languages besides English with reasonable fluency, and have varying degrees of proficiency in eight others . . . On my first day of studying language pedagogy at the Monterey Institute of International Studies, the dean said to the veritable U.N. General Assembly of students gathered in the auditorium, 'If you speak more than two languages, stand up. Three? Four?' I stayed on my feet until he stopped counting and asked the last ones standing about their backgrounds. They replied with fascinating stories like, 'I was born in Switzerland to a British father and a Greek mother, and went to high school in Japan . . .' and when my turn came, I had to confess to my undistinguished white-bread origins. The dean's jaw almost hit the lectern as he exclaimed, 'You're *American* and you speak all those languages? You get free tuition!' If only he had been serious!"

(Kowalski, 2009: 171)

Thomas & Collier (2002) report that two-way immersion programs are the most successful in promoting language minority students' long-term academic achievement, as measured by standardized tests across all subject areas. As a group, students in two-way programs maintain grade-level skills in their first language throughout their schooling and reach the fiftieth percentile in their second language after four to five years of schooling in both languages. Similarly, Oller & Eilers (2002) compared two-way immersion with English immersion in Miami using 952 bilingual and monolingual students from kindergarten to grade 5. They found that while the two-way immersion students initially showed a lag in English performance, this gap was minimal by the time the students reached fifth grade.

Other evidence of the effectiveness of dual immersion can be seen in a study by Sohn & Merrill (2008), which compared the academic performance of Korean speakers in three types of programs—(1) two-way immersion, (2) modified bilingual with minimal Korean language support, and (3) English-only. They found that two-way immersion programs provide the greatest benefit to participating students. Students in Korean-English two-way immersion performed equally well in English language skills, as measured by standardized test scores, as Korean children in English-only programs. They also found that students in dual immersion scored higher in Korean language and general academic skills than students in modified bilingual programs. Similarly, Bae (2007) evaluated narrative English writing skills of Korean-speaking students and English-speaking students in a Korean-English two-way immersion program in Los Angeles during an early phase of elementary immersion (kindergarten to grade 2). She found that both the Korean-speaking and English-speaking groups in the two-way program had comparable writing skills to English speakers in English-only classes.

Despite the many benefits however, two-way immersion programs face a number of challenges. A major difficulty stems from asymmetrical power relationships between the languages. Although two-way immersion programs strive for a balance between the languages, classroom-based research shows that use of the minority language is frequently undermined by the presence of English. For example, Sra. Soto, a kindergarten teacher in Renée DePalma's (2010) study of language use in a two-way immersion program, reflects on the low status of Spanish in the surrounding community: "You have to remember environmentally where they are living . . . We are in a very depressed economic area, our school is. And they see Spanish as the lower echelon language. The language of people they do not like" (p. 62).

As one of two dual immersion kindergarten classes in an otherwise English-dominant school, Sra. Soto's classroom followed a 50/50 model with Spanish used in the morning and English in the afternoon. All of the other classrooms in the school were either English-only or transitional bilingual, where the use of Spanish was minimal. In this English-dominant school environment, Spanish time was often disrupted by announcements, specials, and occasional auditorium events, all of which were in English. DePalma (2010: 65–66) provides the following example of an intercom interruption during official Spanish time, which happened just as Sra. Soto finished scolding Rashid, an English speaker, for speaking in English:

Sra. Soto:	[In a sharp voice] Mira, Rashid. ¿Por qué sigues tú hablando de eso en inglés? Si tú vas a hablar conmigo en inglés . . . (*Look, Rashid. Why do you keep talking about that in English? If you are going to talk with me in English . . .*)
Unknown woman:	[Voice cuts in over the intercom] Mrs. Soto?
Sra. Soto:	Yes?
Unknown woman:	The number you gave for Kathleen, is it a new number?
Sra. Soto:	No, it's her old number.
Girl:	[to Sra. Soto] What do I have to do?
Sra. Soto:	Tu alfabeto. (*Your alphabet*) [Saying the letters in Spanish] A, B, C, D, E, F . . .

DePalma (2010) notes that the intercom interruption was an unnecessary request for information that was not particularly urgent. The fact that Mrs. Soto was required to respond in English (since the speaker from the office did not speak Spanish) undermined her efforts to encourage her students to use Spanish during Spanish time.

Another difficulty for dual immersion programs is recruiting proficient speakers of the minority language. DePalma (2010) states that many of the Spanish speakers in Sra. Soto's classroom were actually more English-proficient than the two-way model assumes. Of the 11 children who had been officially designated as Spanish speakers, Sra. Soto only identified three as good "Spanish role models." Of the remaining children who spoke mostly Spanish at home, four of them preferred to speak English. Similarly, in a study of a Korean-

English dual immersion program in California, Lee (2007) states that some of the Korean students who grew up in Korean homes did not speak Korean as their first language. Her observations of students in the classroom and discussions with the teacher revealed that only four of the 11 students designated as Korean speakers could be considered proficient in Korean. Naturally, English became the language predominantly used by the children in classroom interactions, despite the teacher's strict implementation of the program's 70(Korean)/30(English) split of instructional time.

Meeting the linguistic and academic needs of both groups can be a problem in two-way immersion programs. With both Spanish-speaking students and Spanish learners in the same classroom, teachers face a dilemma (Crawford, 2004). For instance, if teachers simplify their Spanish too much to accommodate English-speaking students, they may be shortchanging the Spanish speakers. If they do not simplify enough, then the English speakers could be lost. This leads to the question of whether Spanish speakers' needs might be better served in a classroom with only Spanish speakers. Because English speakers in Spanish-English dual immersion programs in the U.S. have far less exposure to Spanish than their Spanish-speaking peers have to English, teachers often lower their expectations for English speakers' progress in Spanish (DePalma, 2010). In the kindergarten classroom in DePalma's (2010) study, English speakers were often praised for minor achievements in Spanish while Spanish speakers had to perform at a higher level in English to earn the same level of appreciation. Crawford (2004: 306) aptly describes the different expectations for the two student groups as follows:

> Bilingual skills, for example, are usually seen as a praiseworthy accomplishment by English-speaking students, while taken entirely for granted among English learners. There is a fine line between treating Spanish, say, as a valuable resource and treating Spanish-speaking students as a resource who are there to "service" the needs of English-speaking classmates. While two-way programs are never consciously organized in this way, the potential for inequity is something they must constantly guard against.

English-speaking children in two-way programs have been shown to dominate classroom discourse and take teacher time and attention away from the Spanish speakers (Valdés, 1997). Likewise, well-educated White parents tend to dominate parent councils in dual immersion schools (Crawford, 2004). Palmer (2008) argues that while diversity in student's race, class, and culture is indeed a benefit of two-way immersion, two-way programs must contend with race and class diversity in more than superficial ways in order to be successful in meeting all students' goals.

SUMMARY

In this chapter, I discussed some program options for educating children for additive bilingualism. We saw that bilingual education can take many different forms depending on the goals of the program, target student populations, and how the two languages are used in instruction. I first referred to Cummins's (1996) distinction between the *means* and the *goals* of a particular program. When defined in terms of the *means*, bilingual education simply refers to the use of two (or more) languages to varying degrees in instructional contexts. Proficiency in two languages is not necessarily a desired outcome. We saw that some models, such as transitional bilingual education in the U.S., are bilingual education in name only, with the real aim of promoting English mono-lingualism. However, when defined in terms of *goals*, bilingual education may actually be delivered in one language for a period of time so as to help students develop adequate proficiency in that language. This chapter was about the so-called strong forms of bilingual education whose explicit goal is to develop bilingual capacities in students.

I discussed two types of strong forms of bilingual education: (1) enrichment programs, which serve relatively privileged language majority speakers learning through the medium of another language, and (2) maintenance programs, which help language minority speakers maintain the use of their mother tongues while learning a second language. We saw that language majority speakers and language minority speakers have different needs when it comes to bilingual development. In order to become bilingual, majority language speakers need to have substantial opportunities to hear and speak the target language—it is simply not enough to have foreign language lessons for half an hour a day. We saw that the opportunity to actually study content material (e.g., math, science, social studies) through a target language offers both academic and linguistic benefits. This is in fact the approach taken by Canadian French immersion and the European Schools. Students in these programs become proficient in two or more languages while making good progress academically.

In maintenance programs, we saw that there is always the danger of the majority language dominating students' academic and social spheres. Because of this, many successful maintenance programs postpone the introduction of the societal language into the curriculum for a few years. And when the second language is introduced, it is done gradually and with plenty of native language support. Effective programs are well aware of the unequal prestige accorded to the two languages and often go out of their way to prop up the weaker language. We also saw that because language shift is accelerating and more and more students come to school not already proficient in their native language, there is a need for programs to teach the native language to the children. In particular, programs need to distinguish the specific language and learning needs of L1 and L2 learners of the minority language (May & Hill, 2005).

Finally, I discussed two-way (dual) immersion which serves both language majority and language minority students in the same classroom with the goal of fluent bilingualism for both groups. We saw that dual immersion offers advantages for both groups by turning the minority language into a resource in the classroom. English speakers benefit from having sustained opportunity to interact with peers who are native speakers of the target language while English learners benefit from learning literacy and academic content in their native language, which in turn helps their acquisition of English. By deliberately mixing students from both majority and minority language backgrounds and requiring them to learn from each other, dual immersion has the potential to offset linguistic inequality present in the wider community. But as Palmer (2008: 664) points out, "moments of English dominance appear in practically every turn of talk" in a dual immersion classroom, and "it is challenging to maintain a strong positioning of the minority language and culture with English-speaking students present." The key to addressing this, Palmer states, is in the preparation, openness, and awareness of the teacher in the classroom.

As with all types of education, there are no quick fixes, no one-size-fits-all models in bilingual education. A program that works well for a given student population may not work well with another group. Educators, parents, and policy-makers should study and learn from good practices but implementation of a successful bilingual education program will invariably require adaptation of models to suit the particular set of needs of the local population. Ensuring successful education in two languages is perhaps more complex than doing so in one language but the resulting gain in individual and societal bilingualism makes the whole enterprise well worth the effort.

FURTHER READING

- Calderón, M.E. & Minaya-Rowe, L. (2003). *Designing and implementing two-way bilingual programs: A step-by-step guide for administrators, teachers, and parents.* Thousand Oaks, CA: Corwin Press.—This practical resource provides school administrators, teachers, and parents with information on all aspects of designing and implementing two-way bilingual programs including research-based instructional techniques, student assessment, staff development, and evaluation.
- Christian, D. & Genesee, F. eds. (2001). *Bilingual education.* Alexandria, VA: TESOL.—The 11 case studies included in this volume cover a wide range of bilingual education program types and illustrate the diverse ways in which program features are aligned with community goals, sociolinguistic situations, and student characteristics in different settings.

- García, O. (2009). *Bilingual education in the twenty-first century: A global perspective.* Malden, MA: Wiley-Blackwell.—In this book, Ofelia García provides a comprehensive overview of the history and current state of bilingual education programs and policies throughout the world. She argues convincingly that bilingual education is the right choice for all children in today's globalized world.
- McCarty, T.L. (2002). *A place to be Navajo: Rough Rock and the struggle for self-determination in indigenous schooling.* Mahwah, NJ: Lawrence Erlbaum.—In this book, Teresa McCarty provides a critical life history of the Rough Rock Demonstration School, the first American Indian-controlled school in the United States.

ONLINE AND VIDEO RESOURCES

- http://speakingintonguesfilm.info/—*Speaking in tongues* is an award-winning documentary that provides an inside look at two-way immersion programs. This companion site features study guides and video extras for educators.
- http://www.thornwoodps.ca/dual/index.htm/—The Thornwood Public School Dual Language Showcase shows samples of bilingual books written by students in various languages.

STUDY QUESTIONS AND ACTIVITIES

1. Visit the website http://speakingintonguesfilm.info/about/video_extras/ and watch the video extras titled, "Integration and Immersion" and "Test Scores." What concerns and fears do parents have about enrolling their children in two-way immersion programs? Why might some Mandarin-speaking families be resistant to Mandarin-English two-way programs? What are the concerns of English-speaking families?
2. What factors contribute to making the strong forms of bilingual education successful? What do they all have in common that are lacking in the weak forms of bilingual education?
3. Interview a teacher in a bilingual education program. What are his/her beliefs about teaching and learning? How does he/she make decisions about using each language? How does he/she assess student progress in each language? What instructional strategies does he/she use to promote students' learning of language as well as academic content?
4. Imagine that your class is participating in a local board of education hearing to consider a proposal to implement a two-way immersion program in the district. Assign specific roles to each student in the class (e.g., two or three bilingual educators and administrators who will present

the proposal, several members of the board of education, superintendent, and various stakeholders such as parents, community members, students, teachers, principals, curriculum specialists, and business representatives who will provide testimonies, comments, and questions). Students should come to the session prepared to play their assigned roles and ask critical questions about the program's potential benefits, feasibility, and drawbacks.

Multilingual Families

Parents can only act as gardeners, showing their children the variety of cultures within each language. Gardeners can aid growth but not cause it. The language seeds sown need watering, tending and fertilizing. . . . There will be many anxious days when tender young shoots do not develop smoothly, and later they are in danger of breaking among the strong winds of peer pressure. The parent as language gardener can help maximize those conditions that are open to influence, but parents cannot control the growth of language.

—Colin Baker (2007: 19, 29)

INTRODUCTION

"Baby Einstein," "Bilingual baby," "Your baby can read!," "Brain building games for your baby," "50 simple ways to make your baby smarter." . . . Children's sections in libraries, bookstores, and Internet sites offer a dizzying array of books, software, DVDs, flashcards, and educational toys aimed at parents who want to give their young children a head start in education. Parents these days are inundated with commercial products that claim to make babies smarter, more ready for school, and better equipped to succeed in life. With so many choices and sometimes conflicting messages about the likely benefits of various products, one is often at a loss as to what really works and what doesn't. Consider the following excerpt from the philosophy statement on the "Baby Einstein" website:

At Baby Einstein, we know that babies are passionately curious. Even the littlest of discoveries are truly fascinating to a baby. The world is a colorful place that is just waiting to be explored. This philosophy is what drives us at The Baby Einstein Company to create products that engage babies and make discovery fun for them and their parents . . .

(Baby Einstein, 2012)

It is difficult to dispute a statement like this, and many parents feel they have no choice but to get on the smart baby bandwagon. Even if a popular product has little scientifically proven benefit, one might ask, "If everyone else is making fun discoveries with these products, would my child miss out on important learning opportunities if I don't do it as well?"

Language is an important part of child development, and in an increasingly global world, more and more parents are drawn to the idea of giving their children the gift of bilingualism. Some parents may hire a babysitter who speaks another language, enroll their children in a language immersion program, or play some foreign language videos in the hope that an early exposure to the sounds of another language will help their children learn it later on. Despite these well-intentioned efforts however, not all children who are exposed to two languages become bilingual. Why do some children become bilingual and others don't? What kind of language exposure is necessary and for how long? What does it take to raise children bilingually in monolingual societies? There are clearly many benefits to bilingualism. But are there are any disadvantages to becoming bilingual? Could bilingual input confuse children? This chapter will address these questions.

In what follows, we will see that bilingual proficiency is very much a result of experience with the languages in question. Children need to be exposed to a language in order to learn it. Contrary to what some people believe however, having children watch foreign language DVDs several hours a day will not make them bilingual. If anything, too much media can have a negative effect on children's development of social skills and encourage an early dependence on media (King & Mackey, 2007). What children need in order to become bilingual are sustained opportunities to interact socially with speakers of the target languages. These interactions need to be meaningful—children will not just learn another language if they know it won't serve the purpose of helping them communicate with people.

There are two major ways in which children become bilingual: (1) by acquiring two languages simultaneously from birth, or (2) by acquiring one language first and acquiring a second language later in childhood. While the so-called **simultaneous bilinguals** (i.e., children who acquire two languages from birth) are far rarer than **successive bilinguals** (i.e., children who acquire one language first and another later in childhood), much of the academic literature on child bilingual development is about simultaneous bilinguals (Grosjean, 2010). Many of these studies are carried out by linguists who are themselves bilinguals and are raising their own children in two or more languages (e.g., Deuchar & Quay, 2000; Yip & Matthews, 2007). With detailed, multi-year data on actual language use, these studies show that young children have the natural ability to process bilingual input and to differentiate the two languages in their environment from very early on (Meisel, 2006). They show that with the right kind of language exposure, simultaneous bilinguals can acquire both languages to native speaker levels.

In contrast to the research on simultaneous bilingual acquisition however, systematic longitudinal studies on successive bilingual acquisition are so scarce that it is currently impossible to draw serious conclusions about its underlying mechanisms (Meisel, 2006). The available studies in child SLA disagree as to the developmental trajectories of children exposed to a second language at different times during childhood. We know that due to brain maturation, child first language acquisition and adult SLA differ in important respects (Gass & Selinker, 2008). The question for child bilingualism researchers is, at what point does acquiring a second language during childhood start to look more like adult SLA?

Some scholars (e.g., Meisel, 2006) conclude that initial exposure to a second language in later childhood (i.e., between ages five and ten) leads to a developmental pattern that looks more like adult SLA than simultaneous bilingual acquisition. Others, like De Houwer (2009), contend that even an earlier exposure to a second language (i.e., between the ages of 18 months and four years, or what she calls "early second language acquisition") leads to developmental patterns that are clearly different from simultaneous bilingual acquisition. Obviously, much more research is needed to answer this question.

These difficulties notwithstanding, I will describe case studies of families that have taken different paths to achieve bilingualism. One strategy for raising bilingual children is the so-called **one-parent, one-language (OPOL)** approach, which is popular among linguistically mixed couples (Barron-Hauwaert, 2004). In OPOL, each parent speaks his or her strongest language (usually, the native language) to the child, providing good language models in each language. In other families, one language may be spoken exclusively by everyone at home, while another language is learned outside. This usually applies to linguistic minority families who speak the **minority language at home**. Still other families may mix the two languages whenever they prefer, or have the speech occasion (e.g., attending a religious service) or the presence of monolingual relatives or friends determine their language choice. Most families adjust their language strategies as children grow up and their needs for each language change with schooling or the onset of adolescence. We will see that raising a bilingual family is a journey that requires great care and effort—many families struggle to maintain a balance between the children's languages.

Colin Baker, the author of *A parents' and teachers' guide to bilingualism* (2007), likens the process of raising bilingual children to gardening. He maintains that while parents, as language gardeners, can promote language growth in children, they cannot control it. As children progress through different stages of development, their preference and dominance in the languages will change. They will move in and out of bilingualism according to their need to communicate and identify with different people in their lives. To successfully achieve bilingualism in the family then, parents need to constantly monitor their children's as well as their own language behavior, and modify their strategies as children grow up. They need to be mindful of the fact that a given strategy that works for one child may not work for another child in the same family. I will discuss the relationship between birth order and language experience and the role of the social context in influencing children's language choice and preference.

First, I turn to a discussion of children who are exposed to two or more languages from birth.

SIMULTANEOUS BILINGUAL ACQUISITION

As mentioned earlier, much of the research on children acquiring two or more languages from birth has been conducted by linguists studying the language development of their own children. Studying one's own children has many practical advantages. Living with the children in the same household, parents can observe children's language development unobtrusively as participant observers. They have the advantage of interacting with the children throughout the day (e.g., during play time, meal time) and night (e.g., during bedtime, bath time)—few outside researchers have regular access to such intimate family settings. They also have privileged access to their participants for a long period of time—it is possible to follow the development of the same children for ten years or more. Parent researchers can keep language diaries and make audio/video recordings to document children's authentic language use in various settings with different people. Information on family background and circumstances, as well as the language histories of each child can also be provided in detail.

The earliest systematic studies of simultaneous acquisition of two languages were carried out by Jules Ronjat (1913) and Werner Leopold (1939–49), who raised their children bilingually. Ronjat introduced the OPOL principle as the most effective method for raising a child bilingually in a home where the parents speak different mother tongues. The OPOL strategy was also used by Leopold who studied his daughter Hildegard's acquisition of English and German in the U.S. Leopold spoke only German to his wife and Hildegard, while his wife spoke only English. Leopold claims that Hildegard initially did not separate the two languages and did not associate the languages with specific persons even though he and his wife spoke to her in different languages. He states that it was only in her third year that Hildegard began to treat the two languages as separate linguistic systems and was able to translate between them.

Leopold's observation led to subsequent claims that simultaneous bilingual children start out with a single linguistic system. Perhaps most influential in this regard, Volterra & Taeschner (1978) argued that a child exposed to two languages becomes bilingual in three stages: (1) the child has one lexical system which includes words from both languages; (2) the child distinguishes two different lexical systems but applies the same grammatical rules to both languages; (3) the child has two language systems, differentiated both in lexicon and in grammar, but each language is exclusively associated with the person using that language. Volterra & Taeschner's argument for the existence of an initially fused system was based on the speech of two German-Italian bilingual children whose words (at ages 22 months and 18 months respectively) had no translation equivalents (i.e., words used in one language that correspond to words with the same meaning in the other language).

However, this model has attracted significant criticisms, and there is now a consensus in the field of child bilingualism that a child's two languages develop separately from the very beginnings of speech production (see De Houwer, 2009; Deuchar & Quay, 1998; Meisel, 2006). Several studies have shown that bilingual children use the two grammars differently as soon as there is evidence of grammar (Döpke, 1997; Paradis & Genesee, 1996; Yip & Matthews, 2007). Furthermore, the claim that bilingual children start out with a single, undifferentiated vocabulary is challenged by research that shows that bilingual children develop a fairly stable rate of translation equivalents as soon as they begin talking (Pearson, Fernandez, & Oller, 1995; Quay, 1995).

When compared to monolingual first language acquisition, simultaneous acquisition of two languages proceeds through the same developmental phases as those observed in the respective monolingual children (Meisel, 2006). Both monolingual children and bilingual children start off their conventionally meaningful language production using single words, then go on to produce two word combinations and multi-word sentences before they produce complex sentences (De Houwer, 2009). Bilingual children's overall rate of acquisition in each of these languages is also comparable to that of monolinguals—there is no evidence that simultaneous bilingual children develop morphosyntax faster or slower than monolingual children (De Houwer, 2009; Meisel, 2006).

Overall, simultaneous bilingual children's development in each language is qualitatively no different from monolingual children's development in those languages, and leads to the same kind of grammatical competence possessed by monolinguals. This does not mean, however, that a bilingual child is "two monolinguals in one person" (Grosjean, 2010). Rather, bilingual children

---

OUT OF THE MOUTHS OF BILINGUALS 9.1

A Two-Year-Old Child is Aware of His Bilingual Identity

Mother:	Daddy hai6 me1 jan4 aa3? "What's Daddy's nationality?"
Child:	Ing1gok3jan4 "English person."
Mother:	Jing1gok3jan4 "English person."
Child:	Ing1gok3jan4 "English person."
	Maa1mi4 hai6 zung1gok3jan4 "Mummy is Chinese."
Mother:	Timmy hai6 me1 jan4 aa3? "What about Timmy?"
Child:	Bilingual!

(Yip & Matthews, 2007: 1)

---

acquire competence and skills in each of their languages according to their specific communicative needs and preferences.

SUCCESSIVE BILINGUAL ACQUISITION

While simultaneous bilingual acquisition proceeds in much the same way as monolingual acquisition in the respective languages, successive bilingual acquisition is qualitatively different from monolingual first language acquisition. Research on young ethnic Turkish children growing up in Germany and in the Netherlands shows that the children show clear signs of morphosyntactic influence from Turkish in their second language production (e.g., Pfaff, 1994; Verhoeven & Boeschoten, 1986; Verhoeven & Vermeer, 1984). For example, Pfaff (1994: 86) notes that a Turkish child produced the following incorrect German sentence: "alle Kinder is Jocken anziehen" (all-children-is-jogging-suit-on-put; "all children are putting on their jogging suits"). This sentence contains a progressive that does not exist in German but does exist in Turkish. While errors like this involving the application of Turkish grammar rules in the production of German were quite common in Pfaff's study, they are normally not observed in the speech of simultaneous bilingual children (De Houwer, 2009). The errors that the Turkish children made in German look more like patterns of SLA of German observed for adults than patterns of first language acquisition of German by monolingual children.

In a study of Turkish immigrant children in the Netherlands, Verhoeven & Vermeer (1984) found that in terms of the size of the receptive and productive

Dutch vocabulary, the Turkish-Dutch bilingual children were at least two to four years behind their monolingual Dutch peers. In addition, the Turkish children scored considerably lower than their Dutch counterparts in Dutch morphosyntax. Verhoeven & Vermeer found that while the Turkish children made relatively rapid progress in certain syntactic structures such as wh- words (e.g., who, what, where, when, why), they had great difficulties with complex noun or verb phrases and embedded clauses in Dutch. The authors attribute the Turkish children's developmental lag in Dutch to the restricted Dutch input they were receiving in school.

The children in these studies live in economically depressed urban areas with high concentrations of Turkish immigrants. Verhoeven & Vermeer point out that the Turkish children in their study started learning Dutch when they entered kindergarten in a "submersion context" with little or no support provided in their first language. Similarly, although Pfaff's subjects attend a bilingual daycare program where half of the teaching staff speaks German and the other half Turkish, the aim of these programs is not necessarily to promote functional bilingualism. In many of the programs serving mostly Turkish ethnic children, teachers are often poorly trained, and the schools have poorer facilities and fewer resources than schools for predominantly German children. The teaching of German as a second language is often inadequate and culturally appropriate teaching materials are in short supply. Largely segregated from mainstream society, the children have little opportunity to practice the second language in peer group contexts outside of school and often suffer from anxiety, low self-confidence, and low teacher expectations. Skutnabb-Kangas (2000: 579) notes that even with a great deal of effort in the family and the community, many of the minority children in these "subtractive non-forms of bilingual education" become virtually monolingual in the majority language.

Contextual information such as this is critically missing in many childhood bilingual acquisition studies, making cross-study comparisons difficult. Since only a few studies precisely describe subjects' linguistic history and exposure patterns, as well as the social context of acquisition, the available research provides insufficient basis for answering many of the important questions such as, "Why do some children develop into bilinguals while others become mono-lingual in the dominant language?" As we will see in the following case studies of bilingual families, socially and culturally detailed accounts of language development are vital in our understanding of why some children become bilingual and others monolingual.

CASE STUDIES OF THREE BILINGUAL FAMILIES

The Fantini Family (Fantini, 1985)

Alvino Fantini is a sociolinguist who documented the bilingual development of his son, Mario, from birth to age ten. Alvino was born in Philadelphia of Italian parents who had immigrated to the U.S. While both English and Italian were spoken in his home during his childhood, the use of Italian diminished in later years when the family moved to a suburban neighborhood, and after the death of his Italian-speaking grandmother who had lived in the same home. To Alvino, Italian was an intimate language spoken with family, relatives, and friends while English was a public language (see Alvino Fantini's characterization of Italian as a private language in "Out of the Mouths of Bilinguals" 3.1, p. 59).

But Alvino's enthusiasm for Italian faded when he entered high school. Speaking Italian was considered a social stigma, and he actively avoided Italian during those years. Building on his knowledge of Italian however, Alvino later acquired proficiency in Spanish quite easily. He spent two semesters in Mexico and another in Colombia and traveled extensively in Italy, Spain, and Latin America. He settled in Vermont just before his marriage to a woman born of Bolivian parents in Rome. She grew up mostly in Argentina, Bolivia, and Peru, was educated entirely in Spanish, and spoke Spanish as her dominant language.

The couple spoke Spanish throughout courtship and after marriage. When their son, Mario, was born, they decided to both speak to him in Spanish so as to bring him up bilingually in their Vermont home. The Fantini household had a series of monolingual Spanish-speaking nursemaids from either Bolivia or Mexico who lived with the family and took care of Mario and his sister, Carla, born four years later. Mario in fact spent more hours each day with the nursemaids than with his parents. Mario also spent time visiting his grandparents, aunt, and uncle, all of whom were bilingual in either Spanish and English or Italian and English.

Given the abundant Spanish input, Mario was Spanish dominant when he entered kindergarten. He also had a clear Spanish accent when he spoke English. Noticing his phonological "deviations," a special education teacher in his school prescribed speech therapy for Mario. But his parents knew that Mario's accent was not of pathological origin, and opposed therapy. Mario soon learned to speak English without a foreign accent—only two years later, his third-grade teacher was surprised to learn that Mario spoke another language at home. Mario was educated entirely in English in American public schools, except for summer vacations spent in Mexico and a semester spent in a Bolivian private school during fifth grade. English became the dominant language of his environment outside the home and his vocabulary and stylistic options in Spanish began to fall behind his developments in English. Most of his peers at school were monolingual English speakers who had not traveled outside the area.

Although Mario became more dominant in English due to schooling in English, Fantini (1985: 77) reports that unlike many language minority children, Mario did not experience any negative social attitudes or prejudices for being bilingual:

> At no time was Mario noted experiencing a difficult or embarrassing situation because he spoke one language or the other, nor did he ever report such incidents. If anything, many of the persons with whom he associated valued his ability to speak two languages and their comments consistently reflected this . . . Mario's self-confidence, in fact —in either language—was so great that he spoke spontaneously and naturally in Spanish to his parents even when they visited him at school, this often being the acid test. The only effect produced when he spoke was amazement in his classmates who seldom—if ever—heard other languages.

Fantini (1985) states that Mario has been fortunate in having had positive experiences in each of the communities in which he has participated. His parents actively valued bilingualism and had the means to provide him with a variety of opportunities to hear and speak Spanish. His English-speaking world also seemed to consider his bilingualism as an asset, which motivated him to maintain his Spanish. It also probably helped that Mario had a great deal of self-confidence and was quite sociable.

The Caldas Family (Caldas, 2006)

Stephen Caldas, an American and his French-Canadian wife, Suzanne Caron-Caldas, raised their three children (John and twin girls, Valerie and Stephanie) bilingual in French and English in their Louisiana home. The couple initially followed the OPOL strategy (Stephen spoke to John in English while Suzanne spoke to him in French). Since Suzanne stayed at home for three and a half months after John was born, John was exposed to a great deal of French during that time. But when Suzanne returned to work, John was sent to English-speaking daycare for eight hours a day, five days a week. In addition to daycare, he was immersed in English through TV, neighbors, and his American relatives. When John turned 18 months old, his parents felt that he was not receiving enough French input and decided to both speak to him in French. John remained in daycare until he was four, when he was enrolled in an English-medium preschool.

When John's twin sisters were born two years later, the family spoke only French. As she did with John after his birth, Suzanne stayed with the girls at home for the first three and half months and then returned to work. The girls entered the all-English-speaking daycare with their older brother. Even though both parents spoke only French from the beginning, the girls were exposed to a lot more English through John, who had an obvious preference for speaking English. Caldas (2006: 44) notes:

> This was somewhat troubling to us, because we had expected him to respond to us in French. This confirmed our suspicions that English was the more predominant force in John's environment, and that our combined French speaking was still not enough to counteract the otherwise monolingual English world John lived in . . . . Suzanne and I were the only mouthpieces for French, and this was only because we made a concerted and continued effort to speak it. Had we been around John all the time, the influence of French would have undoubtedly been greater. But with both of us away from home much of the day, English reigned during the children's waking hours.

Like the Fantini family, the Caldas family tried to provide their children with a variety of opportunities to learn French. John attended one semester of partial French immersion program, and the twins attended five and a half years of French immersion programs in Louisiana. When John was nine years old and the twins were seven, the Caldas family moved from a mostly English-speaking community in Louisiana to a bilingual Cajun community where they heard and spoke a lot more French. This was also when the parents started recording family conversations during mealtimes. The family spent their summers in Quebec where the children had daily contact with several members of Suzanne's family who spoke very little English. The children also attended French-speaking summer camp in Quebec where they learned new vocabulary and Quebec idioms that their parents could not teach them. Caldas reports that the summers in French-speaking Canada were so effective as immersion experiences that the children often had trouble shifting back to English when they returned to the U.S.

As John entered pre-adolescence, his enthusiasm for speaking French began to wane while his younger sisters were ever more enthusiastic about speaking French. For example, Valerie often demanded that John speak French, but he grew increasingly frustrated of these demands. Caldas notes that on one occasion, John fired back at Valerie, "I have the right to speak any language I want to speak!", and on several occasions he screamed at Valerie, "English! English! English!" (2006: 63). Caldas reports that the language conflict between John and his sisters got intense at times. One time, Valerie was so mad at John for speaking English that she threw a cushion at him while screaming, "Parle français!!!" A few weeks later, the children's father heard the girls scream so violently at John to "Parle français!!!" that he feared it would come to blows (2006: 63).

When the family returned to Quebec that summer however, within weeks, John was speaking more French than his sisters. The parents observed that John went from speaking almost no French around the dinner table in May in Louisiana, to speaking almost no English around the dinner table in June in Canada, a pattern which continued for the next seven years. Like John, the girls shifted back and forth between English and French depending on whether they were in Louisiana or in Quebec. But when Valerie and Stephanie entered fifth grade, they also dramatically decreased their French speaking despite their return to a French immersion school program in Louisiana. Although the girls and all of their peers in the French immersion program could speak French, they only communicated in English when not being supervised by their French-speaking teachers. Caldas & Caron-Caldas (2002) conclude that the children's peer environment had a greater effect on their language choice than did the parents or the language immersion programs at school.

As the children moved through mid-adolescence, Caldas notes that they identified increasingly with Quebecois peer culture. The children grew increasingly confident and comfortable in Quebec because English is held with high esteem in Quebec. English is the language of popular culture and the children's Quebec friends knew that they could speak English. Caldas notes that Quebecois youth pepper their speech with English pop-cultural words and expressions, and Quebecois adolescents who linguistically "cross over" into English are perceived as "cool." He notes that "Quebec adolescents were saying 'chilé' in the same sense as their American counterparts say 'chill out.' They were also saying 'Moi too' (me too) and 'Full-cool,' 'Je vais caller' (I'm going to call) and 'Il est yo' (He's 'yo,' or 'cool') (2006: 134). However, once back in the U.S., French became "uncool" for the Caldas children and was quickly abandoned in favor of English. In this way, the story of the Caldas children is typical of the language experience of many bilingual children, who constantly move in and out of bilingualism.

The Matthews Family (Yip & Matthews, 2007)

Virginia Yip and Stephen Matthews are linguists at the Chinese University of Hong Kong and the University of Hong Kong respectively, who are raising their three children, Timmy, Sophie, and Alicia, bilingually in Cantonese and English. Virginia is a native speaker of Cantonese and Stephen a native speaker of British English. The family initially adopted the OPOL strategy but with Alicia, the thirdborn, the mother occasionally used English because the children received more input in Cantonese than in English. The parents speak mainly Cantonese with each other with frequent code-switching, a characteristic feature of educated Hong Kong speech (Li & Lee, 2006). The Matthews children are growing up in an extended family situation, with frequent opportunities to interact with their Cantonese-speaking maternal relatives. At home, regular input in English was provided only by the father and the family's Filipina domestic helper. At home, the children received more input in Cantonese than in English and preferred to speak Cantonese.

A former British colony for more than 150 years, Hong Kong recognizes English, Cantonese, and Mandarin as official languages. However, English is used only in secondary and higher education, the higher courts, and international companies, and is rarely heard on the street, in markets, and shopping malls (Yip & Matthews, 2007). Even though Hong Kong was a British enclave up to mid-1997, the number of native English-speaking residents has never exceeded 5%, and over 95% of the population in Hong Kong are ethnic Chinese, the majority of whom speak Cantonese (Li & Lee, 2006). Although the use of Mandarin has increased since the handover of sovereignty to China in 1997, it is rarely spoken in the home (Yip & Matthews, 2007). The predominant mode of communication in Hong Kong is Cantonese.

The three Matthews children attended preschool in Cantonese and English and primary school in English. Despite the similar language histories, the children's speech data reflect birth order differences (more on birth order later in this chapter). Since Timmy is the firstborn, he had no siblings to talk to for the first three years of his life, and his language input came largely from his adult caretakers. Sophie and Alicia, on the other hand, had older sibling(s) who provided significant additional language input. There were also personality differences reflected in the language data. Timmy and Alicia are more reserved while Sophie is an extrovert, the "talking girl" of the family (Yip & Matthews, 2007: 65). Under normal circumstances, Sophie would speak in either language with minimal prompting, which made for easier data collection.

The children's development in both languages was observed and recorded at weekly or bi-weekly intervals for periods of one to two and a half years: Timmy from 2;01;22 (years; months; days) to 3;06;25, Sophie from 1;06;00 to 3;00;09, and Alicia from 1;03;10 to 3;00;24. On average, each recording session consisted of an hour of audio- and in some cases video-recordings of the children engaged in their daily activities such as playing, reading, and role playing. The parents also kept a diary of the children's language development.

Yip & Matthews show that from the outset, the children's Cantonese and English constituted two separate systems—two different grammars were applied in the production of the two languages. However, they found strong evidence for interaction between the two developing grammatical systems. For instance, Timmy's Cantonese utterances were influenced by English syntax, as in (a):

(a)   M4hou2   baai2   keoi5   dai1   laa1
      don't   put   her   down   SFP
      "Don't put her down!" (referring to a child being carried) (Timmy
      3;09;09)

(Yip & Matthews, 2007: 216)

Here, the pronoun *keoi5* "her" separates the verb *baai2* "put" from the particle
dai1 "down." The correct Cantonese structure requires *keoi5* "her" to be placed
after the particle, as in *baai2 dai1 keoi5* (literally "put down her").

Around the same time, Timmy produced English sentences such as (b),
which were influenced by Chinese syntax:

(b)   Why no light? You turn on it. [i.e., Mid-Autumn Festival lantern]
      (Timmy 3;04;05)

(Yip & Matthews, 2007: 216)

Yip & Matthews note that while syntactic transfer occurred in both directions,
the predominant direction of transfer was from Cantonese to English, consistent with the fact that the children were more dominant in Cantonese.

While both monolingual and bilingual children produce non-target structures during their development (e.g., missing objects, as in "I want to put."),
Yip & Matthews show that their bilingual children produced them more
frequently and over a longer period than did monolinguals. The bilingual
children also produced some structures which their monolingual peers simply
did not. For example, Timmy produced (c), in which a prepositional phrase
hai2 ji1jyun2 follows the verb:

(c)   Ngo5   saang1-zo2   hai2   ji1jyun2   go2dou6
      I   born-PFV   at   hospital   there
      "I was born in the hospital." (Timmy 2;08;07)

(Yip & Matthews, 2007: 190)

But the target order in Cantonese requires the prepositional phrase to precede
the verb, as in (d):

(d)   Ngo5   [hai2   ji1jyun2   go2dou6]   saang1   ge3
      I   at   hospital   there   born   SFP
      "I was born in the hospital."

(Yip & Matthews, 2007: 190)

To monolingual Cantonese speakers, non-target utterances like (c) could be
a cause for alarm since monolingual Cantonese-speaking children never
produce sentences with such word order. Indeed, there are countless stories

of bilingual children who have been referred to speech therapists for their perceived "deviations" in language use (as we saw in the case of Mario Fantini's Spanish-accented English). All too often, these referrals result in recommendations for parents to address the child in only one language (usually the socially dominant language) so as not to confuse the child with input from two languages. But what Yip & Matthews's study shows is that these divergences are merely a reflection of a monolingual bias and that they constitute normal stages in bilingual children's development.

Yip & Matthews's study focuses on the children's preschool years, and it remains to be seen how the children's languages will develop during their elementary school and teenage years. If the other two case studies are any indication however, the Matthews children will continually move in and out of bilingualism depending on their need and desire to communicate in either language. Sure, they may take slightly longer to arrive at target-level proficiencies in each language than monolingual children, but with adequate exposure and support, they will become competent bilinguals able to skillfully navigate both of their worlds. This does not mean however, that the three children will develop equally. Each child is different, with his/her unique preferences and talents. Despite the fact that they are growing up in the same family, personal factors may influence an individual child to develop or neglect either language at different times. In the next section, we look at one such factor—birth order, a child's place relative to other children in a family.

BIRTH ORDER DIFFERENCES IN
BILINGUAL DEVELOPMENT

In her discussion of language policies from around the world, Romaine (1995) notes that the education of linguistic minority children in countries like Australia, the U.S., and Britain often entailed removing them from their parents and their own cultural group. She points out that the Statutes of Iona in Scotland dating from 1609 were designed to promote linguistic and cultural assimilation of Gaelic-speaking children from the Western Isles of Scotland with the Scots (English) speakers of the Lowlands. The Statutes required "everie gentilman or yeaman within the said Illandis to put his eldest son (or daughter) to the scuillis on the lawland, and intertcny and bring thame up thair untill they may be able to sufficientlie to speik, reid, and wryte Inglische" (Romaine, 1995: 243). Why did the drafter of this legislation specify the eldest child? What role did firstborn children play in the linguistic assimilation of Gaelic-speaking children?

Research has shown that firstborn and later-born monolingual children have access to different kinds of language learning experiences (e.g., Barton & Tomasello, 1994; Ely & Berko Gleason, 1995). While firstborn children have more opportunities for one-on-one interaction with a caretaker, later-born children hear less speech directed to them by adults because of the presence of elder siblings (Pine, 1995). Perhaps as a result, firstborn children are typically more advanced in their lexical and grammatical development, which tend to be the aspects of language development most sensitive to variation in experience (Hoff-Ginsberg, 1998). Later-born children tend to produce more personal pronouns (Oshima-Takane, Goodz, & Derevensky, 1996) and to develop more advanced conversational skills; they produce contingent responses to join ongoing conversations between their mothers and elder siblings (Dunn & Shatz, 1989) and use social routines to fulfill their roles in the conversations (Pine, 1995).

Firstborn and later-born bilingual children have access to different kinds of language experiences as well (see also Barron-Hauwaert, 2011). Jarovinskij (1995) investigated 18 children raised in families with Russian mothers and Hungarian fathers in Hungary, and found that most of the firstborn children had much more intensive experience with Russian than did the second- and thirdborns. The Russian mothers normally spoke face-to-face with their firstborn children but seldom addressed their second- or thirdborn children directly. As a result, later-born children were more Hungarian-dominant than were firstborns, even though all the children generally spoke Hungarian among themselves. Wong Fillmore (1991) report similar findings in her survey of immigrant and Native American families in the U.S. Younger children were generally more English-dominant than older ones were and showed greater loss of their home language.

The eldest children in immigrant families typically learn to speak the language of the host country when they enter school, whereas the later-born children begin speaking the second language before entering school because the elder siblings bring it into the home (Fishman, 1991). In my own survey of 251 Korean immigrant parents in the U.S., I found that while 78.8% of the firstborn children spoke Korean with their parents before entering school, only 66.3% of the secondborns and 42.9% of thirdborns did so (Shin, 2002). Exposed to English at an earlier age, the later-born children generally spoke more English than their elder siblings and were also less proficient in Korean. Hakuta & D'Andrea (1992) drew similar conclusions in their study of 308 Mexican American high school students. They found that the students' Spanish proficiency was related to the age at which they started speaking English—the earlier the exposure to English, the less Spanish they spoke.

In immigrant families, parents often rely on the firstborn child to be their link to the outside world (Shin, 2002). Firstborn children are often called on to translate written documents for the parents and serve as interpreters (see also Valdés, 2003). Having received the most amount of native language input among the siblings, the eldest child in the family maintains the advantage of being the easiest child for the parents to communicate with. Later-born children, on the other hand, generally hear fewer utterances in their mother tongue directed to them, which effectively reduces the number of occasions for them to respond in that language.

Older children may also discourage their younger siblings from speaking the mother tongue. Jarovinskij (1995) observed that later-born children were reluctant to speak Russian, the minority language, because their elder siblings often criticized their incorrect usage in Russian. As later-born children are repeatedly corrected for their attempts to speak the home language by their more proficient elder siblings, they become "language shy" and converse less in their mother tongue (Krashen, 1998). Rather than risk error, these less proficient speakers tend to interact less in that language. This pattern sets up a vicious cycle—less interaction means less input, and less input leads to incomplete acquisition. Therefore, later-born immigrant children often fail to attain their elder siblings' level of native language proficiency.

As firstborn children bring the societal language home, they may also influence their younger siblings' language attitudes. In her study of Mexican immigrant children in the U.S., McClure (1981) observed that even the Spanish-dominant children used English to address a young girl who, although she knew Spanish, refused to use it with anyone but monolingual Spanish speakers. Interestingly, this girl had teenage siblings who were highly integrated into the Anglo community. They were observed to be using English almost exclusively, even in the home, despite their parents' strong preference for Spanish as the home language. The girl and her older siblings probably identified more with Anglos and knew English as the language of power. Understanding the power dynamic between languages then, is particularly important for families that speak a minority language at home.

RESISTING LANGUAGE SHIFT

Finally, I turn to what I believe is the most important thing that families living in monolingual societies can do to achieve bilingualism—parents should make it a point to speak the native language at home and have the children respond in that language. Parents are perhaps the single most significant source of heritage language input for immigrant children. Research shows that parental use of the native language is crucial in children's development in that language and that children who maintain fluency in the heritage language into adulthood often come from homes where the language was spoken as a matter of policy (e.g., Bayley, Schecter, & Torres-Ayala, 1996; Portes & Hao, 1998). Because English has such a powerful and overriding influence on children's lives once they begin school, some parents may institute a household ban on English to protect the use of the heritage language.

Consider the story of Monica, a bilingual participant in my study on mixed heritage adults (Shin, 2010). She was born in Seoul to a Korean mother and an African American father who was in the U.S. military. When Monica was around four, her parents divorced, and she and her mother moved to the U.S. Her mother subsequently married a Korean man with whom she had another daughter. Monica explained that her stepfather had a strict Korean-only policy in the home and would ignore her and her sister if they did not address him in Korean:

> [My stepfather] spoke to me only in Korean . . . . He, honestly, won't even acknowledge you unless you speak to him in Korean . . . . He ignores my sister. He'll look at my mother and say, "your daughter is trying to say something." That's how it is, even now . . . . When I look at the method that he used to make me speak Korean, I think it's a little extreme. I'm not bitter about it. My sister is. Because that's her father, you know. And she has no bond with him at all. Because she doesn't speak Korean. He basically just doesn't acknowledge her at all. They're very, very strict. Well, my stepfather is. Very, I mean, very tough. Very, very tough. (p. 210)

Few people are as extreme as Monica's stepfather. Most parents adapt to their children's language preferences by also switching to English to varying degrees. Many people believe that it is more important to connect with their children in whatever language than to insist on one and not communicate at all. While children naturally identify with their peers in the majority language and prefer to speak it at home, the push for parents to shift to the majority language can also come from childhood professionals such as doctors, teachers, and speech therapists.

Some time ago, during a parent–teacher conference, one of my younger son's teachers shared with me that while my son was a delightful boy, he had some writing issues that prevented him from getting an A in class. She asked, "Does Joshua speak another language at home?"

"Yes, we speak Korean." I replied.

"Yeah, I thought so," she said. "I often see problems like this in children who speak another language at home."

The fact that this teacher grouped all the bilingual students in the underperformer category bothered me, but I promised her that I would work with Joshua at home to improve his writing skills. I also explained the importance of our children knowing both languages and asked her for her support.

Bilingual families living in monolingual societies need to make much greater efforts to maintain two languages, and this often means learning to brush off the subtle and not-so-subtle suggestions from teachers, doctors, well-intentioned neighbors, relatives, and friends to abandon the home language

(Baker, 2007). Parents need to remember that they are the greatest source of native language input for their children and overcome their reluctance to speak the language at home. Obviously, having the support of people who believe in the value of bilingualism and are also raising children bilingually can be helpful. But even families with little support in the immediate community may be able to connect with others in similar situations through the Internet (see also online resources at the end of this chapter).

OUT OF THE MOUTHS OF BILINGUALS 9.2

Concerns of a Bilingual Parent

"Usually pediatricians are the only professionals who see kids before they enter school. They are the main source of information and resource for the parents. We were fortunate that our doctor is a bilingual himself and raising bilingual kids, but some of our friends had bad experiences with their pediatricians. We had a friend whose pediatrician had concerns about her kids' social and language development around age 2, because they exhibited selective muteness or did not respond to him. Of course they are completely normal kids who are bilingual, the doctor just did not speak their home language. Their language development was not delayed, he just couldn't assess it. . . . In Emma's case there are no external cues that she might be bilingual (looks, accents, socioeconomic background, etc.), so we notice that it is hard for her teachers to remember that she is a bilingual and that impacts how she learns, what she knows, etc. You worry whether you are disabling your child in some way by making her bilingual. If she is labeled as an unsocial/impolite kid, that can become a self-fulfilling prophecy. Or how her early academic experiences will impact her future love of learning and school, since it takes additional effort to keep up."

(Marta Seres, a Hungarian-English bilingual mother
in the U.S., interviewed by Sarah J. Shin)

SUMMARY

In this chapter, I discussed some of the major issues related to raising children bilingually in the family. We saw that there are mainly two ways in which children become bilingual: (1) by acquiring two languages simultaneously from birth (i.e., simultaneous bilinguals), or (2) by acquiring a second language later in childhood (i.e., successive bilinguals). Although far more children become bilingual by being exposed to two languages in sequence, most of the available research on child bilingualism deals with simultaneous bilinguals. We saw that simultaneous bilingual children's development in each language is very similar to monolingual children's development in those languages, and leads to the same kind of grammatical competence possessed by monolinguals. Despite earlier claims that simultaneous bilingual children start out with a single, fused linguistic system, researchers now agree that the child's two languages develop separately from the very beginnings of speech production. Thus, there is no indication that children are "confused" from bilingual input.

While we know quite a lot about simultaneous bilingual acquisition, we know far less about the nature of successive bilingual acquisition due to a severe dearth of systematic studies. The available research seems to suggest that successive bilingual acquisition is qualitatively different from monolingual first language acquisition. Research on young ethnic Turkish children growing up in Germany and in the Netherlands shows that the children's second language productions are clearly influenced by their first language. In addition, the immigrant children lag behind their monolingual Dutch counterparts in terms of the size of Dutch vocabulary and Dutch morphosyntax. However, it is not clear whether this is due to reasons related to brain maturation or to other factors such as the quality of second language input and the subtractive school and social context in which many immigrant children find themselves. More systematic research is needed to address these issues.

I presented case studies of three families that have taken different paths to bilingualism: a Spanish-English bilingual family in Vermont (Fantini, 1985), a French-English bilingual family in Louisiana (Caldas, 2006), and a Cantonese-English bilingual family in Hong Kong (Yip & Matthews, 2007). We saw that maintaining a balance between two languages is a preoccupation for the parents in these studies. The Caldas family and the Matthews family both started out with the OPOL approach but the Caldas family switched to both parents speaking French after they realized that their eldest child was not receiving enough French input. In the Matthews family, the mother also relaxed her policy of speaking only Cantonese when the third child was born because the parents felt that the children were not receiving enough English input. In the Fantini family, only Spanish was spoken by both parents from the beginning to offset the overwhelming presence of English in the child's surroundings. Both the Fantini and Caldas families took frequent trips overseas to give their children opportunities to be immersed in the socially weaker language, and the Fantini and Matthews families had domestic helpers who provided additional input in the minority language.

The case studies showed that children move in and out of bilingualism throughout their development. We saw that the onset of schooling and adolescence has a huge impact on children's language preference. We also saw that children living in the same household can react very differently to the same language policy. While Valerie and Stephanie Caldas embraced French as the family language, their older brother John clearly identified more with English during his adolescent years, leading to some violent arguments among the siblings. We saw that personality may also factor into children's bilingual development. Mario Fantini's self-confidence and extroverted personality led to his speaking Spanish naturally and openly with his parents even in the presence of his monolingual English-speaking peers. In the Matthews family, Sophie was the most talkative child among the three siblings.

We also saw that firstborn and later-born children typically have different language experiences. While firstborn children spend the first few years of their lives in one-on-one interaction with the caretakers, later-born children have fewer occasions to spend time alone with adults. Depending on the preferred language of the caretaker, the eldest child is thus likely to reach the highest level of proficiency in that language among the siblings. Immigrant parents often rely on their eldest child to serve as a language broker—younger siblings are less often called on to perform this function. The older children also influence the language choice and preference of their younger siblings. We saw that eldest children may criticize the language errors of their younger siblings, discouraging them from speaking that language. Therefore, parents may want to encourage older children to help rather than criticize their younger siblings' attempts to speak in the native language. Parents may also create separate opportunities to spend time alone with their younger children.

In sum, raising bilingual children is a journey which requires hard work, patience, and persistence. While bilingualism has numerous advantages and is desired by many, achieving bilingualism is not without cost. In the short term, children may find it difficult to cope with the school curriculum in either language (Baker, 2007). Bilingual children also make language errors that monolingual children simply do not make. In the long term, children may pass through stages when they reject one of the languages. What is important to remember in all of this is that children's bilingualism is dynamic, constantly changing according to the social circumstances and the need to communicate with different people. Raising bilingual children is perhaps more complicated than raising monolingual children, but the hope of seeing them grow up to be skillful multilingual global citizens proud of their linguistic heritage and respectful of other cultures and peoples makes all the hard work worthwhile.

FURTHER READING

- Baker, C. (2007). *A parents' and teachers' guide to bilingualism* (3rd ed.). Clevedon, UK: Multilingual Matters.—Organized around a set of frequently asked questions about bilingualism and bilingual education (e.g.,

My child mixes the two languages. Is this normal? Is it better to develop two languages together or one language later than the other?), this classic text provides a highly readable and practical introduction to bilingualism in the family and in schools.

- Barron-Hauwaert, S. (2011). *Bilingual siblings: Language use in families.* Bristol, UK: Multilingual Matters.—With data from over 100 international families, this book examines how birth order, personality, and family size influence the ways in which bilingual siblings develop in two or more languages.

- King, K. & Mackey, A. (2007). *The bilingual edge: Why, when, and how to teach your child a second language.* New York: Collins Living.—Written in non-technical language by two linguists who are raising their children bilingually, this book dispels common myths about bilingual development in children. It should be a great resource for parents of all language backgrounds, monolingual and bilingual alike.

- Pearson, B.Z. (2008). *Raising a bilingual child.* New York: Random House.—This book offers an overview of why parents should raise their children to speak more than one language and detailed steps parents can take to integrate two languages into their child's daily routine.

ONLINE RESOURCES

- http://www.multilingualliving.com/—Multilingual Living is the home of the popular *Multilingual Living Magazine*, a publication dedicated to families raising bilingual children. Parents can join a discussion forum where they can share strategies, ideas, and resources.

- http://www.multilingualchildren.org/index.html—The Multilingual Children's Association provides parents with useful resources on raising bilingual children and offers an online space where parents can ask questions, find bilingual playgroups, and share experiences.

- http://spanglishbaby.com/—Created by two Latina moms, this site offers links to many useful bilingual family sites. Readers can also get their questions about bilingual parenting answered by a panel of experts.

- http://www.bilingualism-matters.org.uk/ —A team of researchers at the University of Edinburgh have put together a useful site for parents interested in raising bilingual children.

STUDY QUESTIONS AND ACTIVITIES

1. Interview a parent who is raising a bilingual family. What are the language backgrounds of the parents? What are their reasons for raising children bilingually? What language strategies (e.g., One-parent, one-language;

Minority language at home; Mix two languages whenever) have the parents employed and how have they worked? What difficulties do the parents face? Does the family have access to adequate reading materials in both languages and community support outside the family?

2. Observe parents interacting with their young children at home. Do you notice any differences between the way the parents relate to their eldest child and the way they relate to the younger children? How much of the parents' speech is directed to the eldest child? To the younger children? How does each child's gender and personality affect his/her interaction with parents and siblings?

3. Ask some childcare professionals (e.g., pediatricians, speech therapists, preschool teachers, daycare staff) about their experiences in working with bilingual children. What measures have they used to assess children's linguistic, cognitive, and social development? What difficulties have they faced? What additional resources or training could be helpful in their work?

4. It was stated in this chapter that studying the language development of one's own children has many practical advantages, including privileged access to the children and first-hand knowledge of the children's language experiences and environment. But are there some drawbacks as well?

5. Browse several parenting- and/or language learning-related websites. Based on what you have learned in this book, would you say the information contained on each site is accurate and research-based? What are some ways in which to assess the validity of the claims made on these sites?

Glossary

The definitions and explanations given in this Glossary are only meant to facilitate the understanding of the concepts covered in this book. Different scholars may have different emphases and applications of the terms in various contexts.

Academic English The specialized vocabulary, grammar, discourse, and functional skills associated with mastering content curriculum and instruction. This term is contrasted with **Conversational English**.

Additive bilingualism A situation in which one learns a second language while continuing to use the first language. This is the opposite of **Subtractive bilingualism**.

Audiolingual method An approach to foreign language instruction characterized by extensive use of pattern practice and emphasis on listening and speaking skills over reading and writing.

Bicultural identity The behaviors, beliefs, values, and norms that define a person as a member of two different cultural groups.

Bilingual Someone with the possession of two or more languages. In this book, this term is used interchangeably with the term **Multilingual**.

Bilingual education Education in two or more languages.

Borrowing A word borrowed from a donor language and incorporated into a recipient language (also known as "Loanword").

Code-mixing See **Code-switching**.

Code-switching The alternating use of two or more languages within the same conversation, usually when bilinguals are in the company of other bilinguals.

Communicative language teaching An approach to language teaching that emphasizes interaction as both the means and the ultimate goal of learning a language.

Community language See **Heritage language**, **Home language**, **Minority language**.

Comprehensible input hypothesis The theory that language learning is best facilitated when a learner is provided with a bit of language that is at or slightly above his/her current level of knowledge.

Comprehensible output hypothesis The theory that language learning takes place when a learner notices a gap in his/her knowledge of the second language and modifies his/her output to learn something new about the language.

Contextualization cues Communicative devices like intonation, gesture, speech tempo, and volume, which people use to communicate metaphoric information about how they intend their words to be understood by others in the conversation.

Conversation Analysis (CA) An approach to the study of social interaction in everyday situations, including both verbal and non-verbal behavior.

Conversational English The English used in everyday conversations. This term is contrasted with **Academic English**.

Critical Period Hypothesis The view that there is an age-related point beyond which it becomes difficult or impossible to learn a second language to the same degree as native speakers of that language.

Cultural assimilation The process whereby a minority group gradually adapts to the customs and attitudes of the dominant group.

Cultural pluralism A situation in which smaller groups within a larger society maintain their cultural identities, and their values and practices are accepted by the wider culture.

Cultural stereotype The belief that everyone of the same race, ethnicity, and religion acts the same way.

Deficit-based model of bilingualism Seeing bilinguals as deficient in one or both of their languages, especially when compared to monolinguals in each language.

Developmental bilingual education A bilingual education model that enables students to continue developing in their home languages while learning a second language and academic content.

Dialects   Mutually intelligible varieties of a language which differ in systematic ways (e.g., pronunciation, grammar, or vocabulary) from each other.

Diglossia   A situation in which two language varieties co-exist in a society through different functional uses attached to each language. One variety (called the "High" variety) is typically reserved for use in formal domains such as school, government, and the media while another language (the "Low" variety) is used in informal settings of the home and the community.

Early-exit bilingual education   See **Transitional bilingual education**.

Elite bilinguals   Individuals who, in addition to their mother tongue, are highly educated in a foreign language. This term is contrasted with **Natural bilinguals,** and typically refers to members of privileged social groups in post-colonial societies that have the financial and social means to learn the former colonial language.

English as a Foreign Language (EFL)   Study of English by speakers of different languages in non-English-speaking countries.

English as a Second Language (ESL)   Study of English by speakers of different languages in English-speaking countries.

English Language Learners (ELLs)   See **English Learners**.

English Learners (ELs)   Students who are not fully proficient in English.

Enrichment bilingual education   Bilingual education programs that serve relatively privileged language majority speakers learning through the medium of another language.

ESL pull-out   An educational model in which ESL students are taken out of their regular classrooms for about 30 to 45 minutes a day and given language instruction in a separate classroom.

Ethnic identity   The behaviors, beliefs, values, and norms that define a person as a member of a particular ethnic group.

Focus on form   An approach to second language teaching that explicitly draws learners' attention to the structure of language within a meaning-driven content-based lesson.

Foreign language   A language that is foreign to the learner. A language used in a country other than one's own.

Grammar translation method   A language teaching method that requires students to translate whole texts word for word and memorize grammatical rules and exceptions.

Heritage language This term is used synonymously with **Community language, Native language,** and **Mother tongue** to refer to a language other than English used by immigrants and possibly their children.

Home language Language spoken by linguistic minority populations at home.

Identity The behaviors, beliefs, values, and norms that define a person. The ways in which a person understands his/her relationship to the world.

Immersion A language teaching method which involves using the target language as the means of instruction to teach both language and content.

International language A high-prestige language used as a medium of communication between groups of people that speak different languages.

Involuntary minorities People who were originally brought into another society against their will through slavery, conquest, colonization, or forced labor, and were often denied the opportunity for full participation in that society.

L1 (Language One) The first language learned by an individual. This term is often used interchangeably with **Mother tongue** and **Native language.**

L2 (Language Two) The second language learned by an individual.

Language A collection of mutually intelligible dialects.

Language death Occurs when a declining language loses its last remaining speakers through their death or language shift.

Language (linguistic) majority Speakers of a socially dominant language.

Language (linguistic) minority Speakers of a minority language.

Language maintenance The continued use of a language, particularly among language minority speakers.

Language shift A change from the use of a minority language to the socially dominant language.

Late-exit bilingual education See **Developmental bilingual education.**

Lingua franca A common language used by speakers of different mother tongues.

Linguistic ghetto An area of a city inhabited predominantly by members of a linguistic minority group.

Linguistic interdependence principle The theory that L1 instruction that develops L1 reading and writing skills is not only developing L1 skills, but also L2 reading and writing skills.

Linguistic mismatch hypothesis The notion that students will encounter academic difficulties in every situation where there is a switch between home language and school language.

Maintenance bilingual education Bilingual education programs that help language minority speakers maintain the use of their mother tongues while learning a second language.

Majority language A high-status language spoken by the socially dominant group.

Marked language The unexpected (remarkable) language in a given social setting. This is contrasted with **Unmarked language**.

Maximum exposure hypothesis The view that if children come to school lacking proficiency in English, they require maximum exposure to English in school in order to learn it.

Minority language A low-status language spoken by a minority group.

Minority language at home A family language strategy which involves one language being spoken exclusively by everyone at home, while another language is used outside.

Monolingual A person who uses one language.

Monolingual education Education in one language.

Mother tongue The first language a person has learned from birth. This term is often used interchangeably with first language, **Heritage language**, and **Native language**.

Multilingual See **Bilingual**.

Native language The first language one acquires in life. This term is often used interchangeably with first language, **Heritage language**, and **Mother tongue**.

Natural bilinguals This term is contrasted with **Elite bilinguals** and refers to people who are fluent in two or more indigenous languages and use them as a means of communication in everyday life.

Non-non See **Semilingual**.

Official language A language that is given a special legal status in a particular country, state, or jurisdiction.

One-parent, one-language (OPOL) A strategy for raising bilingual children, in which each parent speaks his/her strongest language (usually, the native language) to the child, providing good language models in each language.

Recast   Reformulation of an incorrect utterance that maintains the original meaning.

Reclassified ELs   English learners that have tested at proficient levels on an English language exam and no longer receive ESL instruction.

Semilingual   A controversial term used to describe people who appear to have two underdeveloped languages.

Sheltered instruction   An instructional program for English learners, in which content area curriculum (e.g., math, science, history) is taught in English at a comprehensible level.

Simultaneous bilingual   Children who acquire two languages from birth.

Sink-or-swim   See **Submersion**.

Societal language   See **Majority language**.

State language   A language that has legal status in a political entity; official language.

Strong forms of bilingual education   Bilingual education programs which explicitly promote additive bilingualism. These are contrasted with **Weak forms of bilingual education**.

Structured English Immersion (SEI)   In SEI, content area curriculum is taught in English at a comprehensible level to English learners.

Submersion   The teaching of linguistic minority children only through the medium of a majority language. This term is used interchangeably with **Sink-or-swim**.

Subtractive bilingualism   A situation in which the socially dominant language replaces the weaker minority language. This is the opposite of **Additive bilingualism**.

Successive bilinguals   Children who acquire one language first and then learn another language later in childhood.

Transitional bilingual education   A bilingual education model whose primary aim is to transition students to an English-only instructional environment. The students' native language is used in instruction only as a temporary bridge to learning English.

Transnational migrants   People who move back and forth between countries.

Two-way (dual) immersion   A bilingual education model which typically involves about equal numbers of language majority children and language minority children learning both languages and academic content in the same classroom. Each group serves as native language models for the other group, and students learn each other's languages through social interaction.

Unmarked language   The expected (unremarkable) language in a given social setting. This is contrasted with **Marked language**.

Voluntary minorities   People who have immigrated to the host country willingly and without coercion.

Weak forms of bilingual education   Bilingual education programs in which proficiency in two languages is not necessarily a desired outcome. These are contrasted with **Strong forms of bilingual education**.

World Englishes   Localized or indigenized varieties of English found in diverse sociolinguistic contexts globally (e.g., Indian English, Singaporean English, Nigerian English).

References

Alfonzetti, G. (1998). The conversational dimension in code-switching between Italian and dialect in Sicily. In Auer, P. (ed.), *Code-switching in conversation: Language, interaction and identity* (pp. 180–211). London and New York: Routledge.

Androutsopoulos, J. (2006). Multilingualism, diaspora, and the Internet: Codes and identities on German-based diaspora websites. *Journal of Sociolinguistics, 10*(4), 520–547.

Androutsopoulos, J. (2007). Language choice and code switching in German-based diasporic web forums. In Danet, B. & Herring, S.C. (eds.), *The multilingual internet: Language, culture, and communication online* (pp. 340–361). Oxford: Oxford University Press.

Appadurai, A. (2001). Grassroots globalization and the research imagination. In A. Appadurai (ed.), *Globalization* (pp. 1–21). Durham, NC: Duke University Press.

Atkinson, J.M. & Heritage, J. (1984). *Structures of social action.* Cambridge: Cambridge University Press.

Auer, P. (1984). *Bilingual conversation.* Amsterdam: Benjamins.

Auer, P. (1995). The pragmatics of code-switching: A sequential approach. In Milroy, L. & Muysken, P. (eds.), *One speaker, two languages: Cross-disciplinary perspectives on code-switching* (pp. 115–135). Cambridge: Cambridge University Press.

Auer, P. ed. (1998). *Code-switching in conversation: Language, interaction and identity.* London and New York: Routledge.

Auer, P. (2005). A postscript: Code-switching and social identity. *Journal of Pragmatics, 37*(3), 403–410.

August, D., Goldenberg, C., & Rueda, R. (2010). Restrictive state language policies: Are they scientifically based? In Gándara, P. & Hopkins, M. (eds.), *Forbidden language: English learners and restrictive language policies* (pp. 139–158). New York: Teachers College Press.

August, D. & Shanahan, T. eds. (2006). *Developing literacy in second-language learners: Report of the National Literacy Panel on Language-Minority Children and Youth.* Mahwah, NJ: Lawrence Erlbaum.

Baby Einstein (2012). About Baby Einstein. Retrieved March 19, 2012 from: http://www.babyeinstein.com/en/our_story/about_us/

Bae, J. (2007). Development of English skills need not suffer as a result of immersion: Grades

1 and 2 writing assessment in Korean/English two-way immersion program. *Language Learning, 57*(2), 299–332.

Baetens Beardsmore, H. (1993). The European School model. In Baetens Beardsmore, H. (ed.), *European models of bilingual education.* Clevedon, UK: Multilingual Matters.

Baker, C. (2006). *Foundations of bilingual education and bilingualism* (4th ed.). Bristol, UK: Multilingual Matters.

Baker, C. (2007). *A parents' and teachers' guide to bilingualism* (3rd ed.). Clevedon, UK: Multilingual Matters.

Baker, C. & Jones, S.P. (1998). *Encyclopedia of bilingualism and bilingual education.* Clevedon, UK: Multilingual Matters.

Barron-Hauwaert, S. (2004). *Language strategies for bilingual families: The one-parent–one-language approach.* Clevedon, UK: Multilingual Matters.

Barron-Hauwaert, S. (2011). *Bilingual siblings: Language use in families.* Bristol, UK: Multilingual Matters.

Bartlett, L. & García, O. (2011). *Additive schooling in subtractive times: Bilingual education and Dominican immigrant youth in the Heights.* Nashville, TN: Vanderbilt University Press.

Barton, M. & Tomasello, M. (1994). The rest of the family: The role of fathers and siblings in early language development. In Gallaway, C. & Richards, B.J. (eds.), *Input and interaction in language acquisition* (pp. 109–134). Cambridge: Cambridge University Press.

Batalova, J., Fix, M., & Murray, J. (2005). *English language learner adolescents: Demographics and literacy achievements.* Report to the Center for Applied Linguistics. Washington, DC: Migration Policy Institute.

Batalova, J. & McHugh, M. (2010). *Top languages spoken by English language learners nationally and by state.* Washington, DC: Migration Policy Institute.

Baumgardner, R. (2006). The appeal of English in Mexican commerce. *World Englishes, 25*(2), 251–266.

Bayley, R., Schecter, S.R., & Torres-Ayala, B. (1996). Strategies for bilingual maintenance: Case studies of Mexican-origin families in Texas. *Linguistics and Education, 8,* 389–408.

Bedolla, L. (2003). The identity paradox: Latino language, politics and selective dissociation. *Latino Studies, 1,* 264–283.

Belazi, H.M., Rubin, E.J., & Toribio, A.J. (1994). Code switching and X-bar theory: The functional head constraint. *Linguistic Inquiry, 25*(2), 221–237.

Bhatia, T.K. & Ritchie, W.C. (2006a). Bilingualism in the global media and advertising. In Bhatia, T.K. & Ritchie, W.C. (eds.), *The handbook of bilingualism* (pp. 513–546). Malden, MA: Blackwell.

Bhatia, T.K. & Ritchie, W.C. (2006b). Bilingualism in South Asia. In Bhatia, T.K. & Ritchie, W.C. (eds.), *The handbook of bilingualism* (pp. 780–807). Malden, MA: Blackwell.

Bialystok, E., Luk, G., & Kwan, E. (2005). Bilingualism, biliteracy, and learning to read: Interactions among languages and writing systems. *Scientific Studies of Reading, 9*(1), 43–61.

Bialystok, E., Luk, G., Peets, K.F., & Yang, S. (2010). Receptive vocabulary differences in monolingual and bilingual children. *Bilingualism: Language and Cognition, 13*(4), 525–531.

Bielenberg, B. & Wong Fillmore, L. (2004/2005). The English they need for the test. *Educational Leadership, 62*, 45–49.

Bokhorst-Heng, W.D. & Caleon, I.S. (2009). The language attitudes of bilingual youth in multilingual Singapore. *Journal of Multilingual and Multicultural Development, 30*(3), 235–251.

Bolonyai, A. (2005). "Who was the best?": Power, knowledge and rationality in bilingual girls' code choices. *Journal of Sociolinguistics, 9*(1), 3–27.

Bournot-Trites, M. & Reeder, K. (2001). Interdependence revisited: Mathematics achievement in an intensified French-immersion program. *Canadian Modern Language Review, 58*(1), 27–43.

Brecht, R.D. & Ingold, C.W. (2002). Tapping a national resource: Heritage languages in the United States. ERIC Digest. EDO-FL-02-02.

Brinton, D.M., Kagan, O., & Bauckus, S. eds. (2008). *Heritage language education: A new field emerging.* New York and London: Routledge.

Butler, Y.G. & Hakuta, K. (2006). Bilingualism and second language acquisition. In Bhatia, T.K. & Ritchie, W.C. (eds.), *The handbook of bilingualism* (pp. 114–144). Malden, MA: Blackwell.

Caldas, S.J. (2006). *Raising bilingual-biliterate children in monolingual cultures.* Clevedon, UK: Multilingual Matters.

Caldas, S.J. & Caron-Caldas, S. (2002). A sociolinguistic analysis of the language preferences of adolescent bilinguals: Shifting allegiances and developing identities. *Applied Linguistics, 23*, 490–514.

Calderón, M.E. & Minaya-Rowe, L. (2003). *Designing and implementing two-way bilingual programs: A step-by-step guide for administrators, teachers, and parents.* Thousand Oaks, CA: Corwin Press.

Callahan, L. (2004). *Spanish/English codeswitching in a written corpus.* Amsterdam: John Benjamins.

Canadian Council on Learning (2007). *French-immersion education in Canada.* Retrieved January 9, 2012 from: http://www.ccl-cca.ca/pdfs/LessonsInLearning/May-17-07-French-immersion.pdf

CBC News (2010). Dieppe bilingual sign law meets opposition, January 19. Retrieved March 10, 2012 from: http://www.cbc.ca/canada/new-brunswick/story/2010/01/19/nb-dieppe-sign-bylaw-meeting-645.html#socialcomments#ixzz16Py8Is30

Celce-Murcia, M. & Larsen-Freeman, D. (1999). *The grammar book: An ESL/EFL teacher's course* (2nd ed.). Boston, MA: Heinle & Heinle.

Center for Applied Linguistics (2010). *Education for adult English language learners in the United States: Trends, research, and promising practices.* Washington, DC: Center for Applied Linguistics.

Center for Applied Linguistics (2011). *Directory of two-way bilingual immersion programs in the U.S.* Retrieved January 3, 2012 from http://www.cal.org/twi/directory

Chamot, A. & O'Malley, J.M. (1994). *CALLA handbook: Implementing the cognitive academic language learning approach.* Reading, MA: Addison-Wesley.

Chanseawrassamee, S. & Shin, S.J. (2009). Participant- and discourse-related code-switching by Thai-English bilingual adolescents. *Multilingua, 28*(1), 45–78.

Charity Hudley, A.H. & Mallinson, C. (2011). *Understanding English language variation in U.S. schools.* New York and London: Teachers College Press.

Chen, R.S. (1996). Obtaining credit from local school districts. In Wang, X. (ed.), *A view from within: A case study of Chinese heritage community language schools in the United States* (pp. 51–54). Washington DC: The National Foreign Language Center.

Cho, G. & Krashen, S. (1998). The negative consequence of heritage language loss and why we should care. In Krashen, S., Tse, L., & McQuillan, J. (eds.), *Heritage language development* (pp. 31–40). Culver City, CA: Language Education Associates.

Chomsky, N. (1965). *Aspects of the theory of syntax*. Cambridge, MA: MIT Press.

Christian, D. (1994). Two-way bilingual education: Students learning through two languages. National Center for Research on Cultural Diversity and Second Language Learning Educational Practice Report 12. Retrieved May 4, 2012 from: http://escholarship.org/uc/item/567256ft#page-1

Christian, D. (2008). School-based programs for heritage language learners: Two-way immersion. In Brinton, D.M., Kagan, O., & Bauckus, S. (eds.), *Heritage language education: A new field emerging* (pp. 257–268). New York and London: Routledge.

Christian, D. & Genesee, F. eds. (2001). *Bilingual education*. Alexandria, VA: TESOL.

Christian, D., Pufahl, I.U., & Rhodes, N.C. (2004/2005). Language learning: A worldwide perspective. *Educational Leadership,* December 2004/January 2005, 24–30.

Compton, C. (2001). Heritage language communities and schools: Challenges and recommendations. In Peyton, J.K., Ranard, D.A., & McGinnis, S. (eds.), *Heritage languages in America: Preserving a national resource* (pp. 145–165). McHenry, IL: Center for Applied Linguistics and Delta Systems.

Crawford, J. (2004). *Educating English learners: Language diversity in the classroom* (5th ed.). Los Angeles: Bilingual Education Services.

Crystal, D. (2000). *Language death*. Cambridge: Cambridge University Press.

Crystal, D. (2003). *English as a global language* (2nd ed.). Cambridge: Cambridge University Press.

Crystal, D. (2006). *Language and the Internet* (2nd ed.). Cambridge: Cambridge University Press.

Crystal, D. (2009). *Txtng: The gr8 db8*. Oxford: Oxford University Press.

Cultural Survival (2011). Why you should care. Retrieved August 5, 2011 from: http://www.culturalsurvival.org/current-projects/native-language-revitalization-campaign/why-you-should-care

Cummins, J. (1996). *Negotiating identities: Education for empowerment in a diverse society*. Ontario, CA: California Association for Bilingual Education.

Cummins, J. (2000). *Language, power and pedagogy: Bilingual children in the crossfire*. Clevedon, UK: Multilingual Matters.

Cummins, J. (2005). A proposal for action: Strategies for recognizing heritage language competence as a learning resource within the mainstream classroom. *Modern Language Journal, 89*(4), 585–592.

Cummins, J. (2008). Teaching for transfer: Challenging the two solitudes assumption in bilingual education. In Cummins, J. & Hornberger, N.H. (eds.), *Encyclopedia of Language and Education* (2nd ed.), *Volume 5: Bilingual Education* (pp. 65–75). New York: Springer.

Cummins, J. & Swain, M. (1986). *Bilingualism in education: Aspects of theory, research and practice*. New York: Longman.

Cutshall, S. (2004/2005). Why we need "The year of languages." *Educational Leadership*, December 2004/January 2005, 20–23.

Danet, B. & Herring, S.C. eds. (2007). *The multilingual internet: Language, culture, and communication online*. New York: Oxford University Press.

DeBot, K. & Gorter, D. (2005). A European perspective on heritage languages. *Modern Language Journal*, *89*(4), 612–616.

Defense Language Institute Foreign Language Center (DLIFLC) (2012). About DLIFLC. Retrieved March 19, 2012 from: http://www.dliflc.edu/about.html

De Houwer, A. (2009). *Bilingual first language acquisition*. Bristol, UK: Multilingual Matters.

De Klerk, V. (2000). Language shift in Grahamstown: A case study of selected Xhosa speakers. *International Journal of the Sociology of Language*, *146*, 87–110.

DePalma, R. (2010). *Language use in the two-way classroom: Lessons from a Spanish–English bilingual kindergarten*. Bristol, UK: Multilingual Matters.

Deuchar, M. & Quay, S. (1998). One vs. two systems in early bilingual syntax: Two versions of the question. *Bilingualism: Language and Cognition*, *1*, 231–243.

Deuchar, M. & Quay, S. (2000). *Bilingual acquisition: Theoretical implications of a case study*. Oxford: Oxford University Press.

Dick, G.S. (1998). I maintained a strong belief in my language and culture: A Navajo language autobiography. *International Journal of the Sociology of Language*, *132*, 23–25.

Dilans, G. (2009). Russian in Latvia: An outlook for bilingualism in a post-Soviet transitional society. *International Journal of Bilingual Education and Bilingualism*, *12*(1), 1–13.

Di Sciullo, A.-M., Muysken, P., & Singh, R. (1986). Government and code-switching. *Journal of Linguistics*, *22*, 1–24.

Döpke, S. (1997). Is the simultaneous acquisition of two languages in early childhood equal to acquiring each of the two languages individually? In Clark, E. (ed.), *Child language research forum 28* (pp. 95–112). Stanford, CA: Center for the Study of Language and Information.

Dorian, N.C. (2006). Minority and endangered languages. In Bhatia, T.K. & Ritchie, W.C. (eds.), *The handbook of bilingualism* (pp. 437–459). Malden, MA: Blackwell.

Doughty, C. & Varela, E. (1998). Communicative focus on form. In Doughty, C. & Williams, J. (eds.), *Focus on form in classroom second language acquisition* (pp. 114–138). Cambridge: Cambridge University Press.

Doughty, C. & Williams, J. eds. (1998). *Focus on form in classroom second language acquisition*. Cambridge: Cambridge University Press.

Dougill, J. (2008). Japan and English as an alien language. *English Today*, *24*(1), 18–22.

Duff, P.A. (2008). Heritage language education in Canada. In Brinton, D.M., Kagan, O., & Bauckus, S. (eds.), *Heritage language education: A new field emerging* (pp. 71–90). New York and London: Routledge.

Dunn, J. & Shatz, M. (1989). Becoming a conversationalist despite (or because of) having an older sibling. *Child Development*, *60*, 399–410.

Dutro, S. & Kinsella, K. (2010). English language development: Issues and implementation at grades six through twelve. In California Department of Education (ed.), *Improving education for English learners: Research-based approaches* (pp. 151–207). Sacramento: California Department of Education.

Economist, The (2008, February 7). Marie Smith. Retrieved January 28, 2011 from: http://www.economist.com/node/10640514

Economist, The (2010, November 13). Multikulturell? Wir? Retrieved May 4, 2012 from: http://www.economist.com/node/17469563

Economist, The (2010, November 27). Adios Arizona. Retrieved May 4, 2012 from: http://www.economist.com/node/17581892

Ellis, R. (1996). *The study of second language acquisition.* Oxford: Oxford University Press.

Ellis, R. (2002). The place of grammar instruction in the second/foreign language curriculum. In Hinkel, E. & Fotos, S. (eds.), *New perspectives on grammar teaching in second language classrooms* (pp. 17–34). Mahwah, NJ: Lawrence Erlbaum.

Ely, R. & Berko Gleason, J. (1995). Socialization across contexts. In Fletcher, P. & MacWhinney, B. (eds.), *The handbook of child language* (pp. 251–270). Oxford: Blackwell.

Facts about Germany (2011). *Immigration and integration.* Retrieved March 5, 2011 from: http://www.tatsachen-ueber-deutschland.de/en/society/main-content-08/immigration-and-integration.html

Fantini, A.E. (1985). *Language acquisition of a bilingual child: A sociolinguistic perspective.* San Diego, CA: College-Hill Press.

Fantini, A.E. (2009). Expanding languages, expanding worlds. In Todeva, E. & Cenoz, J. (eds.), *The multiple realities of multilingualism: Personal narratives and researchers' perspectives* (pp. 243–263). Berlin: Mouton de Gruyter.

Federman, R. (2003). A voice within a voice: Federman translating/translating Federman. In Tokuhama-Espinosa, T. (ed.), *The multilingual mind: Issues discussed by, for, and about people living with many languages* (pp. 235–241). Westport, CT: Praeger.

Ferguson, C.A. (1959). Diglossia. *Word, 15,* 325–340.

Fishman, J.A. (1967). Bilingualism with and without diglossia; diglossia with and without bilingualism. *Journal of Social Issues, 23,* 29–38.

Fishman, J.A. (1971). *Sociolinguistics.* Rowley, MA: Newbury.

Fishman, J.A. (1989). *Language and ethnicity in minority sociolinguistic perspective.* Clevedon, UK: Multilingual Matters.

Fishman, J.A. (1991). *Reversing language shift: Theoretical and empirical foundations for assistance to threatened languages.* Clevedon, UK: Multilingual Matters.

Fishman, J.A. (2001). 300-plus years of heritage language education in the United States. In Peyton, J.K., Ranard, D.A., & McGinnis. S. (eds.), *Heritage languages in America: Preserving a national resource* (pp. 81–97). McHenry, IL/Washington, DC: Delta Systems/Center for Applied Linguistics.

Fishman, J.A. (2006). Language maintenance, language shift, and reversing language shift. In Bhatia, T.K. & Ritchie, W.C. (eds.), *The handbook of bilingualism* (pp. 406–436). Malden, MA: Blackwell.

Francis, D.J., Lesaux, N.K., & August, D.L. (2006). Language of instruction for language minority learners. In August, D.L. & Shanahan, T. (eds.), *Developing literacy in second-language learners: Report of the National Literacy Panel for Language-Minority Children and Youth* (pp. 365–414). Mahwah, NJ: Lawrence Erlbaum.

Friedman, T.L. (2005). *The world is flat: A brief history of the twenty-first century.* New York: Farrar, Straus, and Giroux.

Fry, R. (2008). *The role of schools in the English Language Learner achievement gap.* Washington, DC: Pew Hispanic Center.

Fung, L. & Carter, R. (2007). Cantonese e-discourse: A new hybrid variety of English. *Multilingua, 26,* 35–66.

Furman, N., Goldberg, D., & Lusin, N. (2010). Enrollments in languages other than English in United States institutions of higher education, Fall 2009. The Modern Language Association of America. Retrieved April 4, 2011 at: http://www.mla.org/2009_enrollmentsurvey

Gafaranga, J. (2005). Demythologizing language alternation studies: Conversational structure vs. social structure in bilingual interaction. *Journal of Pragmatics, 37,* 281–300.

Gándara, P. and Hopkins, M. eds. (2010a). *Forbidden language: English learners and restrictive language policies.* New York: Teachers College Press.

Gándara, P. and Hopkins, M. (2010b). The changing linguistic landscape of the United States. In Gándara, P. & Hopkins, M. (eds.) *Forbidden language: English learners and restrictive language policies* (pp. 7–19). New York: Teachers College Press.

Gándara, P., Losen, D., August, D., Uriarte, M., Gómez, M.C., & Hopkins, M. (2010). Forbidden language: A brief history of U.S. language policy. In Gándara, P. & Hopkins, M. (eds.) *Forbidden language: English learners and restrictive language policies* (pp. 20–33). New York: Teachers College Press.

Gao, L. (2006). Language contact and convergence in computer-mediated communication. *World Englishes, 25*(2), 299–308.

García, O. (2005). Positioning heritage languages in the United States. *Modern Language Journal, 89,* 601–605.

García, O. ed. (2008a). Spanish as a global language. *The International Mulitilingual Research Journal, 2*(1).

García, O. (2008b). Teaching Spanish and Spanish in teaching in the U.S.: Integrating bilingual perspectives. In Hélot, C. & de Mejía, A.-M. (eds.), *Forging multilingual spaces: Integrating majority and minority bilingual education* (pp. 31–57). Clevedon, UK: Multilingual Matters.

García, O. (2009). *Bilingual education in the 21st century: A global perspective.* Malden, MA: Wiley-Blackwell.

García, O. & Baker, C. eds. (2007). *Bilingual education: An introductory reader.* Clevedon, UK: Multilingual Matters.

García, O. & Bartlett, L. (2007). A speech community model of bilingual education: Educating Latino newcomers in the U.S. *International Journal of Bilingual Education and Bilingualism, 10,* 1–25.

Gardner-Chloros, P. (2009). *Code-switching.* Cambridge: Cambridge University Press.

Gargesh, R. (2006). South Asian Englishes. In Kachru, B.B., Kachru, Y., & Nelson, C.L. (eds.), *The handbook of world Englishes* (pp. 90–113). Malden, MA: Blackwell.

Gass, S.M. & Selinker, L. (2008). *Second language acquisition: An introductory course* (3rd ed.). New York: Routledge.

Genesee, F. (1981). A comparison of early and late second language learning. *Canadian Journal of Behavioral Science, 13,* 115–127.

Genesee, F. (1987). *Learning through two languages: Studies of immersion and bilingual education.* Cambridge, MA: Newbury House.

Genesee, F. (1988). Neuropsychology and second language acquisition. In Beebe, L. (ed.), *Issues in second language acquisition* (pp. 32–57). Rowley, MA: Newbury House.

Genesee, F. (2006). What do we know about bilingual education for majority-language students? In Bhatia, T.K. & Ritchie, W.C. (eds.), *The handbook of bilingualism* (pp. 547–576). Malden, MA: Blackwell.

Genesee, F., Lindholm-Leary, K., Saunders, W., & Christian, D. (2006). *Educating English language learners: A synthesis of research evidence.* New York: Cambridge University Press.

Gibson, M.A., Gándara, P., & Koyama, J.P. eds. (2004). *School connections: U.S. Mexican youth, peers, and school achievement.* New York: Teachers College Press.

González, N., Moll, L., & Amanti, C. (2005). *Funds of knowledge: Theorizing practices in households, communities, and classrooms.* Mahwah, NJ: Lawrence Erlbaum.

Graddol, D. (1997). *The future of English?* London: The British Council.

Graddol, D. (2006). *English next: Why Global English may mean the end of "English as a foreign language."* London: The British Council.

Grieco, E.M. & Trevelyan, E.N. (2010). Place of birth of the foreign-born population: 2009. American Community Survey Briefs. Retrieved February 16, 2011 from: http://www.census.gov/prod/2010pubs/acsbr09-15.pdf

Grosjean, F. (1982). *Life with two languages: An introduction to bilingualism.* Cambridge, MA: Harvard University Press.

Grosjean, F. (1985). The bilingual as a competent but specific speaker-hearer. *Journal of Multilingual and Multicultural Development, 6,* 467–77.

Grosjean, F. (2010). *Bilingual: Life and reality.* Cambridge, MA: Harvard University Press.

Gumperz, J.J. (1982). *Discourse strategies.* Cambridge: Cambridge University Press.

Gumperz, J.J. & Cook-Gumperz, J. (2005). Making space for bilingual communicative practice. *Intercultural Pragmatics, 2*(1), 1–23.

Gupta, A.F. (1993). *The step-tongue: Children's English in Singapore.* Clevedon, UK: Multilingual Matters.

Hakimzadeh, S. & Cohn, D. (2007). *English usage among Hispanics in the United States.* Washington, DC: Pew Hispanic Center.

Hakuta, K. & D'Andrea, D. (1992). Some properties of bilingual maintenance and loss in Mexican background high-school students. *Applied Linguistics, 13,* 72–99.

Harley, B. (1992). Patterns of second language development in French immersion. *Journal of French Language Studies, 2*(2), 159–183.

Harley, B. & Swain, M. (1984). The interlanguage of immersion students and its implications for second language teaching. In Davies, A., Criper, C., & Howatt, A. (eds.), *Interlanguage* (pp. 291–311). Edinburgh: Edinburgh University Press.

Harrison, K.D. (2007). *When languages die: The extinction of the world's languages and the erosion of human knowledge.* Oxford: Oxford University Press.

Harrison, K.D. (2010). *The last speakers: The quest to save the world's most endangered languages.* Washington, DC: National Geographic Society.

Haugen, E. (1989). The rise and fall of an immigrant language: Norwegian in America. In Dorian, N.C. (ed.), *Investigating obsolescence: Studies in language contraction and death* (pp. 61–73). Cambridge: Cambridge University Press.

Heath, S.B. (1983). *Ways with words: Language, life and work in communities and classrooms.* Cambridge: Cambridge University Press.

Heller, M. (2003). Globalization, the new economy, and the commodification of language and identity. *Journal of Sociolinguistics, 7*(4), 473–492.

Hinkel, E. & Fotos, S. eds. (2002). *New perspectives on grammar teaching in second language classrooms.* Mahwah, NJ: Lawrence Erlbaum.

Hoff-Ginsberg, E. (1998). The relation of birth order and socioeconomic status to children's language experience and language development. *Applied Psycholinguistics, 19*, 603–629.

Hornberger, N.H. (1991). Extending enrichment bilingual education: Revisiting typologies and redirecting policy. In García, O. (ed.), *Bilingual education. Focusschrift in honor of Joshua A. Fishman* (pp. 215–234). Amsterdam and Philadelphia, PA: John Benjamins.

Housen, A. (2002). Process and outcomes in the European Schools model of multilingual education. *Bilingual Research Journal, 26*(1), 1–9.

Howard, E.R. & Sugarman, J. (2001). Two-way immersion programs: Features and statistics. Retrieved January 26, 2012 from: http://escholarship.org/uc/item/6z68j0g2#page-1

Huang, S., & Yeoh, B.S.A. (2005). Transnational families and their children's education: China's "study mothers" in Singapore. *Global Networks, 5*(4), 379–400.

Igoa, C. (1995). *The inner world of the immigrant child.* Mahwah, NJ: Lawrence Erlbaum.

International Organization for Migration (2011). Facts and figures: Global estimates. Retrieved January 14, 2011 from: http://www.iom.int/jahia/Jahia/about-migration/facts-and-figures/lang/en

Isurin, L., Winford, D., & de Bot, K. eds. (2009). *Multidisciplinary approaches to code switching.* Amsterdam and Philadelphia, PA: John Benjamins.

Iwabuchi, K. (2002). Recentering globalization: Popular culture and Japanese trans-nationalism. Durham, NC and London: Duke University Press.

Jarovinskij, A. (1995). On bilingual socialization. In Nelson, K.E. & Reger, Z. (eds.), *Children's language* (pp. 23–40). Hillsdale, NJ: Lawrence Erlbaum.

Jeon, M. (2010). Korean language and ethnicity in the United States: Views from within and across. *Modern Language Journal, 94*(1), 43–55.

Jo, H. (2001). Heritage language learning and ethnic identity: Korean Americans' struggle with language authorities. *Language, Culture and Curriculum, 14*(1), 26–41.

Johnson, J.S. & Newport, E.L. (1989). Critical period effects in second-language learning: The influence of maturational state on the acquisition of English as a second language. *Cognitive Psychology, 21*, 60–99.

Johnson, R.K. & Swain, M. eds. (1997). *Immersion education: International perspectives.* Cambridge: Cambridge University Press.

Kachru, B.B. (1985). Standards, codification and sociolinguistic realism: The English language in the Outer Circle. In Quirk, R. & Widdowson, H.G. (eds.), *English in the world: Teaching and learning the language and literatures* (pp. 11–30). Cambridge: Cambridge University Press.

Kachru, Y. (2006). Mixers lyricing in Hinglish: Blending and fusing in Indian popular culture. *World Englishes, 25*(2), 223–233.

Kamanga, C.M.M. (2009). The joys and pitfalls of multiple language acquisition: The workings of the mind of a simultaneous multilingual. In Todeva, E. & Cenoz, J. (eds.), *The multiple realities of multilingualism: Personal narratives and researchers' perspectives* (pp. 115–134). Berlin: Mouton de Gruyter.

Kamwangamalu, N. (2006). Bi-/multilingualism in southern Africa. In Bhatia, T.K.

& Ritchie, W.C. (eds.), *The handbook of bilingualism* (pp. 725–741). Malden, MA: Blackwell.

Kanno, Y. (2003). *Negotiating bilingual and bicultural identities: Japanese returnees betwixt two worlds.* Mahwah, NJ: Lawrence Erlbaum.

Kanno, Y. & Norton, B. (2003). Imagined communities and educational possibilities: Introduction. *Journal of Language, Identity, and Education, 2,* 241–249.

Kappler, S. (2010). Keeping faith: Sikh soldier graduates basic training, *WWW.ARMY.MIL: The official homepage of the United States Army.* Retrieved on March 30, 2011 from: http://www.army.mil/-news/2010/11/10/47924-keeping-faith-sikh-soldier-graduates-basic-training/

Katzner, K. (2002). *The languages of the world* (3rd ed.). London and New York: Routledge.

Kim, L.S. (2003). Multiple identities in a multicultural world: A Malaysian perspective. *Journal of Language, Identity, and Education, 2*(3), 137–158.

King, K. and Ganuza, N. (2005). Language, identity, education, and transmigration: Chilean adolescents in Sweden. *Journal of Language, Identity, and Education, 4*(3), 179–199.

King, K. & Mackey, A. (2007). *The bilingual edge: Why, when, and how to teach your child a second language.* New York: Collins Living.

Kloss, H. (1998). *The American bilingual tradition.* Washington, DC: Delta Systems & Center for Applied Linguistics (original work published 1977).

Kondo-Brown, K. (2003). Heritage language instruction for post-secondary students from immigrant backgrounds. *Heritage Language Journal, 1,* 1–25.

Kondo-Brown, K. (2005). Differences in language skills: Heritage language learner sub-groups and foreign language learners. *Modern Language Journal, 89,* 563–581.

Koslow, S., Shamdasani, P.M., & Touchstone, E.E. (1994). Exploring language effects in ethnic advertising: A sociolinguistic perspective. *Journal of Consumer Research, 20*(4), 575–585.

Kowalski, C. (2009). A "new breed" of American? In Todeva, E. & Cenoz, J. (eds.), *The multiple realities of multilingualism: Personal narratives and researchers' perspectives* (pp. 171–189). Berlin: Mouton de Gruyter.

Kramsch, C. (1993). *Context and culture in language teaching.* Oxford: Oxford University Press.

Krashen, S. (1981). *Second language acquisition and second language learning.* Oxford: Pergamon.

Krashen, S. (1985). *The input hypothesis: Issues and implications.* New York: Longman.

Krashen, S. (1998). Language shyness and heritage language development. In Krashen, S.D., Tse, L., & McQuillan, J. (eds.), *Heritage language development* (pp. 41–49). Culver City, CA: Language Education Associates.

Krashen, S. Long, M., & Scarcella, R. (1979). Age, rate, and eventual attainment in second language acquisition. *TESOL Quarterly, 13,* 573–582.

Lafuente, D. (2008). Affluent in Spanish: From tennis to tequila, Latinos are going upscale. *Adweek, 49*(23), 26–28.

Lam, W.S.E. (2004a). Border discourses and identities in transnational youth culture. In Mahiri, J. (ed.), *What they don't learn in school: Literacy in the lives of urban youth.* New York: Peter Lang Publishers.

Lam, W.S.E. (2004b). Second language socialization in a bilingual chat room: Global and local considerations. *Language Learning and Technology, 8*(3), 44–65.

Lanauze, M. & Snow, C. (1989). The relation between first- and second-language writing skills: Evidence from Puerto Rican elementary school children in bilingual programs. *Linguistics and Education, 1*, 323–339.

Lanza, E. & Svendsen, B.A. (2007). Tell me who your friends are and I *might* be able to tell you what language(s) you speak: Social network analysis, multilingualism, and identity. *International Journal of Bilingualism, 11*(3), 275–300.

Lee, H. (2010). "I am a *kirogi* mother": Education exodus and life transformation among Korean transnational women. *Journal of Language, Identity, and Education, 9*(4), 250–264.

Lee, Jamie Shinhee (2004). Linguistic hybridization in K-pop: Self-assertion and resistance. *World Englishes, 23*(3), 429–50.

Lee, Jamie Shinhee (2006). Linguistic constructions of modernity: English mixing in Korean television commercials. *Language in Society, 35*, 59–91.

Lee, Jin Sook (2002). The Korean language in America: The role of cultural identity in heritage language learning. *Language, Culture and Curriculum, 15*(2), 117–133.

Lee, Jin Sook (2006). Exploring the relationship between electronic literacy and heritage language maintenance. *Language Learning and Technology, 10*(2), 93–113.

Lee, Jin Sook & Shin, S.J. (guest eds.) (2008). Korean as a heritage language [Special issue]. *Heritage Language Journal, 6*(2).

Lee, Jin Sook & Suarez, D. (2009). A synthesis of the roles of heritage languages in the lives of children of immigrants: What educators need to know. In Wiley, T.G., Lee, J.S., & Rumberger, R.W. (eds.), *The education of language minority immigrants in the United States* (pp. 136–171). Bristol, UK: Multilingual Matters.

Lee, S. (2007). Language policy in a Korean–English two-way immersion setting. *Language, Culture, and Curriculum, 20*(2), 109–117.

Lee, T.S. (2009). Language, identity, and power: Navajo and Pueblo young adults' perspectives and experiences with competing language ideologies. *Journal of Language, Identity, and Education, 8*, 307–320.

Leopold, W. (1939–49). *Speech development of a bilingual child: Linguist's record* (vols. 1–4). Evanston, IL: Northwestern University Press.

Lesser, W. ed. (2004). *The genius of language: Fifteen writers reflect on their mother tongues.* New York: Pantheon Books.

Leung, C., Harris, R., & Rampton, B. (1997). The idealized native speaker, reified ethnicities, and classroom realities. *TESOL Quarterly, 31*(3), 543–560.

Levine, G.S. (2011). *Code choice in the language classroom.* Bristol, UK: Multilingual Matters.

Levinson, S. (1983). *Pragmatics.* Cambridge: Cambridge University Press.

Lewis, M.P. ed. (2009). *Ethnologue: Languages of the world* (16th ed.). Dallas, TX: SIL International. Online version: http://www.ethnologue.com/

Li, D. & Lee, S. (2006). Bilingualism in East Asia. In Bhatia, T.K. & Ritchie, W.C. (eds.), *The handbook of bilingualism* (pp. 742–779). Malden, MA: Blackwell.

Li, W. (1994). *Three generations, two languages, one family: Language choice and language shift in a Chinese community in Britain.* Clevedon, UK: Multilingual Matters.

Li, W. (2005). "How can you tell?": Towards a common sense explanation of conversational code-switching. *Journal of Pragmatics, 37*(3), 375–389.

Li, W. & Milroy, L. (1995). Conversational code-switching in a Chinese community in Britain: A sequential analysis. *Journal of Pragmatics, 23*, 281–299.

Li, X. (2007). Souls in exile: Identities of bilingual writers. *Journal of Language, Identity, and Education, 6*(4), 259–275.

Lindholm-Leary, K. (2001). *Dual language education.* Clevedon, UK: Multilingual Matters.

Lindholm-Leary, K. & Block, N. (2010). Achievement in predominantly low SES/Hispanic dual language schools. *International Journal of Bilingual Education and Bilingualism, 13*(1), 43–60.

Lindholm-Leary, K. & Genesee, F. (2010). Alternative educational programs for English learners. In California Department of Education (ed.), *Improving education for English learners: Research-based approaches* (pp. 323–382). Sacramento: California Department of Education.

Lo, A. and Park, J. eds. (2012). Globalization, multilingualism and identity in transnational perspective: The case of South Korea [Special issue]. *Journal of Sociolinguistics, 16*(2).

Lo Bianco, J. (2009). Being Chinese, speaking English. In Lo Bianco, J., Orton, J., & Gao, Y. (eds.), *China and English: Globalisation and the dilemmas of identity* (pp. 294–309). Bristol, UK: Multilingual Matters.

Long, M.H. & Robinson, P. (1998). Focus on form: Theory, research, and practice. In Doughty, C. & Williams, J. (eds.), *Focus on form in classroom second language acquisition* (pp. 15–41). Cambridge: Cambridge University Press.

Mackey, W.F. (1967). *Bilingualism as a world problem.* Montreal: Harvest House.

MacSwan, J. (2006). Code switching and grammatical theory. In Bhatia, T.K. & Ritchie, W.C. (eds.), *The handbook of bilingualism* (pp. 283–311). Malden, MA: Blackwell.

Mahoney, K., MacSwan, J., Haladyna, T., & García, D. (2010). Castaneda's third prong: Evaluating the achievement of Arizona's English learners under restrictive language policy. In Gándara, P. & Hopkins, M. (eds.), *Forbidden language: English learners and restrictive language policies* (pp. 50–64). New York and London: Teachers College Press.

Marley, D. (2004). Language attitudes in Morocco following recent changes in language policy. *Language Policy, 3,* 25–46.

Martin-Jones, M. & Romaine, S. (1986). Semilingualism: A half-baked theory of communicative competence. *Applied Linguistics, 7*(1), 26–38.

Martinez-León, N., and Smith, P.H. (2003). Education for bilingualism in Mexican transnational communities. *NABE Journal of Research and Practice, 1*(1), 138–148.

Maxwell, L.A. (2009). Shifting landscape: Immigration transforms communities. *Education Week, 28*(17), 1–2.

May, S. & Hill, R. (2005). Maori-medium education: Current issues and challenges. *International Journal of Bilingual Education and Bilingualism, 8*(5), 377–403.

McCarty, T.L. (1998). Schooling, resistance, and American Indian languages. *International Journal of the Sociology of Language, 132,* 27–41.

McCarty, T.L. (2002). *A place to be Navajo: Rough Rock and the struggle for self-determination in indigenous schooling.* Mahwah, NJ: Lawrence Erlbaum.

McCarty, T.L., Romero, M.E., & Zepeda, O. (2006). Reclaiming the gift: Indigenous youth counter-narratives on Native language loss and revitalization. *American Indian Quarterly, 30*(2), 28–48.

McCarty, T.L. & Watahomigie, L.J. (1998). Indigenous community-based language education in the USA. *Language, Culture, and Curriculum, 11*(3), 309–324.

McCarty, T.L., & Zepeda, O. eds. (1998). Indigenous language use and change in the Americas [Special issue]. *International Journal of the Sociology of Language, 132.*

McClure, E.F. (1981). Formal and functional aspects of the code-switched discourse of bilingual children. In Duran, R.P. (ed.), *Latino language and communicative behavior* (pp. 69–94). Norword, NJ: Ablex.

McGinnis, S. (2008). From mirror to compass: The Chinese heritage language education sector in the United States. In Brinton, D.M., Kagan, O., and Bauckus, S. (eds.), *Heritage language education: A new field emerging* (pp. 229–242). New York and London: Routledge.

McKay, S.L. & Bokhorst-Heng, W.D. (2008). *International English in its sociolinguistic contexts: Towards a socially sensitive EIL pedagogy.* New York and London: Routledge.

McKay, S.L. & Wong, S.C. (1996). Multiple discourses, multiple identities: Investment and agency in second-language learning among Chinese adolescent immigrant students. *Harvard Educational Review, 66,* 577–608.

Meier, D. & Wood, G. eds. (2004). *Many children left behind: How the No Child Left Behind Act is damaging our children and our schools.* Boston, MA: Beacon Press.

Meisel, J. (2006). The bilingual child. In Bhatia, T.K. & Ritchie, W.C. (eds.), *The handbook of bilingualism* (pp. 91–113). Malden, MA: Blackwell.

Menken, K. (2008). *English language learners left behind: Standardized testing as language policy.* Clevedon, UK: Multilingual Matters.

Milroy, L. (1987). *Language and social networks* (2nd ed.). Oxford: Blackwell.

Milroy, L. & Muysken, P. eds. (1995). *One speaker, two languages: Cross-disciplinary perspectives on code-switching.* Cambridge: Cambridge University Press.

Miniwatts Marketing Group (2010). Internet world users by language. Retrieved January 9, 2010 from: http://www.internetworldstats.com/stats7.htm

Moody, A.J. (2006). English in Japanese popular culture and J-Pop music. *World Englishes, 25*(2), 209–222.

Mukherjee, B. (2004). The way back. In Lesser, W. (ed.), *The genius of language: Fifteen writers reflect on their mother tongues* (pp. 11–24). New York: Pantheon Books.

Muller, A. & Baetens Beardsmore, H. (2004). Multilingual interaction in plurilingual classes: European School practice. *International Journal of Bilingual Education and Bilingualism, 7*(1), 24–42.

Myers-Scotton, C. (1993a). *Social motivations for codeswitching: Evidence from Africa.* Oxford: Clarendon Press.

Myers-Scotton, C. (1993b). *Duelling languages: Grammatical structure in codeswitching.* Oxford: Clarendon Press.

Nakagawa, U. (2010). The seeds of Hallyu. *The Diplomat,* October 22. Retrieved February 2, 2011 from: http://the-diplomat.com/new-emissary/2010/10/22/the-seeds-of-hallyu/

National Center for Education Statistics (2011). Fast facts. Retrieved October 19, 2011 from: http://nces.ed.gov/fastfacts/display.asp?id=96

Nettle, D. & Romaine, S. (2000). *Vanishing voices: The extinction of the world's languages.* Oxford: Oxford University Press.

Ng-Osorio, J. & Ledward, B.C. (2011). *Aia ke ola i ka ʻōlelo Hawaiʻi: Revival of the Hawaiian language.* Honolulu, HI: Kamehameha Schools–Research & Evaluation.

Nguyen, D.T. & Stritikus, T. (2009). Assimilation and resistance: How language and culture influence gender identity negotiation in first-generation Vietnamese immigrant youth. In Wiley, T.G., Lee, J.S., & Rumbergerm, R.W. (eds.), *The education of language minority immigrants in the United States* (pp. 172–201). Bristol, UK: Multilingual Matters.

Nicholas, S.E. (2009). "I live Hopi, I just don't speak it": The critical intersection of language, culture, and identity in the lives of contemporary Hopi youth. *Journal of Language, Identity, and Education, 8,* 321–334.

Nieto, S. (1992). *Affirming diversity: The sociopolitical context of multicultural education* (1st ed.). White Plains, NY: Longman Publishing Group.

Nieto, S. (2002). *Language, culture, and teaching: Critical perspectives for a new century.* Mahwah, NJ: Lawrence Erlbaum.

Nieto, S. & Bode, P. (2011). *Affirming diversity: The sociopolitical context of multicultural education* (6th ed.). New York: Allyn & Bacon.

Nihalani, P. (2010). Globalization and international intelligibility. In Saxena, M. & Omoniyi, T. (eds.), *Contending with globalization in World Englishes* (pp. 23–44). Bristol, UK: Multilingual Matters.

Norris, J.M. & Ortega, L. (2000). Effectiveness of L2 instruction: A research synthesis and quantitative meta-analysis. *Language Learning, 50*(September), 417–528.

Norton, B. (1997). Language, identity, and the ownership of English. *TESOL Quarterly, 31*(3), 409–429.

Ogbu, J. (1992). Understanding cultural diversity and learning. *Educational Researcher, 21*(8), 5–14 and 24.

Oller, D.K. & Eilers, R. (2002). *Language and literacy in bilingual children.* Clevedon, UK: Multilingual Matters.

Omoniyi, T. (2006). Hip hop through the World Englishes lens: A response to globalization. *World Englishes, 25*(2), 195–208.

Omoniyi, T. & Saxena, M. (2010). Introduction. In Saxena, M. and Omoniyi, T. (eds.), *Contending with globalization in World Englishes* (pp. 1–22). Bristol, UK: Multilingual Matters.

Orellana, M.F., Thorne, B., Chee, A., & Lam, W.S.E. (2001). Transnational childhoods: The participation of children in processes of family migration. *Social Problems, 48*(4), 572–591.

Oshima-Takane, Y., Goodz, E., & Derevensky, J.L. (1996). Birth order effects on early language development: Do secondborn children learn from overheard speech? *Child Development, 67,* 621–634.

Ovando, C.J. (2003). Bilingual education in the United States: Historical development and current issues. *Bilingual Research Journal, 27*(1), 1–24.

Palmer, D.K. (2008). Building and destroying students' 'academic' identities: The power of discourse in a two-way immersion classroom. *International Journal of Qualitative Studies in Education, 21*(6), 647–667.

Palmer, D.K. (2009). Code-switching and symbolic power in a second-grade two-way classroom: A teacher's motivation system gone awry. *Bilingual Research Journal, 32,* 42–59.

Pao, D., Wong, S., & Teuben-Rowe, S. (1997). Identity formation for mixed-heritage adults and implications for educators. *TESOL Quarterly, 31*(3), 622–631.

Paradis, J. & Genesee, F. (1996). Syntactic acquisition in bilingual children: Autonomous or interdependent? *Studies in Second Language Acquisition, 18,* 1–25.

Park, J.S.-Y. & Bae, S. (2009). Language ideologies in educational migration: Korean *jogi yuhak* families in Singapore. *Linguistics and Education, 20,* 366–377.

Pavlenko, A. & Blackledge, A. eds. (2004). *Negotiation of identities in multilingual contexts.* Clevedon, UK: Multilingual Matters.

Pearson, B.Z. (2008). *Raising a bilingual child.* New York: Random House.

Pearson, B.Z., Fernandez, S., & Oller, D.K. (1995). Cross-language synonyms in the lexicons of bilingual infants: One language or two? *Journal of Child Language, 22,* 345–368.

Peirce, B.N. (1995). Social identity, investment, and language learning. *TESOL Quarterly, 29*(1), 9–31.

Pennycook, A. (2007). *Global Englishes and transcultural flows.* London and New York: Routledge.

Pew Forum on Religion and Public Life (2011). *The future of the global Muslim population.* Retrieved March 5, 2011 from: http://features.pewforum.org/muslim-population/

Peyton, J.K., Ranard, D.A., & McGinnis, S. (2001). Charting a new course: Heritage language education in the United States. In Peyton, J., Ranard, D., & McGinnis, S. (eds.), *Heritage languages in America: Preserving a national resource* (pp. 3–26). McHenry, IL: Center for Applied Linguistics and Delta Systems.

Pfaff, C.W. (1994). Early bilingual development of Turkish children in Berlin. In Extra, G. & Verhoeven, L. (eds.), *The cross-linguistic study of bilingual development* (pp. 75–97). Amsterdam: Netherlands Academy of Arts and Sciences.

Phinney, J.S. (1989). Stages of ethnic identity in minority group adolescents. *Journal of Early Adolescence, 9,* 34–49.

Phinney, J.S., Romero, I., Nava, M., & Huang, D. (2001). The role of language, parents and peers in ethnic identity among adolescents in immigrant families. *Journal of Youth and Adolescence, 30,* 135–153.

Pine, J.M. (1995). Variation in vocabulary development as a function of birth order. *Child Development, 66,* 272–281.

Poplack, S. (1980). "Sometimes I'll start a sentence in Spanish y termino en Español": Toward a typology of code-switching. *Linguistics, 18,* 581–618.

Poplack, S. (1981). The syntactic structure and social function of codeswitching. In Durán, R.P. (ed.), *Latino language and communicative behavior* (pp. 169–184). Norwood, NJ: Ablex.

Popovic, R. (2009). A long, adventurous road to (im)perfection. In Todeva, E. & Cenoz, J. (eds.), *The multiple realities of multilingualism: Personal narratives and researchers' perspectives* (pp. 33–51). Berlin: Mouton de Gruyter.

Portes, A. & Hao, L. (1998). E Pluribus Unum: Bilingualism and loss of language in the second generation. *Sociology of Education, 71,* 269–294.

Portes, A. & Rumbaut, R. (2001). *Legacies: The story of the immigrant second generation.* Berkeley and Los Angeles: University of California Press.

Portes, A. & Rumbaut, R. (2006). *Immigrant America: A portrait* (3rd ed.). Berkeley: University of California Press.

Project Based Technology Integrated Learning (PBTIL) (n.d.) Being proud to be bilingual.

Retrieved March 10, 2012 from: http://edutel.musenet.org:8042/pbtil/student_projects. html

Puente, D. (2006). Super Bowl ad may leave viewers asking, "Que pasa?": Toyota will debut the event's first bilingual ad. *ABC News/ESPN Sports*, January 26. Retrieved January 14, 2010 from: http://abcnews.go.com/Sports/story?id=1546206

Quay, S. (1995). The bilingual lexicon: Implications for studies of language choice. *Journal of Child Language, 22*, 369–387.

Rajadurai, J. (2010). "Malays are expected to speak Malay": Community ideologies, language use and the negotiation of identities. *Journal of Language, Identity, and Education, 9*, 91–106.

Rajagopalan, K. (2010). The English language, globalization and Latin America: Possible lessons from the "Outer Circle." In Saxena, M. and Omoniyi, T. (eds.), *Contending with globalization in World Englishes* (pp. 175–195). Bristol, UK: Multilingual Matters.

Ramirez, J.D., Yuen, S., Ramey, D., & Pasta, D. (1991). *Longitudinal study of structured English immersion strategy, early-exit and late-exit bilingual education programs for language minority children* (Final Report vols. 1 & 2). San Mateo, CA: Aguirre International. (ERIC Document Reproduction Service No. ED 330216).

Raschka, C., Sercombe, P., & Huang, C.-L. (2009). Conflicts and tensions in codeswitching in a Taiwanese EFL classroom. *International Journal of Bilingual Education and Bilingualism, 12*(2), 157–171.

Rath, A. (2009). Keeping the native Nipmuc language alive [Radio series episode]. In *All Things Considered*. NPR. Retrieved March 10, 2012 from: http://www.npr.org/templates/ story/story.php?storyId=103028551

Rhodes, N.C. & Pufahl, I. (2009). *Foreign language teaching in U.S. schools: Results of a national survey, executive summary*. Washington, DC: Center for Applied Linguistics.

Robertson, R. (1995). Glocalization: Time–space and homogeneity–heterogeneity. In Featherstone, M., Lash, S., & Robertson, R. (eds.), *Global modernities* (pp. 25–44). London: Sage.

Romaine, S. (1995). *Bilingualism*. Oxford: Blackwell.

Romaine, S. (2006). The bilingual and multilingual community. In Bhatia, T.K. & Ritchie, W.C. (eds.), *The handbook of bilingualism* (pp. 385–405). Malden, MA: Blackwell.

Ronjat, J. (1913). *Le développement du langage observé chez un enfant bilingue*. Paris: Champion.

Rumbaut, R. (1994). The crucible within: Ethnic identity, self-esteem, and segmented assimilation among children of immigrants. *International Migration Review, 28*(4), 748–794.

Rumbaut, R. (2009). A language graveyard? The evolution of language competencies, preferences and use among young adult children of immigrants. In Wiley, T.G., Lee, J.S., & Rumberger, R.W. (eds.), *The education of language minority immigrants in the United States* (pp. 35–71). Bristol, UK: Multilingual Matters.

Rumberger, R.W. & Tran, L. (2010). State language policies, school language practices, and the English learner achievement gap. In Gándara, P. & Hopkins, M. (eds.), *Forbidden language: English learners and restrictive language policies* (pp. 86–101). New York and London: Teachers College Press.

Ryoo, W. (2009). Globalization, or the logic of cultural hybridization: The case of the Korean wave. *Asian Journal of Communication, 19*(2), 137–151.

Santos, F. (2007). Demand for English lessons outstrips supply. *New York Times*, February 27. Retrieved February 16, 2011 from: http://www.nytimes.com/2007/02/27/education/27esl.html?pagewanted=1

Sarkar, M. & Allen, D. (2007). Hybrid identities in Quebec hip-hop: Language, territory, and ethnicity in the mix. *Journal of Language, Identity, and Education, 6*(2), 117–130.

Sarkar, M. & Winer, L. (2006). Multilingual code-switching in Quebec rap: Poetry, pragmatics and performativity. *International Journal of Multilingualism, 3*(3), 173–192.

Saunders, W. & Goldenberg, C. (2010). Research to guide English language development instruction. In California Department of Education (ed.), *Improving education for English learners: Research-based approaches* (pp. 21–81). Sacramento: California Department of Education.

Sayer, P. (2008). Demystifying language mixing: Spanglish in school. *Journal of Latinos and Education, 7*(2), 94–112.

Scarcella, R.C. (2002). Some key factors affecting English learners' development of advanced literacy. In Schleppegrell, M.J. & Colombi, M.C. (eds.), *Developing advanced literacy in first and second languages: Meaning with power* (pp. 209–226). Mahwah, NJ: Lawrence Erlbaum.

Scarcella, R.C. (2003). *Accelerating academic English: A focus on the English learner.* Oakland, CA: Regents of the University of California.

Schafer, S. (2010). Army gets first Sikh enlisted soldier since 1980s. *msnbc.com*, November 10. Retrieved March 30, 2011 from: http://www.msnbc.msn.com/id/40113583/ns/us_news-life/

Schecter, S.R. & Bayley, R. (1997). Language socialization practices and cultural identity: Case studies of Mexican-descent families in California and Texas. *TESOL Quarterly, 31*(3), 513–541.

Schleppegrell, M., Achugar, M., & Oteíza, T. (2004). The grammar of history: Enhancing content-based instruction through a functional focus on language. *TESOL Quarterly, 38*(1), 67–93.

Schola Europaea (2007–2009). Welcome to the website of the Schola Europaea. Retrieved January 13, 2012 from: http://www.eursc.eu/index.php?id=2

Schola Europaea (2011). Facts and figures on the beginning of the 2011–2012 school year in the European Schools. Ref.: 2011-10-D-30-en-1. Retrieved January 16, 2012 from: http://www.eursc.eu/fichiers/contenu_fichiers2/1749/2011-10-D-30-en-2.pdf

Shin, S.J. (2002). Birth order and the language experience of bilingual children. *TESOL Quarterly, 36*(1), 103–113.

Shin, S.J. (2005). *Developing in two languages: Korean children in America.* Clevedon, UK: Multilingual Matters.

Shin, S.J. (2006). High-stakes testing and heritage language maintenance. In K. Kondo-Brown (ed.), *Heritage language development: Focus on East Asian immigrants* (pp. 127–144). Amsterdam and Philadelphia, PA: John Benjamins.

Shin, S.J. (2007). For immigrant students, the ESOL glass is half-full. *Essential Teacher, 4*(4), 17–19.

Shin, S.J. (2009). Negotiating grammatical choices: Academic language learning by secondary ESL students. *System, 37*(3), 391–402.

Shin, S.J. (2010). "What about me? I'm not like Chinese but I'm not like American.":

Heritage language learning and identity of mixed heritage adults. *Journal of Language, Identity, and Education, 9*(3), 203–219.

Shin, S.J. & Milroy, L. (1999). Bilingual language acquisition by Korean schoolchildren in New York City. *Bilingualism: Language and Cognition, 2*(2), 147–167.

Shin, S.J. & Milroy, L. (2000). Conversational code-switching among Korean–English bilingual children. *International Journal of Bilingualism, 4*(3), 351–383.

Short, D. & Fitzsimmons, S. (2007). Double the work: Challenges and solutions to acquiring language and academic literacy for adolescent English Language Learners. A Report to the Carnegie Corporation of New York. Alliance for Excellent Education, Washington, DC.

Singleton, D. (2001). Age and second language acquisition. *Annual Review of Applied Linguistics, 21*, 77–89.

Skutnabb-Kangas, T. (2000). *Linguistic genocide in education—or worldwide diversity and human rights?* Mahwah, NJ: Lawrence Erlbaum.

Slavin, R.E. (2003). Foreword. In Calderón, M.E. & Minaya-Rowe, L., *Designing and implementing two-way bilingual programs: A step-by-step guide for administrators, teachers, and parents* (pp. ix–x). Thousand Oaks, CA: Corwin Press.

Snow, C.E. (1990). Rationales for native language instruction: Evidence from research. In Padilla, A.M., Fairchild, H.H., & Valadez, C.M. (eds.), *Bilingual education: Issues and strategies* (pp. 60–74). Newbury Park, CA: Sage.

Snow, C.E. & Hakuta, K. (1992). The costs of monolingualism. In Crawford, J. (ed.), *Language loyalties: A source book on the Official English controversy* (pp. 384–394). Chicago: University of Chicago Press.

Sohn, S.-O.S. & Merrill, C.C. (2008). The Korean/English dual language program in the Los Angeles Unified School District. In Brinton, D.M., Kagan, O., & Bauckus, S. (eds.), *Heritage language education: A new field emerging* (pp. 269–287). New York and London: Routledge.

Spada, N. & Lightbown, P. (2008). Form-focused instruction: Isolated or integrated? *TESOL Quarterly, 42*(2), 181–207.

Statistics Canada (2004). Reading achievement of students in French-immersion programs. *Education Quarterly Review, 9*(4), 25–48. Catalogue no. 81-003-XIE. Retrieved January 10, 2012 from: http://www.statcan.gc.ca/pub/81-003-x/81-003-x2002004-eng.pdf

Su, H.-Y. (2003). The multilingual and multi-orthographic Taiwan-Based Internet: Creative uses of writing systems on college-affiliated BBSs. *Journal of Computer Mediated Communication, 9*(1). Retrieved July 5, 2012 from: http://jcmc.indiana.edu/vol9/issue1/su.html

Suárez-Orozco, C. & Suárez-Orozco, M. (2001). Children of immigration. *Harvard Educational Review, 71*(3), 599–602.

Suárez-Orozco, C., Suárez-Orozco, M., & Todorova, I. (2008). *Learning a new land: Immigrant students in American society.* Cambridge, MA: Harvard University Press.

Swain, M. (1985). Communicative competence: Some roles of comprehensible input and comprehensible output in its development. In Gass, S. & Madden, C. (eds.), *Input in second language acquisition* (pp. 235–253). Rowley, MA: Newbury House.

Swain, M. (1998). Focus on form through conscious reflection. In Doughty, C. & Williams, J. (eds.), *Focus on form in classroom second language acquisition* (pp. 64–81). Cambridge: Cambridge University Press.

Swain, M. & Lapkin, S. (1982). *Evaluating bilingual education: A Canadian case study.* Clevedon, UK: Multilingual Matters.

Swan, D. (1996). *A singular pluralism: The European Schools 1984–1994.* Dublin: Institute of Public Administration.

Swiss Federal Statistical Office (2011). Languages and religions: Data, indicators. Retrieved May 29, 2011 from: http://www.bfs.admin.ch/bfs/portal/en/index/themen/01/05/blank/key/sprachen.html

Taft, R. & Cahill, D. (1989). Mother tongue maintenance in Lebanese immigrant families in Australia. *Journal of Multilingual and Multicultural Development, 10,* 129–43.

Tan, A. (2004). Yes and no. In Lesser, W. (ed.), *The genius of language: Fifteen writers reflect on their mother tongues* (pp. 25–34). New York: Pantheon Books.

Tavares, A. (2000). From heritage to international languages: Globalism and Western Canadian trends in heritage language education. *Canadian Ethnic Studies, 32*(1), 156–171.

Thomas, W.P. & Collier, V.P. (2002). *A national study of school effectiveness for language minority students' long-term academic achievement.* Santa Cruz, CA: Center for Research on Education, Diversity and Excellence.

Todeva, Elka. (2009). Multilingualism as a kaleidoscopic experience: The mini universes within. In Todeva, E. & Cenoz, J. (eds.), *The multiple realities of multilingualism: Personal narratives and researchers' perspectives* (pp. 53–74). Berlin: Mouton de Gruyter.

Tse, L. (1998). Ethnic identity formation and its implications for heritage language development. In Krashen, S.D., Tse, L., & McQuillan, J. (eds.), *Heritage language development* (pp. 15–29). Culver City, CA: Language Education Associates.

Tse, L. (2000). The effects of ethnic identity formation on bilingual maintenance and development: An analysis of Asian American narratives. *International Journal of Bilingual Education and Bilingualism, 3*(3), 185–200.

Tse, L. (2001). *Why don't they learn English?: Separating fact from fallacy in the U.S. language debate.* New York: Teachers College Press.

Tucker, J. (2006). *The ESL logjam: Waiting times for adult ESL classes and the impact on English learners.* Los Angeles: National Association of Latino Elected and Appointed Officials Educational Fund.

Turnbull, M. & Dailey-O'Cain, J. (2009). Introduction. In Turnbull, M. & Dailey-O'Cain, J. (eds.), *First language use in second and foreign language learning* (pp. 1–14). Bristol, UK: Multilingual Matters.

Turnbull, M., Lapkin, S., & Hart, D. (2001). Grade 3 immersion students' performance in literacy and mathematics: Province-wide results from Ontario (1998–1999). *Canadian Modern Language Review, 58*(1), 9–26.

United States Government Accountability Office (2010). Foreign language capabilities: Departments of Homeland Security, Defense, and State could better assess their foreign language needs and capabilities and address shortfalls. [GAO-10-715T] Retrieved March 30, 2011 from: http://www.gao.gov/new.items/d10715t.pdf

Uriarte, M., Tung, R., Lavan, N., & Diez, V. (2010). Impact of restrictive language policies on engagement and academic achievement of English learners in Boston public schools. In Gándara, P. & Hopkins, M. (eds.), *Forbidden language: English learners and restrictive language policies* (pp. 65–85). New York and London: Teachers College Press.

U.S. Census Bureau (2005–2009). American Community Survey. B16001. Language spoken at home by ability to speak English for the population 5 years and over—Universe: population 5 years and over. Retrieved May 18, 2012 from: http://factfinder2.census.gov

U.S. Department of Education, National Center for Education Statistics (2011). *The Condition of Education 2011* (NCES 2011-033), Table A-20-1. Retrieved May 4, 2012 from: http://nces.ed.gov/fastfacts/display.asp?id=16

U.S. Department of Education, National Clearinghouse for English Language Acquisition and Language Instruction Educational Programs (NCELA) (2011). The growing numbers of English learner students. Retrieved October 19, 2011 from: http://www.ncela.gwu.edu/files/uploads/9/growingLEP_0809.pdf

U.S. Department of Education, Office of Vocational and Adult Education (2011). *National Reporting System.* Retrieved February 16, 2011 from http://wdcrobcolp01.ed.gov/CFAPPS/OVAE/NRS/reports/index.cfm

Ustinova, I.P. (2006). English and emerging advertising in Russia. *World Englishes, 25*(2), 267–277.

Valadez, C.M., MacSwan, J., & Martínez, C. (2000). Toward a new view of low-achieving bilinguals: A study of linguistic competence in designated "semilinguals." *Bilingual Review, 25*(3), 238–248.

Valdés, G. (1997). Dual-language immersion programs: A cautionary note concerning the education of language minority students. *Harvard Education Review, 67*(3), 391–429.

Valdés, G. (2000). Introduction. In *Spanish for native speakers: AATSP professional development series handbook for teachers K–16*, vol. 1 (pp. 1–20). Orlando, FL: Harcourt College.

Valdés, G. (2001). *Learning and not learning English: Latino students in American schools.* New York: Teachers College Press.

Valdés, G. (2003). *Expanding definitions of giftedness: The case of young interpreters from immigrant communities.* Mahwah, NJ: Lawrence Erlbaum.

Valenzuela, A. (1999). *Subtractive schooling: U.S. Mexican youth and the politics of caring.* Albany, NY: State University of New York Press.

Van Deusen-Scholl, N. (2003). Toward a definition of heritage language: Sociopolitical and pedagogical considerations. *Journal of Language, Identity, and Education, 2*, 211–230.

Verhoeven, L.T. & Boeschoten, H.E. (1986). First language acquisition in a second language environment. *Applied Psycholinguistics, 7*, 241–256.

Verhoeven, L.T. & Vermeer, A. (1984). Ethnic group differences in children's oral proficiency of Dutch. In Extra, G. & Vallen, T. (eds.), *Ethnic minorities and Dutch as a second language* (pp. 105–132). Dordrecht, Holland: Foris Publications.

Viadero, D. (2009). Research hones focus on ELLs. *Education Week, 28*(17), 3–5.

Volkman, T.A. ed. (2005). *Cultures of transnational adoption.* Durham, NC and London: Duke University Press.

Volterra, V. & Taeschner, T. (1978). The acquisition and development of language by bilingual children. *Journal of Child Language, 5*, 311–326.

Wang, S.C. (2007). Building societal capital: Chinese in the U.S. *Language Policy, 6*, 27–52.

Warschauer, M., El Said, G.R., & Zohry, A. (2002). Language choice online: Globalization and identity in Egypt. *Journal of Computer Mediated Communication, 7*(4). Retrieved January 6, 2011 from: http://jcmc.indiana.edu/vol7/issue4/warschauer.html

Waters, J.L. (2005). Transnational family strategies and education in the contemporary Chinese diaspora. *Global Networks, 5*(4), 359–377.

Weinreich, U. (1963). *Languages in contact: Findings and problems.* The Hague: Mouton de Gruyter.

Wentworth, L., Pellegrin, N., Thompson, K., & Hakuta, K. (2010). Proposition 227 in California: A long-term appraisal of its impact on English learner student achievement. In Gándara, P. & Hopkins, M. (eds.), *Forbidden language: English learners and restrictive language policies* (pp. 37–49). New York and London: Teachers College Press.

Wesche, M., Toews-Janzen, M., & MacFarlane, A. (1996). *Comparative outcomes and impacts of early, middle and late entry French immersion options: Review of recent research and annotated bibliography.* Toronto: OISE/UT Press.

Wiley, T.G. (2001). On defining heritage languages and their speakers. In Peyton, J.K., Ranard, D.A., & McGinnis, S. (eds.), *Heritage languages in America: Preserving a national resource* (pp. 29–36). McHenry, IL/Washington, DC: Delta Systems/Center for Applied Linguistics.

Wiley, T.G. (2005). The reemergence of heritage and community language policy in the U.S. national spotlight. *Modern Language Journal, 89,* 594–601.

Wiley, T.G. & Lee, J.S. (2009). Introduction. In Wiley, T.G., Lee, J.S., & Rumberger, R.W. (eds.), *The education of language minority immigrants in the United States* (pp. 1–34). Bristol, UK: Multilingual Matters.

Wiley, T.G., Lee, J.S., & Rumberger, R.W. eds. (2009). *The education of language minority immigrants in the United States.* Bristol, UK: Multilingual Matters.

Wiley, T.G. & Valdés, G. (2000). Heritage language instruction in the United States: A time for renewal. *Bilingual Research Journal, 24*(4), i–v.

Wong Fillmore, L. (1991). When learning a second language means losing the first. *Early Childhood Research Quarterly, 6,* 323–346.

Wong Fillmore, L. (2000). Loss of family languages: Should educators be concerned? *Theory into Practice, 39*(4), 203–210.

Wong Fillmore, L. & Snow, C.E. (2000). What teachers need to know about language. Washington, DC: ERIC Clearinghouse on Languages and Linguistics.

Working Group on ELL Policy (2010). Improving educational outcomes for English Language Learners: Recommendations for the reauthorization of the Elementary and Secondary Education Act. Retrieved December 15, 2011 from: http://ellpolicy.org/wp-content/uploads/ESEAFinal.pdf

Wright, W.E. (2005). Evolution of federal policy and implications of No Child Left Behind for language minority students. Policy Brief (EPSL-0501-101-LPRU), Education Policy Studies Laboratory, Arizona State University.

Wright, W.E. (2007). Heritage language programs in the era of English-only and No Child Left Behind. *Heritage Language Journal, 5*(1).

Yi, Y. (2009). Adolescent literacy and identity construction among 1.5 generation students: From a transnational perspective. *Journal of Asian Pacific Communication, 19*(1), 100–129.

Yip, V. & Matthews, S. (2007). *The bilingual child: Early development and language contact.* Cambridge: Cambridge University Press.

Young, R. & Tran, M. (1999). Language maintenance and shift among Vietnamese in America. *International Journal of the Sociology of Language, 140,* 77–82.

Zentella, A.C. (1997). *Growing up bilingual: Puerto Rican children in New York.* Oxford and Malden, MA: Blackwell.

Author Index

Subject Index